10,000 Hills
A Little Boy's Journey

10,000 Hills
A Little Boy's Journey

Written by
C.T. Wilson, Esq.

First Edition: August 2013
Printed in the United States of America
ISBN-10: 1495463230
ISBN-13: 9781495463235

Forward

"This book is powerful because it's true. It's a real look at the horror and struggle many boys and girls go through in the foster care system. We can have psychiatrists and therapists write about the lives of these youths, but CT Wilson proves nothing is more potent than hearing it from someone who experienced these horrors first hand. The fact that he is so revealing, provides us all with something that all people in foster care, adopted or not, can, should, and need to receive - the understanding of how and why we need to repair the broken pieces of the foster care system.

CT still bears the scars of the terrible journey he went through, but to see him educate and arm himself with the power to overcome his obstacles and then go back to the frontline and fight for all the others going through what he has been through, is so inspirational. I encourage all to read this book and learn something about a side of life that's hard to believe exists in this world. Maybe we can all begin to do what is needed so all can be soldiers fighting the good fight like CT."

Darryl "D.M.C." McDaniels
–legendary rapper and member of the pioneering hip-hop group Run-D.M.C.

Lesser Demons

When a dark memory resurfaces, it is like a weight that buckles my knees. To be violated and forced to commit such humiliating acts, I treat these memories as single instances of the horrors I faced. This is how I deal with them; this is always how I view them. My childhood has become compartmentalized in that way, for my own good. Each event is singular, stand alone; something I can deal with. That's how I keep the impact from becoming overwhelming, how I keep the demons at bay.

I can only pray that nothing happens to completely destroy the barriers that I have carefully put in place to separate the dark events of my childhood. Each time I moved, each time I thought my mother was going to come for me, each day worrying about my sisters, the guilty feelings of not being there for my siblings, and each night worrying that I would find my bags packed the next morning with the fear of being sent to yet another home unwillingly...If taken as a whole, these feelings would be too much.

The memories of betrayal at the hands of someone who 'loved' me; all the days I was beaten past the point of tolerance, my body wanting so badly to just quit; and the nights that held much worse in store. The terror of feeling that as a child, my only value was to provide for the voracious appetite and dark desires of a sick and violent adult; I was made to feel unwanted or less than human. If the reality of these individual memories ever falls upon me as a whole, if I am ever forced to deal with the emotions caused by all of those tortures at one time, I will surely break.

That is what is so scary about dealing with mental anguish. If the flood gates are ever allowed to open completely, it can cause you to literally break apart. In writing this book, I was forced to actually piece parts of my childhood abuse together just to describe it. The feelings of shame and humiliation have been almost overwhelming. The recollection of loneliness and abandonment, desertion and betrayal, have seemed too much to handle. This was not truly reliving <u>all</u> of the emotional damage; I was only skimming the surface. This is just getting close enough to provide a description, like viewing a pencil shaded imprint instead of seeing a real grave marker. While the paper version can elicit some pain, it is nothing compared to seeing the name of a loved one on a headstone.

When I hear of adults taking their own lives after years of dealing with the pain of childhood abuse, I am reminded of my own mortality. I again realize there but for the grace of God I go. After beginning this book and intentionally exploring the damage done by the neglect and abandonment in the system, and the pain caused by 'loved ones,' I see just how dangerous these feelings and memories really are.

How does a person with all that inside survive? What is placed on the other end of the scales to provide balance with the chaos of anguish in MY soul? How can I ever be normal or expect to have anything but the heart of a merciless violent sociopath?

Thank God for his strength and salvation.

Introduction

I am not a writer by trade, nor do I feel I am gifted with the ability to draft an awe inspiring manuscript filled with colorful language and creative twists, all while weaving a tapestry of interconnected and sweeping story lines that come together in an exciting and fulfilling denouement! Rather, I am writing from the heart and this book depicts events in my life, plain and simple. It sets out to describe my troubled childhood and how that childhood impacted, and continues to impact, my adult life. What may seem like professional commentary and self-diagnosis is just how I feel and cope with my situation, nothing more. These chapters recall childhood memories germane to the subject matter at hand. It is not my goal to be redundant but to show you specifically how the struggles I have today tie back to my childhood.

This is not written as a search for applause or accolades or pity. I can go an entire lifetime without getting that from anyone. I am reliving and revealing my childhood's painful secrets to illustrate a shameful tragedy in our community, to remind people that abused and neglected children DO exist. They grow up, and many remain alone and directionless, full of angst, apprehension and pain. Children in the care of social services can be easily overlooked, neglected and victimized. This book provides insight into my life as an adult to show the numerous ways the impact of child abuse has not ended at adulthood, and that some of the methods I use to survive the pain become a detriment to having a normal existence.

I want each person who reads this book to understand that I am not unique; that you do not need to graduate law school or join the military to overcome childhood abuse and past suffering. I want you, the reader, to understand that I am no one special. I am not extraordinary because of my survival. I am just a regular person. There is no one experience or person in my adult life that "made all of the difference," and there is no silver bullet to overcoming the legacy of abuse and pain.

So please, do not feel that there are things missing just because I do not go into detail about my first marriage, or my time in the Army, college, or law school. There is not going to be a lot of character development of good people in my life who saved me...because they weren't there. In my experiences, I have learned the human mind often refuses to fully comprehend the true nature of the evil humans can do to one another, especially when victims are young and helpless.

I want my story to shed light on the plight of an abused child. This is not only to bring awareness of the very real impact of child abuse, but to also change people's perspective of abuse victims. In truth, we look just like everyone else. We fit in as best we can and hope no one notices, but in fact you may be working with a victim of abuse, friends with one, or you might have married a victim of child abuse. The haunting pain and quiet suffering are common throughout all the adult survivors I have encountered. Maybe my story will help you understand what most will never talk about.

My message to all victims of suffering, abuse and neglect is this: know that you will not always have to endure the pain you may be going through right now...and that you are not alone! The wounds do eventually heal and the past does not have to dictate the future. Pain does not have to be the dominate emotion in anyone's life and shame does not have to be carried forever. Abuse should not stigmatize you. Rather, victims of abuse should be proud to have survived events as a child that would have broken most adults. In fact, it is that very difficult childhood journey that has prepared each of us for greater things. You have survived the crucible and your very existence speaks wonders of the spirit and inner strength that is inside of each victim of child abuse.

Truly, life is a journey, and the road to success and happiness is a long and arduous one. The only way to reach your goals is to keep moving forward, keep walking. Many times, obstacles are placed in your path, and you must either circumvent or go over them, lest you be stopped in your tracks. The life of a neglected or abused child is a journey over rough and uneven ground. In most cases it is just a long string of hills that must be overcome. These hills can slow you down or even stop you if you tire, give up, or simply lose faith.

Because of the unspoken horrors that many of us victims have faced, we are forced to walk these hills alone, without help or even inspiration. Even while those around are gliding forward on an easier road, we are forced to overcome obstacle after obstacle, hill after hill.

Never forget that those laborious and numerous hills you have climbed demonstrate your strength and resilience. Each of the events you have survived, each obstacle overcome is its own little victory, its own success. If you see yourself in my story, know that I am just a regular person who never gave up, even when everyone gave up on me. Just like you, I was worth saving, even if I was forced to save myself. This is the story of a little boy's journey, my path and these 10,000 hills.

TABLE OF CONTENTS

PART I...1

1. The Special Day...3

2. Birth and Foster Care 13

3. Adoption and Becoming a Wilson.................................... 41

4. Freeburg - Home Life 81

5. High School & Moving Backwards 107

PART II..121

6. The Long Road...123

7. Loving Your Abuser...129

8. Effects of Abuse on Sexuality 145

9. Race and Racism..157

10. Religion 171

11. Relationships 189

12. Family 203

13. Parenthood and the Impact of Abuse 215

14. To Lie..227

PART III..245

15. Social Services 247

16. Abused Children in the Foster System 263

17. Closure..271

18. Message to Survivors 281

19. 10,000 Hills...291

PART I

1. The Special Day

It is finally morning and today is the big day. My excitement has prevented me from getting much sleep, but that is just fine. I have had difficulties getting proper rest for as long as I can remember and this time there is at least a positive reason for my sleepless night. I reach over to my right and find that my wife has already exited the bed. As usual, she gets a jump on the day and the task of corralling my three little hellions into the bathroom to make them at least appear well-behaved and well-mannered. I hear her whisper to them that, "today is a special day for your daddy, so I expect you to be on your best behavior." Then I hear yelps of pain as the hair brushing begins. You'd think they were in there getting poked and pinched, but it's just my three little girls going through the morning ritual of teeth brushing, face washing and hair styling.

My wife is used to me having difficulties sleeping, so she tries to give me an extra few minutes of rest while she gets the children ready. Hearing the tumult going on down the hall in my girls' bathroom is like my second alarm clock. However, this is a daily ritual that seems to stand the test of time, no matter what the weather or season. Always the same.

In fact, if it were not such a special day, I could predict with almost 99% certainty what this day would bring. There is a ritual that is followed: getting our three children up, dressed and fed, driving them to school, rushing to work, and then working through lunch each day so you can leave work on time. The daily ritual continues by picking my girls up from school, taking them to their different events, be it soccer, singing, dance, piano, gymnastics, girl scouts, or play practice.

There might be a different event, but always the same sequence of hustling around, then getting dinner ready so we can at least eat as a family. Sometimes we watch Dora, or SpongeBob, or even Fosters Home for Imaginary Friends; whatever the littlest one decides, since she is the loudest. Then it is bath time, laying out clothing for tomorrow, Bible stories, iPad games, and bedtime for the little ones. Then it is daddy and mommy time - time to make lunches, do a few loads of wash and prepare for tomorrow's court appearances.

Some say this is a rut or monotony, but to me it is paradise. This predictability is like sweet music to my ears after a childhood of never knowing if I was going to eat, where I was going to sleep, or what home I was going to be placed in. Finally, I have a life that I can depend upon. Far from a rut, this repetition is soothing and reassuring. It's dependable.

But, today is different, today is special for me. The kids are not going to school today, they are going to see Daddy make history. Since my three little alarm clocks have gone off in various forms of yelps, squeals, or grumpy morning complaints, I know that it is time for me to rise out of bed and start my day.

I look into the mirror as I wash my face and decide if I need to shave (the answer is NO, much to my wife's chagrin). As always, the mirror shows the details and hidden defects that are not apparent to anyone else. But I see them all. I always see them each time I look into the mirror - the scar over the bridge of my nose, the gash near my hairline, and the crease in the corner of my left eye. These imperfections on my face are nothing compared to the scars left on my soul from a childhood long gone. While the physical wounds have healed, the emotional and mental damage

4

remains. As I do almost every day, I splash that cold water on my face and suck it up. I take all of that self-loathing, shame, doubt, and humiliation and swallow it down. In fact I focus those negative emotions into a finely honed edge that is my passion and drive to never be a victim again, and to remind others that they do not have to be victims either. I will make these scars mean something.

As I pull out my favorite suit and tie, I begin to feel the excitement building. Not that I am a stranger to wearing a suit, since I have been doing so for eight years as an attorney and a division chief in the prosecutor's office. Since it is a "special day," my wife insists that I wear a French cut shirt with cuff links. While not exactly my cup of tea, I put the shirt on and struggle to fit the cuff links into their slots. She is right, as usual, that I should treat this day with more than my normal nonchalance and enjoy the experience. Now, this day does have significance.

Today I get to take my family to our state's capitol in Annapolis, Maryland so they can witness my swearing in as the first African-American to EVER represent Charles County, Maryland in any state office. After 350 plus years, this is indeed an achievement. I want my children to see that their Daddy is making a difference or at least trying, and that there is always a chance to create history.

I walk down the stairs to see my girls at the breakfast table eating their cereal and pop tarts. Again, I cannot help but marvel at their beauty. My wife has done a great job of getting them ready, but they are always pretty little girls. However, today I focus on the fact that my little girls all look just like their daddy. While this may not be amazing to most people, it is something special for me.

Growing up, I honestly cannot recall being around anyone who looked like me. I never shared their family features or even their skin color. Now I have three little brown babies that look just like me, walk like me, and have my high strung temperament. Unless you grew up without a birth family, you may not be able to understand my joy.

After packing the family up and getting them all settled, we start the long ride from Southern Maryland to Annapolis. As I do quite often, I take the time to look at the house as we pull out - our house! It is a modest house by D.C. area standards, but to me it is a mansion. This is a far cry from my childhood. The living and family rooms are larger than the entire house in which I was born. I cannot help but be grateful that I no longer have to sleep with roaches and mice crawling on me, or have to share a couch with family members. Many times, I just sit there looking at my house through the mirror of my car in complete wonderment. However, today I have to be on time, so I simply thank God for my gifts and keep it moving.

As usual, Daddy's car, Daddy's music. The type of music depends on the day or mood I'm in. This day is kind of melancholy yet happy, so I turn on some soft rock. As we drive down the road, the 'Boxer' from Simon and Garfunkel begins playing. It seems like a very fitting song for this day. Looking at me, you might not think that I know that song, but I know it very well. Sadly enough, I knew that song growing up and was able to understand the underlying theme of being alone and beaten, yet never giving up. It is a shame that by 10 years of age, I felt the pain and anguish in every note of that song. By that tender age, I had experienced a lifetime worth of disappointment, rejection, humiliation, and suffering but yet had to keep on going even though I felt so very alone.

I look in the back of the car to see my youngest daughter in complete disagreement with my musical selection. Her constant booing breaks me from my reverie. She is not really a big fan of my music anyway, and she knows if she keeps booing, I will eventually let her pick a song when my choice has concluded. I listen to her voice, so deep for a little girl and see those perfect pursed lips with that furrowed brow. I take a mental snapshot of that moment, of her playful petulance, trying to drown out the music with her booing. Even though I tell her to stop being rude, in my mind I capture the moment, allowing the little things in life to bring me joy. So we listen to my music, but I throw in some songs I know the little one would like. Some consider forcing your children to listen to music from yesteryear a mild form of torture, but I consider it fun and enjoy her chagrin each time an old song comes on. Carpe Diem ... Seize the Day!

I try so hard to ensure that I don't miss a single second of my life, that I appreciate each and every thing, and that I stop to smell the roses, each and every one. Finally I have a life that I can enjoy. I do not have to look to tomorrow, hoping things will get better. I do not have to erase day after day, splintering my memories in order to appear normal. No longer do I have to create a false reality where I am loved and valued. I now have a family that wants me, and loves me, and will not hurt me. I finally trust enough to let myself be loved and put my past behind me. I don't want to miss a minute of it.

The events of that momentous day are kept in my memory bank like so many snapshots: trying to find seats for my family; sneaking them down on the house floor during the ceremony; making sure my children use the proper hand to cover their heart during the pledge; walking the same stairs George Washington used when he came to Annapolis to resign his commission; and raising my hand and being sworn in as a member of the Maryland House of Delegates, an Elected State Official! While my daughters may never truly appreciate the significance of that day, I do, and I appreciate that I now have a family to share that modicum of success with. Because I have intentionally forgotten so much of my past for reasons that will become readily apparent, I try to absorb and lock in as much of my life as it now exists.

What People See

The saying that 'you should not judge a book by its cover' is true.

Many times we look at people who look a certain way and immediately mistrust them. We see teenagers with tattoos and dreads, or skinned heads, homeless people with ragged clothes, and bikers with long grey beards and leather, and we judge them by their appearance. These people are often dismissed as the lunatic fringe, the wastrels, and the bottom of society. We never really get to know these people and may be shocked to discover their fine qualities and pleasant dispositions. Similar judgments are made for many of those that are educated, have high powered jobs, or hold political office. There is an assumption that these people are lucky, born with a silver spoon in their mouths, are the products of a good family, and have no compassion or idea of what suffering really means. These assumptions are usually wrong and short change the individual being judged.

On paper, I appear to have been blessed with every opportunity (which is kind of true), but not without struggle. I have had the pleasure of serving my state and serving my country, both as a prosecutor and a soldier. I have had a chance to protect my country and my community. I did not serve in a hands-off role; I was an enlisted soldier and a line attorney. In both cases, I served at the pleasure of my commander or my elected official. Neither was a job for glory or money, they were both jobs of public service, jobs of sacrifice and dedication to justice. Today, I am fortunate to be a person in a position to help others. I did not run for office because I thought I deserved to be elevated above people, far from it. Becoming a state delegate means that I am duty bound to be a public servant, accountable to my constituents – not for just the title of elected official, but the opportunity to serve and make a difference.

As a prosecutor, I rose to the level of division chief. I actually became chief of a prosecutorial unit I created. I wrote grants and employed dozens of people in the office of the state's attorney, while building my unit. I did this with the idea that you cannot merely lock people away to solve crimes. Citizens have to be involved in the criminal process to protect communities. Instead of just trying cases, our team also attended community meetings and acted as grassroots level problem solvers assisting citizens in their protection. One of my murder trials was turned into a televised one-hour documentary, showcasing my success and community work.

As an elected official, I serve on several committees and sit on a multitude of boards for non-profit organizations. I work with both the legislative and judicial branch to create a safe environment for foster children. I work with churches around the region to identify families in need and help those that remain homeless. I work on behalf of victims of crimes to ensure that they receive justice and their day in court.

As an experienced trial attorney, I now own my own budding law practice. People see a young black attorney who appears to be well-spoken, intelligent, and confident (some would say cocky). I drive a nice car and have a nice house. I wear a suit and tie almost every day and control my own schedule.

I have a wondrous family with three little girls and a beautiful wife. My wife is a corporate owner who is a great role model for our children. She takes time out to cook (occasionally) and care for the girls, including doing homework, extra-curricular activities and guiding them as only a mother can.

Reality

By appearances, many people just assume that I came from good family stock or that I was just gifted and never really suffered and struggled in life. Since I have wavy hair and am light-skinned, people also assume that racism never really affected me, that I was always the exception to the stereotype. I may come off as confident and self-assured because I laugh out loud and do not seem to care what others think of me. None of these things are even close to who I really am or what I have been through. What you see is only a part of me. Like many of the children in our community, I am so much more than I appear.

Like many foster youth and children who have suffered egregious and humiliating abuse at the hands of those who were entrusted to care for them, my life was spent struggling just to get to normal. When you are let down by a system or a person who is supposed to take care of you, value you, and protect you, you struggle just to be viewed as average. The fact of the matter is children that struggle through a state foster system and children that have suffered abuse are starting out in a hole. Most of us spend our entire lives just trying to dig our way out, many of us never make it, and some of us never try. When you start life out with normal being a goal, happiness and success seem unattainable.

The pain of a lifetime of neglect and abuse doesn't go away simply because of time. Growing up and escaping a horrible childhood does not erase what occurred. However, society does expect for you to simply put your past behind you and move forward. This is not so easy. Once you have suffered these unimaginable horrors it is hard to find a reason to move on or to find any value in yourself. Without value, there is little hope that your life will get better; in fact many don't even think they deserve a good life...or even an average life.

Going through life with this dark secret of abuse has been difficult, to say the least. This is a burden I bear alone, yet share with thousands upon thousands of children and adults in our country. The reminders of my childhood are everywhere and show up when I least expect them to. In fact, these are more than reminders - they are problems and neurosis I have inherited from my childhood. As such, there is a constant underlying thought that no matter how much I achieve or how far I have come, I do not deserve to be happy and I can lose everything in a moment. Just to know that at any time, some part of my past can manifest itself in an unexpected manner, take me off guard, and disrupt everything I have tried to build is frightening. To lower my defenses and allow myself to be happy, instead of keeping my guard up and waiting for the other foot to fall, makes me nervous. And I know I am not alone.

10,000 Hills

2. Birth and Foster Care

Birth Family – Qualifier

I am the oldest of 17 children by the same mother, born in Missouri. This much I know as fact. But before I go on, I must clarify how this story will be presented. For me, one of the many problems of being put up for adoption is that there was very little record of my existence. I mean, it is obvious that I was born; however, the details were sketchy at best. Couple that with relying on childhood memories and the confusing and contradictory input from relatives I met much later. The end result was a somewhat murky tale of my birth and early childhood. I rely on the facts as I understood them. Many of these facts were told when I was a child, while others were my actual memories of events that have remained etched into my brain. The human mind will often fill in the blanks to make the story complete and understandable, but this is the truth to the best of my knowledge.

I know that when you are a child, people tell you things that are not exactly true. Sometimes it is for your benefit, like the tooth fairy and Santa Claus. Other times it is for your protection, like your father just hasn't settled down yet. However, every child is building his world of truths from the knowledge imparted by those he loves and trusts. As such, many things that may not be true are taken to heart and believed. They become that child's reality. When a child is then put up for adoption, many of his most vivid memories may be made up of lies he was told. This adds a layer of difficulty in my attempts to be truthful and factual. In trying to recall the events of my early childhood, I oftentimes run into facts I have believed my entire life, but are in direct contradiction with one another. As I relate the events, I will try to keep to the facts that are most realistic and proven.

Mother

The events leading up to and including my birth are clouded in mystery. I went through life believing one thing, only to find that another was true. In many cases, there were just multiple and differing points of view for the same event. As clear as I understand it, I was born around the end of 1971 or early 1972 (since I do not have access to a birth certificate, even this is vague). I was born to Mary Wilson, who was the middle child of 14 children. While I am not sure in which town my mother lived during the time surrounding my birth, I do know it was in the foothills of the Ozark Mountains in the middle of Missouri.

I was told many years later that my mother was a troubled teen and had some developmental disorders. She could not talk without moving her hands. When she used her right hand, her left hand would mimic that movement. She also had a habit of disappearing for long periods of time without contacting her family. She would eventually come back home with no excuses or explanation as to where she had been.

I was Mary's first born child. She was a teenager when she became pregnant with me. By all accounts my mother was indeed married at the time. She was a white teenager married to an older white man. This was apparently not that uncommon in the Midwest at that time. I was told she may have also been the victim of sexual abuse from one of her trusted caretakers in her childhood. Apparently, she had a difficult start in life and marriage was not solving any of her problems. Either way, the fact is that I am part African-American, not a product of two white folks. The only information I was ever able to find about my birth father was from my grandmother who told me that Mary liked "coloreds and cops." I'm guessing my birth father was a black cop? Later conversations with my aunts and uncles did little to clear this mystery up. Either way, one thing is certain; I was not the biological son of Mary's husband. My mother stepped out.

I grew up believing the story of my birth that was told to me by social service workers. I was told that my mother hid her pregnancy from her husband and her family. She eventually disappeared when she was nearing the time of giving birth to me. At that point, she hid in a ragged shack down the road from my grandmother's house until she gave birth. It was described like she was trying to keep a secret puppy, hiding me away and trying to feed me without anyone knowing. While she tried to keep me safe and fed, it became apparent that she could not do so without help. I became deathly ill and refused to take in any food or breast milk. She then contacted one of her sisters and they took me into town to a hospital. It was at that point that her husband was made aware that she was ever even pregnant. This was the version I grew up with.

Years later, I was told by my grandmother that while my mother did hide her pregnancy, I was born in a hospital somewhere. She had gone to the hospital to give birth to me, and my grandmother was told once I was born. My mother suffered from blood loss or some sickness from childbirth, so I was actually released from the hospital before she was. Since she was married, her husband was notified to pick me up from the hospital. He took me back to my grandmother's house and left me on her front porch. My grandma related that there was quite a stir at the hospital when her husband repeatedly denied that I was the right baby. Somehow I was taken from the hospital before I had a legal name assigned to me or a real birth certificate. (When my grandmother told me this story several of my aunts just looked at me and shook their heads, letting me know that it wasn't that straight forward).

Whether she sneaked off to give birth and hid me in a shack, or sneaked off to have me in a hospital is irrelevant. The point is that I was obviously unplanned. I am sure my mother did not want to have a constant reminder of her unfaithful acts. I am sure her entire family was in complete shock at her bringing home a black baby. So, I started life as an unwanted product of an adulterous affair.

Early Childhood

I don't remember much about my birth (I was awful young then). So I will fast forward to my earliest memories. Early memories begin at my grandmother's house. As I already mentioned, my grandmother lived in the country backwoods. Her home was not much more than a one bedroom shack that was elevated off the ground to prevent flooding. There was a small kitchen right off the living room and a single wood burning stove to heat the entire house. This is where 14 children were raised, my mother included. Her property was miles from any other houses or businesses. This meant that my mother and her family lived mainly off the land, gardening, farming, and raising farm animals and livestock. Despite my grandmother's limited means, it was a family setting surrounded by her 14 children.

By the time I was around four years old, I had three sisters - Heather, Holly, and Candy Lynn. We were separated by approximately nine to 12 months. My three sisters were all the product of her first marriage. Yes, this is the same husband that she had when she gave birth to me. It was the same white man that she cheated on and never told that she was pregnant. Apparently he was forgiving. However, by the time that I was old enough to remember, he was out of the picture. He finally left her. She was alone with four children and no true means of supporting any of us.

At some point, my mother moved to Rolla, Missouri to raise her family. This was considered the city, although it was not much more than a small town back then. The little house she found was somewhat decrepit and run down. However, it was near more resources than our grandmother's house. There were at least stores nearby, and churches that would give out food and clothing to families in need. My mother was finally no longer surrounded by her family. Whatever she was running from, she was finally free to live by herself.

From my earliest memories I was hungry, always hungry…and always dirty. While my mother finally had her own place, she did not keep it clean, nor did she keep us fed. We were very poor. I also remember that my mother was always pregnant. Every memory, every picture that I have of her, she is pregnant or holding an infant.

Our level of poverty was awful. Even as small children we would sometimes have to root through trash in the neighborhood to find edible food. We would go long periods without eating. Being the oldest, I was the last to eat. My mother did receive some kind of government assistance, but that wasn't enough. I found out much later that she was somewhat proud and would often refuse government help, unless she was absolutely unable to get food elsewhere. Even when we did eat, it was usually unhealthy filler food. These cheap foods usually contain the least amount of nutrients for healthy development.

We slowly became dependent upon the church and neighbors for food. In fact, they were the main reason that we survived. It was the kindness of strangers that allowed us to eat when my mom was gone. Different people would come by the house and leave food on the porch. Sometimes it was even cooked. They would call in through the door to let me know that they were going to leave it for me. They knew that I would not open the door until they were gone, but they would leave it anyway.

My mother also had a boyfriend or two while I lived with her. One of her boyfriends, Kenneth, worked at Sambo's. That was the time when we were able to eat at least one good meal a day. No matter what time he would get off work, we would all wake up and have a meal of uneaten leftovers that he was able to take out of the restaurant. Many nights I would lay in bed with my stomach hurting from hunger just hoping that Kenneth would be coming in with food. I stayed awake many nights just hoping, because he did not come home that often.

The house we lived in was a wreck, filth from floor to ceiling. Instead of cleaning up the place, there were just paths through the trash to walk between the rooms. We learned from an early age to deal with roaches, rats and mice. I remember Heather would sometimes wake up screaming in her bed because she felt a bug on her. I would let her come and sleep on the couch with me and tried to stay awake all night just to protect her from these little bugs.

The sink was always dirty and filled with dirty dishes…and those dishes were filled with roaches. There were dirty diapers everywhere. We were always covered in dirt and usually running around in diapers or underwear. As a little boy, I did not actually know we were living in deplorable conditions; it was really the only life I knew. Sure it was different than Grandma's, but it was just how we lived. But, there was more.

When my mother was around, she was very loving and affectionate, but she also slept a lot. She would sleep all day long on the couch used as my bed. Oftentimes she would lay on that couch naked and asleep. When my sisters would cry for food or because they needed to be changed, it would fall upon me to help them. She would be in such a stupor that she would not even stir while they screamed and cried. I hated to hear my sisters cry. Not because it got on my nerves, but because I knew they were not happy or that they were in pain. I quickly learned to change diapers and feed little ones while I was still wearing diapers myself.

Caring for my sisters also meant cooking for them. Now, cooking is a strong word. All I could do was prepare Gerber oatmeal, crackers, or hotdogs. (Yes I know that you cannot give an infant a hotdog, but I was only four years old at the time). I would run the hot water from the tap and mix it with the oatmeal from that square green box. To this day, I still get nauseous from the smell of that stuff! We would eat raw bacon from the refrigerator, or any kind of meat I could get my hands on. Those dishes in the sink were there because my sisters and I had to learn to feed ourselves. All the while, my mother would be on the couch sleeping, when she was at home.

Many times she was not home. Usually, she was gone during the night, while we were asleep, leaving us alone in that house. The problem was that infants and small children wake up all through the night. I would have to get off the couch to console one of my sisters who would wake up scared or just hungry. All I could do was give them what we had in the house to eat, which wasn't much. So, many nights they would just cry in my arms until they were too tired to cry, and then they would finally fall asleep. I would hold onto them until morning, even if we all slept on the couch together.

While my mother would leave on many nights, other nights she would throw "parties" in the house and in the back yard. As I got older, I remember a constant stream of strangers coming into the house when my mother was around. I have several memories of my mother "dancing" in a see-through dress with a group of men and women. I remember some of the women and men were naked or in their underwear. As a child, I just thought she was dancing. As an adult, I realize the mounds of people my mother would 'dance' and 'wrestle' with were not just there to party.

My mother would not always know where her friends were. Many times they would leave the backyard and come into the house to wake us up. Mostly it was to play with us or have a look at us. Other times it was for more nefarious reasons. She never seemed to know or care what happened to us while these parties would go on. The mornings after would find a large number of men and women naked and asleep in my mom's bed and around the house. We would watch them, one by one, wake up and stumble out of the house until there were only us kids left. Sometimes, my mother would stumble out with them.

Even with all of this, I always had fond memories of my mother. My love for her was unconditional. The filth we lived in was merely a byproduct of being poor and her being a teenage mother. I always remembered my mother as a beautiful woman. Her hair was kind of unkempt and stringy, but that was okay. Her teeth were missing or rotted out, but that just meant she had a different look. She was always pregnant, but that was because she was making more sisters for me. A child's reality is seldom based in truth, and often based in emotion. And, I loved my mom. Her every flaw was just another part of her that I loved. But, the truth was, she was a drug addict and she chose her addiction over her family.

Strangers

My mom would leave us in the house with complete strangers. These were supposedly my mother's friends, but I did not know them. They always acted really odd, with slurred speech that I could not understand. These people would not always be friendly to me and my sisters. I remember having a pet kitten I used to play with. I watched one of her "friends" pull out a pocket knife and throw that knife at my kitten while I was petting it. The knife stuck the kitten right in the middle of its back. I watched that kitten run off with the pocket knife sticking out of its back until its back legs gave out. It just laid there in the middle of the backyard crying out.

My mother and her friend were just standing there laughing and laughing. That poor kitten did not die immediately, and we got to hear it cry out in our backyard for what seemed like hours. I could not stop crying, and I rarely cried at all. My mother could not understand why I was so upset. It was like she didn't even know what happened, even though she was standing right there when it was happening. Even worse, she laughed along with the man who threw the knife. I guess she was so out of it, she could not see how wrong it was. Not only did I witness this man kill my pet, but he was allowed to stay the night in our house. I did not understand why my mother laughed while I was crying so intensely. Why she still let that man stay with us.

I saw another man "changing" my sister Heather. She was screaming so loud that I pulled her out from under him and just hid in the closet with my hand over her mouth to stop her crying. I also remember waking up to a complete stranger sitting on the couch doing something to his penis, later I understood that he was masturbating. I woke up to witness this odd behavior. While he did not touch or harm me in anyway, it was still a very confusing moment.

Other times, my mother's friends would put me and Heather together in sexual positions with our clothes off and tell us to "move like this" while laughing and joking. It seemed that these people got a kick out of making me and my sister perform for them. While they never harmed me, I am not so sure what happened to my sisters. They just seemed to want to be entertained. I realized that there was one thing I could do to keep these strangers from messing with me and my sisters. My mother loved what would now be considered classic country music. She always asked me to sing for her friends when they were acting normal. So I figured if I sang these folk songs to her friends when they would come around my sisters, they would stop doing these things to us. I would just sing song after song, while they laughed or just sang along. I would do this during the middle of the night for hours on end for their entertainment...to protect us. This did not always work, but it worked enough for me to remember doing it.

We were poor, dirty and hungry, but we had each other. When Mom was sober and present, we had her attention. She would try to play with us. She would cook us little eggs made of cooked sugar. We would play hide and seek in a house full of trash. We would sit outside in the sun and let chunks of chocolate (Chunky's) melt in our hands, and then we would lick the chocolate off our fingers. I remember how much she loved honey and wanted to be a beekeeper. She even dressed me in her beekeeper outfit. We would listen to country music, Tammy Wynette, Don Williams, Elvis, Patsy Cline, and even some of the folk music of the day such as Peter Paul and Mary, or Simon and Garfunkel.

She loved to sing and loved me to sing with her. She was so proud of me when I knew the lyrics to a song she liked. She would sing along with me to songs I can't even remember now (although the song would come on the radio and I would know each and every line). We watched television together, as a family. Hee Haw was one of her favorite shows. I remember crying with her when the television program was interrupted by the death of Elvis Presley. When she was awake and sober, our lives were great. We were poor and sometimes hungry, but we were loved.

At other times, my mother would act like a totally different person. She would stumble and move erratically. Her speech was slurred to the point where I could not understand her, but, she would still ask me to sing for her. As time moved on she began to ask for much more. She would lay on my couch naked and asked me to sit there between her legs. She would tell me that I was her little man and that she loved me so much. She would ask me to touch her or put things inside of her. These memories were never abusive in nature and she was never violent or mean. Her affection was different from normal. As a child, I never knew why she would go through these drastic changes.

Now, it's plain to see as an adult that my mother was a drug addict. When I look back at her pictures, it is obvious. In reflecting on her actions, it is obvious. Although I cannot remember ever seeing her consume any drugs, the lifestyle she led was the life of a drug addict. The drastic changes in her personality, the inappropriate contacts she would have with me when she was in that state and the fact that she would let other people come into contact with her children who meant us no good made it apparent. She could have been a loving and giving parent, but her choices made her a neglectful and poor excuse for a mother.

The good times seemed to come less and less. My mother began to disappear for days at a time, leaving us alone. Sometimes the neighbors would call social services when they noticed we were alone. We had each been removed from the house several times and placed in temporary homes because of my mom's absences. We learned to be very quiet when mom was gone and not attract any attention. There were times when we were so hungry I would have to go and ask neighbors for food because my sisters could not stop crying due to their hunger, even though this meant we would be taken again.

My mom started moving around more often. She would take us on trips to California and Arkansas to avoid social service visits. We would travel in the camper of a pickup truck with my mother and her friends. We would stay away for weeks, only to come back to that dirty house. She was living this gypsy/commune lifestyle and subjecting her children to this unbalanced and ever-changing existence. It was not enough that we were hungry, neglected and left on our own. We were now being moved around from place to place, sleeping in the back of a pickup truck with my mother and her addicted friends. She seemed more out of it than ever and her friends were being more and more inappropriate.

Her drug use was getting worse and the impact on her children was becoming even more apparent. We were becoming malnourished from a constant lack of healthy food. My mother was leaving us with strangers more and more. When she was around she was always naked and always asleep. I tried to fulfill my role as the "man" of the house, protecting and feeding my sisters, even while we were on the road.

Eventually we came back to the house in Rolla. Since things were getting worse, social services was becoming more of a regular fixture in our lives. We had been removed from the house previously, but now we seemed to have a dedicated social worker who was trying to fix our family. However, my mother would not or could not fix her issues. The filth we were living in was getting worse. She never even tried to clean up anymore. Her boyfriends moved in, but that did not last long. She continued to have strangers over to the house, some for the night, and others for a few days. She would still leave us alone, even though she knew social services was watching. It seemed as if the state was giving her plenty of chances, but she just could not quit her habit.

The loving and caring side of my mother was disappearing. She was coming home less and less. Her actions were becoming increasingly more erratic when she was home. We now saw a woman who was unkempt and disheveled most of the time. She was sleeping more and more, passed out and naked on the couch that I used as a bed. She was such a mess, stumbling around the house, slurring her words, totally out of it.

I didn't even know my mother's drug of choice. I remember the house having beer cans and empty liquor bottles around. I remember seeing people drinking in the house and in the backyard, but I know it was more than just liquor. Whatever she was doing would drastically change her personality. It would make her sleep so hard that she could not even hear her children crying at night. It made her forget to feed us. It made her forget to change my sisters' diapers. It made her forget us.

I was informed much later that my mother may also have been the victim of sexual abuse as a child. I guess she was trying to find ways to hide the pain. Relationships didn't work; her husband and boyfriends kept leaving. Creating a family and having the unconditional love of her children did not numb the pain she was dealing with. Like so many others, she may have turned to alcohol and drugs to cope. But, like so many others, self-medication solved nothing and only created more problems. Instead of dealing with the pain of her childhood, she now also had to deal with the pain of her children going without, the pain of slowly losing her children.

The Last Day/First Night

While some of my memories were clouded due to my age, I can still vividly recall the last moments I spent with my mother. It was just me and her. She was back to her old loving self for the first time in a long while. My sisters were off visiting my grandmother, so we had time to just sit around watching television and singing our favorite songs. We even ate sandwiches and potato chips together. It was such a great day. I had mom all to myself. I did not have to take care of my sisters. I had no responsibilities and no stress for once. I wasn't hungry or worried about my mother being gone or my sisters being scared. I had not seen my mom being so attentive in a long while. I was the center of her world again.

As it began to get dark, my mother stood me up from the couch. She went to my sisters' room and grabbed my stuffed dog that Kenneth had brought from Sambo's some time ago. I did not really understand what was going on. I thought we were going somewhere together. It had been a long time since we went anywhere together. I could not figure out why we needed my puppy. I do remember realizing that she became very sad when she approached me with my stuffed animal.

She grabbed my hand and walked me toward the door, holding my stuffed puppy close to her chest with the other arm. When we got to the door she opened it and then knelt down in the threshold. She said "buddy, it is time for you to be a man. I love you very much." Then she gave me my stuffed animal, hugged me, and gave me a kiss. Then we walked out onto the porch. I felt her let go of my hand, so I turned around and she was gone. The door was closed. She had gone back inside without me. I went to the door and banged and banged on it. I was crying so hard for her to let me back in. I did not know what was happening or what I had done wrong. We had had such a good day together! But, she did not open the door. I was barely five years old.

Moments (or what could have been hours) later a Social Services worker, Martha, pulled up in her truck and put me in the front seat. I was still crying when we drove away. I was trying to keep that door in sight to see if my mother was going to open it, to see if she was going to come for me. She never did. That was the last day I ever saw my mother.

The next evening, I was taken to a building where my sisters were already waiting. My grandmother was there with them. I still did not know what was going on. Where was mom? We had been removed from her before, but this seemed different. I remember sitting in that wood paneled room holding Holly and Candy in my arms, with Heather sitting at my side. My grandmother left without saying goodbye. We were huddled together, we were so scared. I remember just sitting there numb, feeling that things were going bad. I don't remember being told anything else that night, but I do remember that my sisters and I were separated. This was the first night in my memory that my sisters weren't with me, that I wasn't there to protect them.

Apparently, we were considered at-risk children. We had dirt crusted under our nails, filthy matted hair and threadbare clothes. We were all underweight and suffering from various stages of malnutrition. Because I always let my sisters eat first, I was in the worst shape. We were sickly, coughing and weak. I would suffer from bouts of pneumonia for years to come. The state thought we were all fetal alcohol babies. As a result, we were placed in facilities to determine our mental deficiencies and needs. As it turned out, only Heather and Holly were fetal alcohol babies; Candy and I were 'normal.'

I was placed in a facility with other boys my age and given a bed. I don't remember being able to fall asleep at all. I was so worried about my sisters. I still did not know what was happening. The next day, Martha picked me up and told me we were going to visit my Grandma. Now things were making some sense. We were being taken until mom could get herself back together again. Martha asked me if I wanted to have my sisters come with me. Of course I wanted to see them again! However, Heather was still wetting the bed, and I knew that Grandma would spank her with a flyswatter if she peed on herself.

I told Martha that I didn't want Heather to get a spanking, so I went to visit Grandma alone. It was my last opportunity to ever see my sisters again, and I missed it. I was just trying to protect my sister! I didn't know we were going to be apart forever. I didn't know we were going to be separated and taken to other cities. I was just trying to be a good big brother.

Into The Foster System

I soon found out that a child going through the system has no control over his or her life. They have no input, no voice, and no idea of what will happen next. I know children born into their biological home have no input or idea of what their future will bring, but it is not the same thing. Those children at least have faith in their parents, unconditional love. They are not just a number at their home, they are important. Many times they are the single focus for their parents' existence.

I had the added burden of knowing that I had a family and being totally separated from them. My mother had 13 brothers and sisters, many of whom were of age to care for children. However, I was never placed with any of my relatives. My grandmother was available, as were the rest of my family, but I was not lucky enough to have them in my life, to have some tie to my past. In hindsight, I realize my mother's family was so impoverished that they would not qualify to have foster children. I now understand there would have been little benefit in placing me right back into poverty, especially when I was physically sick and suffering from malnutrition. As a child, I did not know why my grandmother or my aunts and uncles would let me be taken away.

Why didn't they try to place the four of us together? It makes sense now that Candy and Holly would have fared better as a single adoption. After all, everyone wanted a white baby girl, especially one that was under two years of age, who did not have any true memories of their birth family, and who could be integrated into another family without disrupting that child's life. Many infants that were adopted never found out that they were not born into the family. It was much simpler for the child and the parent. However, Heather and I were old enough to remember our birth families, old enough to remember each other. I still don't understand why they did not try to keep any of us together. So, that fateful night was the last night I ever saw my sisters.

Being a black child in need of a home in the middle of Missouri was a difficult sell indeed! This was the early 70's and black boys were definitely not in demand. In fact, I worked real hard on keeping my hair straight and sounding as proper (or white) as possible. I remember being in a group or boys home and being asked to make a book about my life. I was given green cardboard paper to make this book. I had two pictures of my mother and a few pictures of my sisters and family. Since I had no picture of my father, I was told to cut out a picture of a black man from a magazine and tell people that was my dad. This was a bit confusing, but I did as I was told. I told the other boys this was my dad. Just like them, I had a mom and a dad. That was a lie, and not the first one I had to tell to try to fit in, to try to be normal.

I cannot recall how long I was at this first facility or how old I was, but it seemed like a long time. I guess it was a boy's facility as it had a mix of boys of all ages. Although I was the only black kid, there were children of all sizes and appearances there (I remember the other boys made up a song about me being the "little black bird"). While some of the younger boys were busy trying to look good and get placed, others were angry and could not be successfully placed in foster care. Some of these children were put up for adoption because they had learning disabilities or behavioral problems. No matter how normal they looked, the anger and pain they felt from being abandoned was too much. Many of these boys knew they had families and would not be happy until they were returned to their families.

I missed my mother, but I knew this time was not like the times before. Since I was not going to see my mom or my Grandma, I just hoped someone would see fit to take me in. Maybe, if I was lucky, I would again be reunited with my sisters. If they found a home, maybe they would come for me. That never happened.

Eventually, I was placed in my first foster home (actually, it was my fourth or fifth foster family, having been removed several times before when I was still with my mother). I cannot remember the name of this family, or what these people looked like. I know there were other foster kids in this home. I know it only lasted a few days, maybe a week. I don't know the reason I was sent away, but I know it was not a good fit. I just remember a white family that was very religious. We prayed all of the time. But, for the life of me, I cannot remember anything else, not even a face. I just remember the disappointment of being sent away. There was no warning, no time to even ask why. I was just removed. From that point, I was taken back to a different facility, to sit and wait for another family to take me in.

I was soon taken in again by another family, the 'Bombers.' This family, I do remember. They lived on a large farm. There were cattle and corn. This was another white Christian family (apparently not uncommon in the Midwest) with one little blonde headed boy. He was about a year younger than I was. I remember he and I got along very well, but there was a definite difference in treatment. I guess I should not have expected to be treated as a son right off the bat, but I was young and trying to find acceptance, and still had hope beyond hope to recreate the family I lost and missed so much.

I remember the time with the Bombers was very stressful. Although, I did not know it at the time, they were losing their farm. Maybe they thought the extra money from taking in a foster child would help them get by. Maybe they really did want another child, but it felt more like a burden than a blessing. I remember the mother crying in the kitchen and pulling her hair out. I mean literally pulling her hair out. I could hear the husband and wife arguing at night while we were supposed to be asleep. Arguing about me, about how much it cost to feed me, about how difficult it was to care for me and keep the farm running.

The Bombers did give me my first Christmas, so to speak. When I lived with my mother, I never remembered having a Christmas. I didn't even know what Christmas was. I had never decorated or even seen a proper Christmas tree. We just didn't have the money. It just wasn't something that was brought to my attention. Now I was hearing about this wondrous event. There was the birth of Christ, but also there were presents... for me! I could not even imagine such a day - Santa Clause, elves, dinner and singing. It was just too much to believe. As the day came closer, I could see that it was true. We were singing songs at school. People were telling stories about Santa and the reindeer. This was going to be a dream come true.

Of course I was still somewhat sickly. My body was still suffering from malnutrition. I was still well under my proper body weight and I was still getting colds more and more as the weather got colder. I remember seeing the stockings, and one had my name on it the morning of Christmas Eve. It was finally happening. I was so excited, so nervous, so dizzy. I passed out on Christmas Eve. I woke up days later in the hospital with pneumonia. In fact, I had to stay there for several weeks until my lungs cleared up, sleeping in an oxygen tent. I had slept right through my first Christmas.

After I returned home, I remember sneaking down the steps to see if the Bombers were arguing about me, to see if they were discussing whether or not they would keep me. Anyone who has spent time in the foster care system or has been put up for adoption remembers that sneak. We have all sneaked around the house at night trying to hear what the adults were talking about; trying to figure out if they were talking about you; trying to figure out if they were talking about keeping you or sending you away.

This was always my greatest fear as a foster child; not knowing what was going to come next, not knowing if I should even want to stay at the home. I was trying to figure out if I should continue to allow my feelings for that family to grow, and trying to get some hint about what my future held and where I would be sleeping tomorrow. Every time I heard any of my foster parents talking, I worried that it was about me. I wanted to know what they thought about me. I just wanted to know what was coming. Even if the answer was to send me away, I just wanted to know!

I must have been in pre-k or kindergarten at this point. Needless to say, I wasn't a good student. An average child needs a few things in order to be successful: a structured life, dependable environment and faith in himself. I had none of these. It's not that the Bombers were unstructured, far from it. They were rigid about time management and proper etiquette. As farmers, they were meticulous about how we spent our time. There was playtime, but there were also chores and Bible study. We had to ask to be excused before leaving the dinner table. We had to read the Bible before going to bed. It was very organized. However, it still wasn't a dependable existence because I was in constant fear of being sent away again. There was nothing being done to support any sense of self-esteem or faith in myself.

I was taking phonics in school and had no desire to learn how to read. I didn't want to do any schoolwork! The Bombers were very attentive to any homework we had, so I had to remedy that. I came up with a genius idea on the bus ride home from school one day. If I did not have any books, how could I have any schoolwork? Childhood genius. Following that line of reasoning, I grabbed the first opportunity I could to dispose of the cause of my woes and lost playtime. I threw my schoolbooks out of the window as soon as the bus left the house that morning. I told my teacher I could not do any work because I no longer possessed the means to perform...I had no books! Success.

I remember the walk up to the house, opening the door and finding my meager belongings packed and stacked up against the door. Apparently throwing my books away was not the best idea. In hindsight it was obvious that they had known for a few weeks that it was going to be my last day. It was devastating to me. I cried and begged them to forgive me. I promised to pay for the books and never skip out on my homework again. I am sure they were a little confused at some of the statements, but they still said their goodbyes. A social worker came to pick me up and take me away again.

I quickly learned to deal with my emotions as a little boy. I was dealing with a great deal at a young age. Imagine being ripped from everything you are familiar with - not only your mother and father, but your siblings, your aunts, your uncles, grandparents and friends. Even more, the fact that you were being removed from everything that is familiar to you. You no longer had your room or your bed, your kitchen, your house, or your neighborhood. When you are a child, these things are yours. Of course a child cannot buy them, but a child does have a possessory interest in them.

Today, I watch my four-year old walk around my house with impunity. Her dirty little handprints are in every room of the house, even in rooms she is not allowed. She opens the fridge to get a drink, goes into the pantry to get a snack, and changes the channel on the TV when she wants to watch SpongeBob. She is never concerned that she will be offending someone or touching something that is not hers. In her mind, it is all hers, because this is her home and she knows she belongs there. In fact, she knows all that we have is here for her as well. Home is not just a place; it is a comfortable state of mind, with a feeling of safety.

When a foster child has to share a room with another child, it's not really sharing. When I was with the Bomber's, I slept in a bunk bed over their son. It was never *my* room. The toys were never *my* toys. Oftentimes the son even resented the fact that he had to share with me at all.

"What do you do at night when you are hungry?" This seems like a general question with an easy answer to most people. Last night my oldest daughter was downstairs eating goldfish and drinking milk at midnight. She didn't even think to wake me up to let me know she was hungry. But, when I was in foster care I never felt comfortable enough to even go to the fridge, more or less go to the fridge in the middle of the night without permission. The Bomber's, like some other foster families, kept their fridge out of bounds. No, I was never starved. It was, however, very clear that the Bomber's house was not my house.

I was dealing with the constant anxiety of not being good enough and being moved. Each time I would get used to a new environment or get to know the people around me, I was moved. I had to appear to be a good child and try to be part of any family I was placed in, yet realized that I was not part of that family. I had to be prepared for any disappointment, yet always put my best foot forward and put on a good show. I had to learn to hide what I was really feeling inside if I wanted anyone to want me.

The Apsher's

I vividly remember the day I showed up at my next foster home. It was a warm sunny day. The social worker was driving me to my next home.

In my heart I hoped it would be my last home. I just wanted to stay in one place, to have a place I could call home. We drove down this long driveway that split a large meadow. There were horses and ponies in the pasture. It was scenic and beautiful. We drove across a small bridge to a large country house with a circle driveway surrounded by the woods. I could not believe how big and beautiful this house was. As we pulled around the circle, the family started coming from the woods.

They had three girls, Bethany, Tammy and Ladonna. It had just rained earlier, so the family was out picking mushrooms. I got out of the car and grabbed my belongings. They took me inside the house and showed me to my room…for the first time in my life I had my own room. Then, we all went back outside and the daughters took me back out to hunt for mushrooms.

We were ushered back some hours later to the dinner call with our bags full of mushrooms. Jodie Apsher, the mother, was calling out that it was dinner time. We came to the table and there was a place setting for me. Each plate had vitamins on it, including mine. We had lemonade and country fried steak with potatoes. It was wonderful. I had only been there for a few hours, but felt at home for the first time since leaving my mother's side.

Alvin Apsher was a Chemist for the federal government. Jodie was a stay-at-home mother. They were a conservative Christian family in word and in deed. The house was not ostentatious, but it was nice. There was an upright piano in the living room where Jodie would play church music from time to time. The daughters were so friendly and loving right away. They asked me questions and told me about themselves and what they liked. They all seemed so excited to have me there. Finally, I did not feel like I was being a burden or that I didn't matter. I had value and people actually cared about me. I thought I would never again be a part of a family, but maybe I was wrong.

34

Apparently, social services made a point to tell the Apsher's that I never had a chance to be a child, that I had never had a chance to have fun. They were told I had been suffering from the guilt of not being able to care for my sisters and that I needed an opportunity to be care free and just be a normal child. The Apsher's gave me some of my childhood back. It seemed as if every day was eventful and full of fun. They had a chicken coop in the back and taught me how to feed the chickens and gather the eggs. I learned how to pick string beans from the garden in the front of the house. We grew all sorts of vegetables that were eaten fresh. They would take me on trips to the vineyard to pick grapes for grape preserves. Sometimes it was strawberry picking, other times it was apple picking. We were always doing something fun and productive.

I couldn't wait to get home from school each day to see what was in store. I loved running from the bus stop, through the trailer park and down the hill to see our house. They got me my first bike, although I remember it was definitely a girl's bike complete with the banana seat and a basket, but I was thrilled just to have it. We even got a baby pig for a pet. We raised that pig until it was big enough to ride. In true mid-western Fashion, that pig "ran away" one day and we had bacon, sausage and pork chops to last us for a year.

Mr. Apsher would hunt deer and we would eat deer meat. Sometimes he would bring home squirrel or rabbits and we would eat those too. We would eat! Not gluttonous, but we always had food, always had fresh food and meat. Not that they could not afford to buy groceries, they just wanted us to be healthy and eat the best things.

The Apsher's were also very religious. We prayed at every meal and Jodie or Alvin would always come into my room at night to pray with me. Sunday's were the Lord's Day, the entire day. We would go to church in the morning, have lunch at church and then go to church again until it was time for supper. There were Sunday school and Bible readings. We would even read the Bible together at home. We ate all meals as a family, each person sitting at the table in their spot. Everything was done as a family, always.

I was included on every family outing, taken to visit all of their relatives, and treated just like their three daughters. They had a nephew named Byron who became my best friend. We were the same age and bonded quickly. The house and surrounding forest was one big adventure. We would play in the creek behind the house looking for crawdads. We would search the rocks for spiders and beetles or run around collecting fireflies in a jar at night. Byron and I would climb trees and ride our bikes all over the property. I was again the only black child in the area, but I did not notice. This was the best time I had ever had, the best time I would ever have as a child.

Kenneth Patton

One Sunday after church, Mr. Apsher told me that I had a visitor waiting for me near the trailer that was used for Sunday school. I walked over to the area and saw my mother's old boyfriend Kenneth Patton. My first reaction was terror. I had finally found a place where I could be happy, where I could be safe, where I could eat until I was full, and he was going to take me back to my mother. My second thought was guilt. Why would I not want to see my mother again?

I had forgotten about my past. For the first time in my life I was not thinking about my mom coming for me or worried about where my sisters were, I was just being a child. Seeing him again reminded me of my responsibilities to my birth family. Funny enough, he had just come by to see how I was doing. He did not stay long. He could not tell me where my mother was or how my sisters were doing. He just wanted to say hello.

That night I felt so bad. In my head I had abandoned my mother and my sisters. In reality, I never really let anyone replace them. I felt guilty because I was happy. I never forgot I had a mother. In my mind, Mary was still my mother. Jodie was a very kind and patient woman. While I never let her replace my mother, I loved her nonetheless. Since I never had a proper dad, Alvin was a good guy to be around.

He wasn't overly affectionate, but he was strong and caring. He would put his hand on my shoulder while we were walking and would explain some of life's lessons to me. Sometimes it was which mushrooms were safe to eat, what poison ivy looked like, and why you should not approach a horse from behind. Other times he would tell me why it was important to take my vitamins or why we all had to pull together and do the chores we were assigned. He showed that he cared by teaching me how to be strong and responsible. I never had a father figure before and he seemed to want me as his son.

End of My Childhood

Everything was going so well. I was happy and loved. I felt part of the family, and I felt safe. I remember one night asking Mr. Apsher if they were going to keep me. He averted his eyes and said something like he was going to try. That was good enough for me, but I could tell that something just wasn't right. Some weeks later, I was surprised to have another visitor from my past. My social worker was waiting for me at the Apsher's house. She sat me down and told me that there was another family that was interested in meeting me.

Inside I was devastated. I found my family, so why did I want to meet another family. Then it hit me, the Apsher's did not want me anymore! I was so hurt. I was angry. I was curious. What did I do wrong? I thought everyone was happy. I knew Jodie had just given birth to her fourth daughter, Samantha, but I thought she was going to be one more sister for me to play with. Now I realized I was just wrong, that this was just another foster home, and I was still not part of their family.

In that split second I learned what pragmatism meant. Just go with it. So I feigned interest in the possibility of having a new family. Of course I did not want to leave, but I wasn't going to make a scene. After all, the Apsher's had been very good to me and I did not want to hurt them by asking them why. I did not want to make them feel bad for sending me away. So I said okay. I might as well make the best of the new situation, I thought.

My social worker told me that this new family wanted to adopt a little boy. This wasn't going to be a foster home. This wasn't going to be temporary. This was going to be my chance to finally have a home and family that were legally mine. The problem was, this was not what I wanted. I already had what I wanted. Now, I was going to be sent away again. I had allowed myself to be happy and content. I had let my guard down. I was in such emotional pain because I was being rejected again. Just like my mother, the Apsher's did not find me worth fighting for. They were not going to try to keep me. I should have known that all of this was too good to be true, that a boy like me did not deserve the things the Apsher's had. I wasn't one of them, so why should I expect to have the happiness they had?

The transition to Tom and Millie Wilson was altogether different. First, I did not go right away. It was even unusual that I was being told that I was going at all. Usually, my bags were packed one day and it was on to the next home. But this time, it was gradual and all the more painful. The Wilson's came to visit me at the Apsher's home. They took me out on a date, if you will. We went to see a movie; I think it was the "Bird Man of Alcatraz" or something that a child would not want to see. We walked out when they started showing scenes of naked prisoners in the shower. They came back a few weeks later to first take me out to eat, then to the park.

This was a sad time for me, I wished they would have just removed me from the Apsher's and let me stay somewhere while the process took place. To go back and see the family I wanted so much to be a part of was torture. To sit at the dinner table, knowing I wasn't wanted, hurt me so much. Everything around me was crumbling and I could do nothing about it but watch. I never thought I could hurt that much as a little boy. I swore that I would never hurt that much again, that I would never *allow* myself to be hurt that much again. Just because someone says they love you doesn't mean they will fight to keep you.

I cannot remember much about the last day. I purposefully forgot most of it. I just remember them saying that they would call and visit. I remember Ladonna and my other two sisters crying. I remember being sad. I remember leaving the Apsher's for the last time, still holding on to that stuffed dog my mother had given me years earlier, with tears silently rolling down my cheeks. I had come to terms with the fact that the Apsher's did not want me, that Jodie and Alvin were not going to be my parents, and that LaDonna, Samantha, Tammy and Bethany were not going to be my sisters. This would never be my home. It was not what I wanted, but it was what I was going to get. So I had to deal with it.

So, I sucked it up, and grabbed my bags and walked to that green Dodge Aries the Wilson's drove. At least I had a glimpse of happiness; at least I had a small respite from the tough world. For a moment, I was able to forget that my mother had given me away and that my sisters and I were separated. For a little while I was allowed to be a child. That would have to do.

Much later in life, Mr. Apsher explained to me that they were worried that I was the only black child in their community. They thought it would have been cruel to keep me when there was a family in the city that wanted me. They thought I would be happier around a diverse population. Unfortunately, I was 35 years old before I found out that they really wanted me, and thought they were doing what was best for me. By then, I was too jaded to believe them.

10,000 Hills

3. Adoption and Becoming a Wilson

The Wilson's

At first glance, it may have seemed that the Wilson family was similar to the Apsher family. They were both white couples in their mid-thirties that had only female children. However, this is where the similarities end. This new home was completely different from the home I had allowed myself to become attached to. In fact, I had never been around a family like this before. Each home I can remember always had a working father and a stay-at-home mother. There was always a parent around to care for the children in the house. There was no all Sunday church with Tom and Millie, just a quick, 45 minute service!

I was even more surprised at the way this couple interacted. Millie was a short and tough woman who always seemed to be the decision maker. She would regularly have a can of beer with dinner. Since she was catholic, the whole family was catholic and attended mass. She liked to watch football on the weekends with a six-pack and her feet up. When her team was not doing well, she had no problem letting a few curse words fly. She was not the nurturing type of woman who constantly catered to her husband and children. Most days, she would rather sit on the couch after a long day's work and have Tom bring her a beer, than interact with the children.

Tom, on the other hand was a mild-mannered short and chubby

elementary school teacher. He wore glasses with a strap on the back to keep them in place. He played the accordion and baritone saxophone for fun instead of watching any sports. He never drank, but still made sure to buy Millie her favorite beer. Although he was not raised Catholic, he became Catholic once he and Millie were married. He gave his checks to Millie every other week. In turn, she gave him some of his money as an allowance. He appeared to be an unassuming person, soft spoken and jovial. He loved to play practical jokes and liked music from the 40's, 50's, and show tunes. He appeared to be very loving, constantly playing and interacting with his children.

This was very different from any of the homes in which I had previously been placed. All of the women in the previous households were nurturing and caring homemakers. I never heard any curse words from the other foster parents. I never witnessed anyone consuming alcohol, and to see a woman drinking and cursing during a football game was simply shocking! The men I had known before were always in charge of the house, controlling the finances and making all of the major decisions. They were rugged and hard-working, constantly doing yard work, hunting and any home repairs. Tom was just the opposite. He took on the responsibility of doing the dishes and laundry, instead of the yard work. It seemed like he placated Millie; she was the dominating force in this home.

They had two daughters, Mary and Jennifer. The older teenager, Mary, was a product of Millie's first marriage, while Jennifer was the youngest and their only child in common. The girls seemed friendly enough when I first met them. They did not receive me like the Apsher's girls, but I had experienced much worse in the past.

The Wilson home was strikingly different from any home I had been in before. I was raised in the foothills of the Ozark Mountains. Each previous foster home was in a rural setting, with forests, streams and farm land. The Wilson's lived on the south side of St. Louis, right smack in the middle of the city. There were no horses or cows, no fields or forests.

The closest I had been to an urban environment before was in the small town of Rolla. This was my first up close view of the city, the traffic, the bright lights, and few visible stars at night. The house the Wilson's owned was a quaint old brick two-story with a flat roof, a sizable yard, and an alley to the rear. The house was in the German part of town, mixed with Polish and Irish families. Again, there were no people that looked like me. I was again in an all-white area with an all-white family. I guess there were not enough black families looking to adopt. Then again, I never really cared since I had never been around black people.

While I was devastated to leave the wonderful life I had enjoyed with the Apsher's, it was hard not to be excited. For the first time in my life, I had a family that wanted me. They wanted to adopt me. They had even put in the effort to come and visit me, to get to know me. I wasn't just placed on their doorstep in the middle of the night; they actually sought me out. I had a chance to finally stop moving around and leave my uncertainty behind me. If I made this work, this could be my family. It had to work!

Before Adoption

The adoption didn't happen right away. There was a nine-month waiting period to see if things would gel. It was during this time that I learned about the Wilson family and how I fit in. Tom was extraordinarily affectionate, something I had never experienced from a man before. He doted over me, showing me to all of his co-workers, neighbors and friends. Now, Millie was somewhat distant from the beginning. Some of this could be because I still held out hope that my mother would come back, so I probably did not take to her that quickly. At that age, I still believed I already had a mother. I never had a permanent father, so I quickly warmed up to Tom. I could not wait to call him Dad.

Since Tom and Millie were blue-collar workers, money was never abundant. Coming from the Apsher's, the Wilsons appeared to be poor. Not as impoverished as my birth mother, but it was still a struggle and we lived paycheck to paycheck. It felt kind of odd to be going back to poverty, when I had been removed from a carefree existence where I wanted for nothing. While I never went hungry at the Wilson's, we never had the money to dine out or buy anything but the basics. Grocery shopping was always predicated by coupon clipping and taking advantage of double coupon days. Other times, we would simply have to buy the dented cans and no name brands of food.

Their Dodge Aries was one step away from the junk pile. While it looked okay, it ran poorly. Tom was not handy with tools, so we depended upon the neighbors to help keep that car running. Their house was also not what it first appeared to be. It was replete with structural issues, a leaky roof, and a flooding basement. While there were two bathrooms, the upstairs shower did not work very often and the toilet would clog and run over regularly. The house was also constantly cluttered and dirty. I guess having both parents working meant that cleaning was not always on the top of the priority list. This meant I was once again living with roaches and mice, and there was no room set up for me when I got there. I spent the first few visits sleeping in the hallway, not knowing I would be sleeping there for almost a year.

By that time I was no stranger to poverty. I never complained about the conditions of the house or the food we had to eat. I wasn't spoiled like that. But, I did not understand why I would be taken from a family with the means to take care of me, and placed with a family that was barely making ends meet. While I was young, I could still recognize that the Wilson's were struggling financially.

I wondered why my social worker thought this was okay. Of course, when she came to visit me, the house was cleaned up. But, did she ever even look in the basement? Did she not see that old rusted out metal pool in the back yard that always had a thick film of algae growing in the brackish water? Could she not see the cracks or water spots in the ceiling? Didn't she wonder why I was still sleeping in the hallway while my sisters had their own rooms? Maybe this WAS the only family left and she had to make it work too?

My new school also struck me as odd. They were inner city schools with all of the typical problems of classroom overcrowding, fights, and truancy. It was a difficult adjustment coming from a beautiful campus-like elementary school with small classrooms and strict teachers who knew your name. Now, I was just a number. The books were old, the teachers were underpaid and non-attentive, and the students were belligerent. It was not an easy environment in which to learn.

Given the Wilson's work schedule, Jennifer and I were latchkey kids from the outset. They left for work before we went to school and got home much later than we did. So we were responsible for catching the bus on time when I was still in third grade. There was no one to see us off in the morning, and no one to make sure that we got home safely. I know this was not uncommon for many children during that time, but it still struck me as odd. If they didn't have the time to care for their children, why would the Wilson's want another? Why would the state place me in a family that would have me spend so much time without supervision? Again, I just figured this was the best I was going to get, this was as much as I deserved, so I just went with it. After all, somebody finally wanted me!

Instead of looking at the bad, I focused on the good. I had a roof over my head, food to eat and a family that actually wanted to adopt me, or at least a father that seemed to want me. While this house was not the best, I knew what it was like to be without a home and without a family. I never wanted to be in that situation again, no matter what the cost. I never really imagined as an eight to nine-year old, just how much I would have to pay to have a family.

To be honest, I was having fun with the Wilson's in the beginning. Social Services was still involved in my life at that point. There were regularly scheduled visits to check on me and see if I was happy. This was a trick question considering the circumstances…happy compared to what? What choice did I have? I had to be happy or I was going to be homeless, and I was making the best of it. I was determined to make this work and to be happy.

As I said before, the Wilson family was a white family. And, when I say white, I mean WHITE. Millie was German. Both of her parents came from Germany after WWII. While Tom was Irish, the whole family embraced the German culture. We regularly ate Braunschweiger and knockwurst with sauerkraut, and Millie had a great recipe for German potato salad. We celebrated Oktoberfest, manifest, and all other German festivals. They both played in a German Umpa band. More specifically, Tom played baritone and accordion in the band and Millie danced. They were really into the culture.

Tom wore the traditional German Lederhosen with ankle socks and matching calf covers and a Bavarian hat to complete the set. Millie would dance the polka in a German Polka group with her traditional Dirndl dress, right out of the sound of music. They danced in parades and festivals all summer long. Tom even collected beer steins from around the world. This was a weekly event during the warmer months and band practice all year round. They even got me into dancing around the Maibaum or "May pole" in my little uniform. I was always the only black kid on the entire dance team, but why not? Again, it was so different from the life I had lived, but it seemed fun.

Tom had a thing for old Broadway musicals and introduced me to all of them. From Oklahoma to the West Side Story and Hello Dolly, we would watch all of these movies and listen to the records. Music was a huge part of Tom's life and he even wanted me to play in the band with him. I was so moved by the fact that he wanted to do things with me. He even borrowed a baritone from one of his friends so he could teach me how to play. Unfortunately, as the months went by he realized I was not that good at reading music and this seemed to make him more upset than normal. I noticed he would curse under his breath when we tried to go over the notes because I still could not understand. I brushed that odd reaction off, maybe he just liked music, and maybe I wasn't trying hard enough.

The Wilson's were also big in the boy scouts. Millie was a Cub Scout leader and Tom was a Boy Scout leader. I received my Cub Scout uniform a few weeks after I moved into the house. They told me it was their goal for me to become the youngest Eagle Scout in Missouri. This was monumental! They were planning a future with me! No one ever talked to me about my future. No one ever made long term plans for me before. If they were willing to PLAN to make me an Eagle Scout, then I was going to make them happy. (I actually received my Eagle Scout badge at the age of 13, though not by choice). By the time my adoption date arrived, we had already been on several camping trips and scout jamborees. I was having fun and doing things I had never done before. While things were not perfect, it seemed as if I had finally found a permanent home.

Early Issues

Even though I was trying to make the best of things, I couldn't help but notice some red flags popping up as my adoption date grew closer. Tom did have a temper when I let him down. If I didn't read the music correctly, he became very frustrated and angry. He would curse and turn red. When I asked to play a sport instead of just doing cub scouts, he and Millie became furious and said I was ungrateful for all they were doing for me. Sometimes I could actually see Tom bunching up his fist, as if he were barely able to contain himself. My relationship with Millie seemed to sour quickly. I could not understand why she was not loving or affectionate towards me. Maybe I did not warm up to her as quickly as she wanted me to? But, for whatever reason, she became increasingly distant, almost annoyed that I was still there. I began to believe she really did not want to adopt me.

In fact, I received my first spanking before my adoption was finalized because I didn't say good night to her after saying good night to Tom. This was not a violent or angry beating, but to me it seemed somewhat unfair. It was just a paddling across the backside with a wooden paddle, but it hurt. There were quite a few misplaced smacks, but that was nothing new. I had been switched by my grandmother, but I had never been spanked by a foster parent before. The closest time I came to a spanking was when I got popped on the leg for negligently knocking Mr. Apsher's jeep out of gear with my knee. (Years later I was told that the Apsher's also let me go because they were told they couldn't spank me as they spanked their children. They thought this was unfair to me and that I was being robbed of the discipline their children received). So naturally, I was somewhat caught off-guard by the physical punishment and the reason behind the spanking.

Tom came up to my bed the night I was paddled and sat there rubbing my head while I cried. He said he didn't want to hurt me, but that I had to do the right thing. He promised if I did the right thing, I would never get a spanking again. He stayed there until I went to sleep. While the spanking was not an issue, Millie's dislike of me was not getting any better. In fact it seemed to be getting worse.

While Millie was getting more distant, my relationship with Tom was becoming more affectionate. He was always doting on me. He seemed to shower me with affection. Of course he lost his temper, but that was because I let him down, had disappointed him. When I did the right things, he was so proud of me. He was always at my side. He was always sitting beside me on the couch or having me sit on his lap. He always wanted me to come with him when he went to band practice, even though he never invited his daughters. We even peed together, in the same bowl at the same time. He said it was how men did it. I didn't see anything wrong with it. In fact, I was just happy that someone wanted to spend time with me and wanted to be with me that much.

Things progressed from peeing together to him monitoring my bowel movements. I suffered from headaches as a little boy and as Tom would say, my headaches were a result of me being backed up. So, I began to receive enemas or a suppository every time I complained about a stomachache or headache. Even if I had a slight fever, I received an enema or a suppository. While it was uncomfortable and painful, Tom was an adult and he was my father, so I believed him.

Tom would always insist on performing the enema or placing the suppository himself. I figured he performed them because Millie was a girl and she was not supposed to see me naked. He told me I would get use to them and then it could be fun. Again, who was I to question him? In fact, I believed that could be a cause for headaches well into my thirties. (It is amazing just how much credence we give our parents, how much we believe even after we become adults.)

These were uncomfortable times and I learned not to complain about headaches to avoid things being pushed inside of me. Whenever I spent more than five minutes on the toilet, Tom would tell me I was backed up, and out came the suppositories for that, too. Suppositories were soon replaced by enemas, and again, he insisted on being the one who "helped" me with the enema tube.

I remember just how uncomfortable it was to have an enema, to have so much warm water forced into me; to be forced to hold it for 15 minutes to be sure it worked. My response to each enema or suppository was always tears, and lots of them. No matter how often it occurred, I never got used to it. It never got better, no matter how many times I had to go through it. I did not resist, I didn't even think it was wrong. I just thought of it as another kind of medicine I had to take so I would feel better. And no child ever wants to take medicine.

Tom also started coming into the bathroom while I was in the tub or try to get me to shower with him in the upstairs bathroom when no one was home. He would usually just make sure I was clean, soaping up and washing every inch of my body. He always checked to see if I was clean, making sure I did a good job. While I had never had anyone do this before, I figured it was okay. Tom was more affectionate and attentive than any other foster parent, and I trusted him. After all, he loved me, and he told me so all of the time.

Adoption Day

On that fateful day, I went into a courtroom and told the judge I wanted to be a Wilson, and that I wanted to change my name and have my birthday on February 20. If someone would have taken the time to ask me what was going on, maybe I would have been spared the turmoil and humiliation that was to come. If someone would have provided me with options or told me that the Apsher's wanted me back, I might have changed my mind. But that did not happen. To me the choice was simple, this was my last hope. Tom told me he loved me every day. I had a house, although it was dirty and in disrepair; I had food, even if some of the canned goods were dented or without labels; and I had a family, even if was not the best home I had been in.

After all, what child is totally happy? What little black boy would say no to a guaranteed family at nine years old, with no chance of ever finding another family willing to take him in? So I gave the only answer I could provide. I said "yes." After all, this family could never be worse than spending my life alone. Could it?

Being a Wilson in St. Louis

Once I was adopted, everything became official. I was a Wilson. I was no longer a foster child. I was no longer without a home or without a family. I was finally going to get my chance to live a normal life, or as normal as a black child can live in a white household. No more worries about being sent away. No more sneaking around at night in an attempt to overhear adults talking about my future or their disappointment in me. I finally had security. It seemed too good to be true. Maybe I was finally valuable enough to have a family that wanted me. Maybe I did deserve to have a good life.

However, it did not take long for me to realize that security is not all it's cracked up to be. It seemed my quest for a home had a heavy cost that I was going to pay for, with interest. I guess I didn't deserve a normal life after all. It was almost as if the Wilson's were performing for social services just to get through the adoption process. I no longer had visits or contact from any social worker. I was no longer a ward of the state. I could not avail myself to any helpful services. I just had the Wilsons.

First Beating

It wasn't long before the thin veil of normality and decency was torn away. I remember my most valuable possession was a single photograph of my mother with me sitting on her lap. This was the only thing I had from my past. Somehow the stuffed dog my mother gave me was "lost" when I transitioned from the Apsher's. I kept that dog for years and through many moves, but somehow it got lost shortly after the move to the Wilson's. Tom came to the rescue of course and bought me a stuffed bee to remind me of my mother's affinity for beekeeping, but it was HIS gift to me, not a keepsake from my mother.

I treasured my photo of me and my mother and kept it downstairs on the kitchen shelf. This way I could at least see my mom every day before I went to school. A few months after officially becoming a Wilson, I remember coming downstairs to find my picture cut into a bunch of pieces. I was crushed to lose the last vestige of my birth family.

51

As I walked into the living room I asked Tom what happened and he replied in the oddest way. While I was devastated, I never thought in a million years that he would have been the one to cut it up. I was not accusing him, but I did demand to know what happened. He told me I probably did it! Why would I do that? He insisted that I was the one who did it and that I was just mad at my mom for abandoning me. I responded by saying, "Father, I would never do that. I love my mom." He flew into a rage, not because I questioned him, but because I called him father, not dad. I never referred to him and Millie as Mom and Dad, always mother and father. He asked me several times to call him dad, but I always forgot. There wasn't a real reason I was aware of for using mother and father, I just did it. But that morning calling him father set him off.

He immediately struck me in the face with the back of his hand. I was stunned and scared. I had never been hit like that before. As I fell to my knees he kicked me in the stomach with his hard soled work shoes. He must have struck me at least a half dozen times before I knew what was happening. I just remember him yelling, "What did I tell you to call me? What did I tell you to call me?" I was finally able to stand up, trembling and wracked with pain and said "I'm sorry, Dad."

He calmed down and told me to go get a rag for my nose. It was bleeding pretty badly and swelling. I did as I was told. He didn't have to tell me not to tell the school what happened. He knew I wouldn't tell on him. Later that night, he came into the hall where I was staying and told me he was sorry, but I had to learn to listen and do what I was told. I replied by saying "I'm sorry, Dad. I'm sorry. I'm sorry I let you down." After all, he told me many times to call him dad but I did not listen. I felt it was really my fault and I drove him to it.

Scouts

It was obvious Tom really wanted a son. Both Tom and Millie wanted to have an Eagle Scout in the family. So my early years with the

Wilson's were consumed by scouting. As mentioned earlier, both Tom and Millie were scout leaders before I became a part of the family. They tried to help our neighbor Ritchie through scouts, but he was getting older and struggling to get his Eagle Scout before the deadline of his 18th birthday. I, on the other hand, was fresh and young. So I was pushed through cub scouts and Webelo scouts in record time. I didn't really want to be a scout anymore, but I did it to make Tom and Millie proud of me.

My scouting accomplishments seemed to be the only things that made them happy. Each time I received a new badge or award, both of them would just be beaming with delight. They were so proud to tell the other parents that their son received his arrow of light patch at the earliest age, or that I became a boy scout at 10½ years old. When I was performing, scout activities seemed to be the only time Millie was interested in me. I was just happy to have parents that were proud of me and wanted me to be successful at something.

However, scouts slowly became the bane of my existence. I was never allowed to play sports when we lived in St. Louis because it would interfere with my scouting. Tom would spend night after night forcing me to learn about different subjects and preparing me for my next badge. He would get very angry when I didn't get the subject matter or became confused. It was all too much and coming too quickly. Farming, sewing, leatherwork, sailing, swimming, knots, land navigation, semaphore, sign language, and Morse code. I was drilled on all of these subjects relentlessly. I nearly drowned trying to get my lifesaving badge, since I barely earned my swimming badge only weeks earlier. Tom pushed the lifeguard to pass me for both.

I am not an overly intelligent person today, and was not an overly bright child. I could get subjects, but it took a while and Tom was not a patient man. He was extremely book smart and could memorize and master subjects instantly. As such, he felt as if I was simply not trying. His anger would always get the best of him and I would pay dearly for my mistakes and inability.

Scouting did provide one positive aspect to my life. Although we were poor, my parents would spare no expense when it came to scouts. I was able to go on camping trips that would last a week or more. This was my great escape. I could just be a boy again. I could get away from the stress and the increasingly improper attention from Tom. He always made me give a detailed accounting of events when I returned home from these camping trips. I thought he was just trying to live vicariously through me and ensure that his hard earned money was well spent. However, he would always ask me the same question at the end. "Did you boys sit in a circle and play with each other yet?" I would always respond the same, "No." I didn't believe that boys would want to do that to each other.

Less Money – Failing Household

It became clear that the Wilsons were struggling financially. I guess they didn't figure the cost of another mouth to feed. While we were in transition before the adoption, they were receiving a stipend to care for me. Now that I was adopted, the money stopped coming in and I was just a burden. The old Dodge Aries finally broke down and they were forced to purchase an old red van that ran marginally better than the Dodge.

The disrepair to the house was getting worse. Even before I was adopted I noticed the basement would flood during a heavy rain storm or snow. I don't mean this to say that some items just got a little wet, I mean there was one to two feet of water in the basement, sometimes more. The basement was generally used for storage since it was uninhabitable due to the rain water. The house was also in a general state of filth. This brought roaches and mice. We would try to keep the roaches out, but as anyone who has been poor can attest, once you have roaches they are nearly impossible to get rid of. Especially when the house is always messy and the basement is stocked full of wet boxes and trash.

To supplement the household income, we would collect cans on the weekends. We would drive around "Forest Park" and other areas of the city looking for aluminum cans. We had a magnet to discern the steel cans from the aluminum cans. Tom would have me and Jennifer rummaging through trash cans and dumpsters to get enough to recycle for money. This was a weekly event and we were happy to help out. It was exciting to find a trash can full of empty beer cans and Tom would be so proud of us. It became a competition between Jennifer and me to see who could fill up the most bags on a weekend for our parents. However, we also had to look through dumpsters in our neighborhood. It was very embarrassing to have someone you knew see you rummaging through their trash at night. It also made us targets of laughter and jokes at school when those same children told our classmates.

We very seldom got to go out to eat. Even fast food was a rarity. When we did go, we were instructed to grab all the free ketchup, mustard, and salt packets we could get. We never ate anywhere without coupons or special sales. All of our food shopping was done at the discount grocery stores. We always bought the dented cans of food and the off brand cereals. I never had any brand named food until I was in high school. Our clothes were usually second hand from the Salvation Army or the church donation box. While Tom seemed not to care, Millie usually refused to collect cans or have anyone see her going to the donation box to receive handouts. (It is a sad state of affairs that a person cannot raise a family on a teacher's salary, and this is still true today.) I was happy that we were able to eat at all, so it was no bother to me. I had been through worse.

Being Mixed

Early on, the Wilson's explained to me that I was unique. I was not white, but I was not black. This seemed especially important to Millie. I was supposed to tell everyone that I was mulatto. Since my birth parents were of different races I did not argue, but no one else seemed to believe me, or even care. I wasn't white. I was brown with curly hair. That made me black.

When we went out in public, there were always people staring at us. I wasn't even close to being white, but my parents tried to make me look as white as possible. My hair was always combed out in big curls and sprayed with hair spray which dried my hair and scalp something fierce. No matter how much the Wilson's may have denied it, I was black and could not fit into the mold this white family was trying to put me in. No matter how I was dressed and how I spoke, I was still stared at. When we were out as a family, we were always a spectacle. I still stood out as a black boy with a white family.

Physical Discipline

After the first serious beating, I became very scared of Tom. I did not want to make him lose his temper again. I was still a young kid who was bound to mess up and the next severe beating came less than a week after the first. I accidentally fell asleep on the bus and missed my stop after a field trip. I woke up at the bus depot and had to find someone to call Tom to pick me up. He told me I worried the whole family and they were scared someone had taken me. Millie was worried that they were going to get in trouble for child neglect.

The entire car ride home I apologized but Tom said that I was still going to be punished. I didn't have a chance to get out of the car before he pulled me out by my hair and began dragging me up the stairs of the porch. He was punching me and slamming me against anything in my way. The entire time Millie was telling Tom to calm down because we were out in public. Once I was inside Tom kept asking me why I would do such a thing. Why would I put the family through this? When I could not give him an answer he just kept punching and kicking me. He would knee me in the chest and face until I fell. Then he would kick me and yell at me to get up. When I stood up he punched me in the face again and again until I fell to the floor. I don't know how long this lasted, but it seemed to go on forever. This would not be my last beating.

56

Even before I was adopted, we always had chores. Of course they were simple to start out with. I had to make my bed and take out the trash. Sometimes I had to help with the dishes. Soon after my adoption the chore list became much more grueling. It went from making our lunches for school to also making lunches for Tom and Millie. We also now had to make their breakfast and dinner as well as wash all of the clothes. We even had to iron Tom's shirts and lay out Tom and Millie's clothing for the next work day. While our household responsibilities were a bit much for kids 10 to 11-years old, that may not have been that uncommon. After all, they both had to work and we were just in school across the street. The repercussions for not properly finishing our chores, however, were swift and painful.

It was clear to me that I was helpless now and Tom would lose his temper and beat me often. If I forgot to make his breakfast or put his clothes out for the next morning, I was beaten. If I couldn't find all 42 pairs of Tom's socks, I would get beaten. If the knives were in the wrong drawer or some spoons were missing, I would get a beating for that, too. I am not talking about a spanking. I don't remember ever getting a spanking after I was adopted. There was never any measured discipline meted out. It was rage and anger, spite and malice. It was always out of control. I was hit with whatever was close. The attacks devolved into bar room brawls with only one person fighting. What started as punching and kicking moved on to attacking me with objects like plastic cutting boards, wooden spoons, and glass bottles; whatever he could lay his hands on. I would get beaten till I lost consciousness, and when I came to, Tom would still be beating me, yelling at me to get up and stop pretending.

Sexual Contact

It seemed like once it was official, once I was a legal Wilson, Tom's affection and attention quickly transformed into sexual deviancy. I had already received more enemas and suppositories in those first nine-months than most people receive in a lifetime. Tom also peed in the same toilet with me more often than I would care to remember. But that was just the beginning. Sometimes, if I had to go really badly, we would just pull off the road and we would pee together. This did not strike me as odd; I had peed in the snow with Byron (my friend at the Apsher's) before. In fact, I kind of thought it was neat that Tom was doing something with me that was kind of juvenile, kind of a silly game boys played. Sometimes we would see who could pee the farthest or who could pee the longest. We were just goofing around.

Things changed when he offered to hold my penis for me. He said it was what real men do. It didn't seem right, but I let him. What possible harm could come from that? He was just holding it. He eventually demanded that I hold his penis while he peed, and I did as I was told. I definitely didn't want to do that. He said it was just in fun and we could try to aim for each other.

Shaving

The peeing together moved on to more invasive contact. I remember the first time Tom offered to teach me how to shave. As a little boy I was thrilled. He lathered my face up and gave me a razor with no blade in it for practice. I was nine or 10-years old at the time. Once we were done, he told me the hair on my face would grow faster if I shaved more often. I had no hair on my face, but I sure wanted some. Every little boy wants to have a manly beard and mustache, just like their father. This was a typical father and son moment.

The next day he told me we were going to shave again. Of course I was excited. I had a father that wanted me to shave with him - every boy's dream. A few days later he told me it was time to shave again. It was early in the morning and everyone else was asleep, but this time there was no feeling of a father and son bond. This time he said he was going to shave my testicles.

Tom told me early on that a boy's biggest danger was a hernia. Since I had no idea what a hernia was, he showed me, or more precisely, I showed him. He had me pull down my pants and show him my testicles. He told me that if one was hanging lower than the other there might be a problem. However, at that point I didn't have any testicles. They hadn't dropped yet. So in my best interest, he would check me at least once a week to see if my testicles had dropped. Sometimes he missed a week, but since I was receiving regular enemas and suppositories, he apparently was able to keep up.

Once my testicles dropped, he explained that I needed to be shaved. If I wanted to hurry the hair growth down there, I needed to shave often. I really didn't want him to do this. When my eyes began to well up, he immediately told me to "shut the &%#@ up before I wake everyone." He took a real razor and shaved me down there even though I didn't have any pubic hair. From that point on, he never offered to help me shave my face again, but he ritually shaved my testicles. Needless to say, it was quid pro quo soon enough. Eventually I was forced to return the favor and shave his scrotum. There was a constant threat of violence if I accidentally cut him. It became his little ritual that played out for a time. He would shave me and then I would be forced to shave him.

Unfortunately for me, handling his testicles would get him aroused. In fact, he was already aroused by handling mine. Shaving me wasn't enough. After one of the early morning shavings, I sat naked while he wiped the remainder of the shaving cream off of my body. I tried to stand up because I knew I had to shave him next. I was so miserable, but did not want to do anything to set Tom off. He pushed me back down into a sitting position on the toilet. I did not know what to expect or what I had done wrong, I was just startled. He immediately shoved his face right into my crouch and began sucking my penis! I was paralyzed. I had never had anyone ever do that to me. I didn't even know what he was doing, really. He was not gentle or kind. It did not feel good and I did not get aroused.

After a few minutes he just stopped. He then told me that since my testicles had dropped I would start to enjoy that soon. I was horrified. There was nothing pleasant about what he did. I just couldn't stop crying, even at school. I knew he was wrong. How could I ever enjoy that? How could this be happening?

Changing Rooms

Eventually a room was cleared for me. It really wasn't a room, just a sitting area off Tom and Millie's bedroom. They put some beads up to create a door of sorts. Tom said since I was a part of the family now, I deserved my own room. It had been over a year since I had arrived. This also put me closer to him at night. Even more strange was that it put me closer to Millie, too. However, Tom did not seem to mind.

I guess once he crossed that line and made it obvious about his sexual desire, he felt little need to mask his intentions. From that point on he would sneak into my bed at night and try to suck my penis while grabbing my hand and placing it on his genitals. He would place his hand over my mouth to keep me from making noise while he held me down. Sometimes his hand would be covering my mouth and nose so I could not breathe. I would struggle and panic and he would become more forceful and more invigorated. I knew this was wrong. I was so scared; so scared of getting caught. I knew Millie already had a dislike for me, if she saw this, she would have every reason to hate me and I would be sent away again.

I was helpless in that bed, just waiting to hear those beads jiggling in the middle of the night. Dreading that sound! It seemed now he had no filter and no need to pretend. There was no more peeing together, he didn't need to do that now. He no longer tried to make his sexual affection playful; he just did what he wanted. Conveniently for him, I was always right in the next room. All he had to do was get up out of bed and I was there. The only thing I could do was cry silently in my "own room" while he assaulted me.

Coughing

Unfortunately, I was also very sickly when I was around that age. I caught pneumonia when I was with the Bombers, mostly because I was so malnourished that my body could not fight off any type of infection. Therefore, winter time was always bad for me. I was constantly sick, and would cough all through the night. Having my bedroom so close to Tom and Millie's meant they were awakened in the middle of the night by me coughing. The sicker I got, the more difficult it was to stop coughing at night. Instead of getting up to take care of me or give me some cough syrup, they would just get mad.

Somehow they both believed I was doing this on purpose, that I was too lazy to get out of bed. They both had to work in the morning and I was intentionally stopping them from getting any sleep. Apparently, I was supposed to get up, go down to the kitchen and gargle with warm salt water to stop my cough. The problem was that I could never hear myself cough because I was asleep. But they never saw it that way.

So Tom would come in and begin punching and kicking me while telling me that I knew I was disturbing them. He would then throw me down the stairs into the kitchen where he would make me gargle with salt water. I would try to stay awake. I would try not to cough. I would even eventually fall asleep, and no matter how hard I tried to stay awake, no matter how many pillows I put over my head, or how far I would duck under the covers; they could still hear me cough. This meant waking up to a beating, without knowing why. I would sometimes wake up as I was airborne. Being thrown down the steps, crashing at the bottom in pain, trying to get my bearings.

We had one of those restaurant style big wooden shakers and this is what I was supposed to use to get my salt water. Instead I would get beat in the face and head while in the kitchen trying to get the warm water to gargle. After one severe beating with that salt shaker, Tom split my skull.

Now, I am not talking about the lumps and small lesions I would get during the winter months from being beat with the salt shaker, or the handheld wooden cutting board. This was a great big gash in the front of my skull. To this day, it still looks like premature balding because hair will not grow there. I used to sometimes look at my bloody pillow when I made my bed in the morning. I would see mostly small little blood marks on the pillowcase or sheet. Some were old and brown, and some were still red. They never once thought to buy some cough syrup to help my cough!

Dominance

Obviously, Tom was not the meek and gentle man he first appeared to be. He was not letting his wife control the house, far from it. His mood set the tone for all of the children in the house, and that tone was usually fear. Since I would do anything to keep Tom from being mad, it is a logical conclusion that I would also do anything to keep him happy. Once Tom established his control over me, it was simple for him to continue his sexual advances. Within a year of being adopted I was in constant fear of his physical abuse. The discipline was so random that I was never sure when I was going to be beaten. This atmosphere quickly wore down any resistance I once had. It was easy for him to take advantage of such meek prey.

What started out with him performing oral sex on me in my bed or the bathroom evolved into something much more perverted. He performed oral sex on me for months. Each time he would force my hands onto his genitals to stimulate him while he did it. It is sad to say that eventually my penis would get erect with his stimulation. I hated myself for this reaction, but there was nothing I could do about it. I was too young to have an orgasm, but I still became aroused when he performed this on me. It seemed like every night he would find an excuse to wake me up or take me on a ride in order to fondle me. By then, this wasn't done as punishment, but it was coerced. If I resisted, he would just hold me down, smother me to where I couldn't breathe, or hold me by the throat until I would almost black out.

It seemed each time he became more aggressive and agitated. He became more and more forceful, as if he couldn't get enough or wasn't getting enough out of forcing himself on me. He began coming at me more and more often, regardless of the time of day or night. He would just snatch me up and drag me into the basement or drive around the corner to the alley. I really didn't understand what he was trying to do. I didn't enjoy it and he didn't seem to be satisfied because he just kept coming at me more and more, even multiple times in one day.

New Punishment

As time went on in St. Louis, the beatings were more and more severe and increasing more frequently. It seemed as if I was being beaten multiple times a week for a variety of reasons. The list of chores was becoming longer and longer. It was now my responsibility to remove the water out of the basement after it rained. This meant I had to take a pail or bucket and literally throw water out the window into the alley or dump it in the yard. We were now doing everything for Tom and Millie, from washing and cooking, to dishes and lawn work. Of course, the more we had to do, the more chances we had to mess up. It was impossible to complete everything we were supposed to complete in a timely manner. As a result, we would be punished when we failed to complete our list of chores.

The morning after a very bad night of punishment, Tom woke me up early for another "shave." It was clear that I was still very upset and did not want any part of this, so he grabbed me by my throat and carried me down the stairs. I could not breathe! I remember seeing stars and flashes of light. Everything went black and white, but I could not get him to release my throat so I could breathe.

Finally, he let go of my throat once we were in the downstairs bathroom. He insisted that I shave him first. I noticed he was instantly aroused even through his underwear. I remember lathering him up and trying to be careful with the razor. Somehow I made a mistake and cut him on his belly. He was furious, but it was very early in the morning. He couldn't start hitting me without waking everyone so he just grabbed my head and face and forced his penis into my mouth.

I was crying and gagging, but he would not stop. He kept moving my head back and forth with his penis in my mouth until he ejaculated in my mouth. I immediately began to throw up, but he grabbed my throat with one hand and covered my mouth with the other. The vomit came out of my nose.

That fateful event opened up a new and horrific chapter in my life. Now, he had found a new punishment for me. Something that was even worse than the beatings. The escalation of molestation was now paired with the physical abuse. Eventually, the physical and sexual abuse coalesced into a single form of discipline. Sometimes one, sometimes the other, usually both. I would get my second special round of discipline after everyone else went to sleep or once we left to go on a drive.

It was a form of punishment. He would even kick me in the testicles during my beatings just to have a reason to "look" at them later. At this time his physical abuse became consistently tinged with some sexual overtones. Many times he would even forcefully and painfully grab my genitals when he could get away with it. He knew he had carte blanche to do whatever he wanted to do to me. I was too little and too scared to do anything to stop him.

During this new discipline, he was always the recipient. Prior to this, he performed sexual acts on me and I thought my life could get no worse. I cannot describe how bad it made me feel inside. I had never been more humiliated and embarrassed. Even if no one else knew, I knew. Now it had taken a turn for the worse. I didn't even think it was possible to get worse, but I was wrong.

It had come to the point that now when I was being punished he always forced me to perform oral acts on him. Unlike all the times in the bed or the van, this was always about forcing me to please him. He found a new use for his toy and he used me as often as he could. I was now in trouble for the smallest thing, not making my bed, not tying my shoes when I walked, scuffing my church shoes, or going to school without a belt. Of course, all of these minor infractions now enraged him beyond reason. The beatings didn't always last as long as before, but he raged and hit just enough to send a message that I deserved what would come next and it would be my fault.

Fun Parent

I know it sounds impossible to believe, but I really thought he loved me. Even with the unreasonable discipline, beatings and sexual assault, he was still my favorite parent. In fact, once he ejaculated he immediately became remorseful and loving again. I would receive a reprieve from the torrent of violence and abuse, but it was more than that. Tom was a fun parent. He loved to play practical jokes and tricks. It would not be out of character to find him running through the house with the garden hose to squirt his children when we were not expecting it. He was the one who taught us how to play cards and even made cards a way to learn math and money. He brought home little pets like hamsters and guinea pigs.

Even with little money, we found ways to have fun and enjoy ourselves. He would get out his accordion and play us a tune. He was the one who would get Jennifer and me out of school early to watch the St. Louis Cardinals walk in their victory parade after winning the World Series. He would take us out to watch a baseball game from the bleacher seats.

If you took away all the abuse and molestation, he appeared to be a good father, if those words even belong in the same sentence. He sang songs about his children while we drove in the car. He constantly bragged to his friends and co-workers about my accomplishments in the scouts. He tried to school me on black history, bringing home African themed calendars and even bought me a black power hair pick. (Kind of useless with my hair texture, but he didn't really know.) In fact, Friday was our favorite day of the week. That was the day Millie had to work until 6:00 p.m. This meant we may have a chance to do something fun with Tom.

Yet, there remained the constant threat of physical abuse. I could be beat at any moment and for any reason. I had no idea when or for what I was going to be in trouble, but I always knew everything that happened to me was my fault. The immense stress of knowing I was the cause of all my pain kept me confused and uncertain. Finally, Tom used my emotions. He knew I desperately wanted a family. I was living in a constant state of fear: fear of violence, fear of sexual assault, and fear of disappointing him. He was the only father I had known and I still loved him.

He used my love for him. The kindness and love he showed me between the beatings and abuse was just too much. I was terrified of him and I was terrified of losing him at the same time. I remember many nights when he was late coming home from work or a band practice. I would be so fearful that something happened to him. I would pray to God to keep him safe. I promised I would do anything if he would just be okay. I was so confused at this point that I did not know what to think. I did not want this to keep happening, but I also did not want to be alone again, with no one to care for me or call me their son.

Trying to survive under all of this pressure was difficult, to say the least. After a few years of being with the Wilson's, I was in a constant state of shock. What happened to me? What did I do to deserve this? At that point, I hadn't adjusted to all of the abuse yet. I still had hope that someone would come and rescue me. Surely my mom or the Apsher's would check on me. Martha or family services must want to know how I was doing. It wasn't that I wanted to be without a family. I didn't want to leave the Wilson's and be alone again, but I did not want this either. I was in shock of what my life had become.

Since I never knew what was coming, I was constantly on edge. One might think with all the threats of violence and unreasonable punishments that I would have been the model child. You would think that I would do anything to stay out of harm's way, that I would do anything to keep Tom from getting mad. That does make sense, but all of that abuse and fear had the opposite effect. As the punishment became more severe and the molestation became part of my discipline, I seemed to get worse.

Tooth

I messed up the easiest of tasks. I couldn't find things that were right in front of my face. At one point, I was supposed to organize canned goods from Aldi's to put in the cupboard, but no matter how hard I tried, I just kept making mistakes, and this day was no different. I told him I was done, but I forgot to open the other side of the cupboard and I only organized one side. How stupid of me. I honestly did not think! He immediately flew into a rage and started pulling all the canned goods out of the cupboard and throwing them at me. I was so scared that I forgot to duck. One can hit me square in the face and broke my front tooth clean out of my mouth. This was a permanent tooth. (Every time I smile, and in every picture I take, I see that blacked outline where my tooth used to be.) Later that night, Tom pulled me to go into the basement and told me that I did that on purpose, that I was intentionally trying to make him mad. It may have appeared that way, but my brain honestly could not function with the fear he induced.

Math

Many times we would sit at the table and go over my math

homework. I was never good at math anyway, and dreaded these times when he did math work with me. He would look over my shoulder while I worked and within minutes I was messing up. Then he would sit down beside me to watch me work. Each time I messed up he would pinch my leg very hard. This would totally destroy my ability to focus. After messing up over and over, he would stop me to quiz me on my times tables. He would tell me that I was making him mad on purpose.

At that point, I couldn't even tell him what 2x2 was even if he just told me the answer. I would panic and blurt out anything. This would infuriate him to no end. Then he would start punching me on the side of my head for each mistake I made. Eventually, I couldn't even tell him my name if I wanted to. In the end, he would decide that I was just trying to make him mad and wanted him to lose his temper.

When he had enough of my mistakes, he would tell me that I obviously wanted another type of discipline. He would then pull his penis out right there at the table or I would be pulled out to the car for a "ride." During the entire drive he would be rubbing his penis and telling me that this must be what I wanted, otherwise I would have told him what 2x2 was.

Anytime he tried to work with me I became mentally incapable of completing even the simplest tasks. I would have to prepare to get merit badges. I was only doing this to make him happy, but he wanted me to be perfect. Even though I read the books and was prepared to go in front of

the merit badge counselor, it would all fall apart once he started asking questions.

As we drove to the counselor's house, I couldn't remember anything, and I had studied so hard! I honestly knew the subjects, but was too scared to think. I remember this specifically with my Animal Science merit badge. I knew Tom was going to quiz me before I went to the counselor, and I knew what was in store for me if I started missing answers. I was ready this time. I knew each pig, cow, and horse by appearance and what they were all used for. Tom began to quiz me and I answered each question correctly and with confidence. I got them all on the first try. Then he went back to ask about one type of pig that I was a little hesitant on.

Although I answered it right the first time, I now could not remember. He became frustrated and told me the answer. He then showed me the exact same picture and I could not remember. He started showing me other pictures and I could not remember any of them! I had no idea what was happening. He started getting more and more upset. I was panicking now. He was yelling and screaming as he pointed to the different photos and I could not identify one of them. It was now time for my appointment. During the drive he threatened to beat me to death if I didn't get this badge. The only reason why he didn't strike me was because I was getting ready to go in front of someone he knew.

I had to go in to see the counselor by myself to be tested. I answered all the questions and waited for the grade. I broke down and cried before the counselor could even tell me how I did. I begged him to let me pass. I told him that I needed this badge and that I really had prepared for it. He told me that I got every answer right and awarded me the badge. I came out of that house relieved and happy. I was going to make Tom proud of me. I did it! When I told him I was successful, he just got angry all over again. He said I was trying to make a fool out of him and got him angry for nothing. I tried to sit in the back of the car, but he made me sit in the front passenger seat for the ride back to our house. He punched and punched me the entire ride back. I knew when we drove past the turn off to our house my night was going to get much worse. And I was right.

The Bottles

Another morning we were on our way to the recycling bin and Tom asked me to bring all the bottles from around the house. That was one of my chores, one of my household and family responsibilities. We were a family and I had my duties, as did each member of the household. After collecting the bottles, it became obvious that one was missing! I was terrified to bring the bottle carrier into the house with one bottle missing. I knew how mad he would get. Tom told me to go out to the car to get the last bottle.

While still panicking, I was relieved the bottle would be found and I would not have to bear the brunt of his anger for not completing my job. I went to the car and opened the trunk of the green Dodge Aries to get the bottle. I could not find it! I didn't see the bottle in the trunk! I know Tom said it was in there, but it was so cluttered and I just didn't see it. I meekly went into the house after searching the whole car. I told Tom it wasn't in the trunk and I could see him getting mad. He sent me back out to the car and said he was giving me another chance before he came outside.

By this point I was in tears and was gripped by fear of what I knew would happen if I didn't produce that bottle. I again searched the entire car, not just the trunk, but the bottle was nowhere to be found. He must have been mistaken, but how could I tell him he was wrong. I immediately ran around the outside of the house to see if I could find another bottle to complete the six-pack in the carrier. I was in luck; I found an empty beer bottle in the ally. One bottle was just as good as the next, so I thought, and I brought it to Tom.

He immediately lost it. He began screaming at me to get him his bottle. Did I think he was stupid, was I trying to make a fool out of him? At that point he began punching and kicking me while dragging me out to the car. He opened the trunk and told me to get the bottle. We were outside in the street now, so he had calmed down, lest the neighbors notice his ranting and violent behavior. Once he opened the trunk, he calmly told me to get the bottle out so we could go. I looked inside and still couldn't see the bottle. I was blinded by my tears and was pleading with him that it was not there. He reached down and grabbed the bottle. It was there, right in front of me! I was paralyzed with fear. I didn't want to stand back up and go into the house because I knew what was waiting for me. He became so enraged, yelling and kicking, pushing my head into the trunk and asking me why I was trying to embarrass him outside like this. I looked up to the side and tried to apologize, and that's when he slammed the trunk on my face.

The trunk latch hit me right in the corner of my eye. The pain was so excruciating, and there was blood everywhere, everywhere. Millie started yelling…at me. She told me to get inside before the neighbors saw me. I was dizzy, bleeding and in a great deal of pain. Instead of taking me to a hospital, they tried to put a butterfly bandage on the cut. It was swelling up so badly that the bandage popped off. I was in so much pain, but they would not take me to the hospital. For two painful days I was kept home from school and forced to put ice on my face. Only because the swelling kept getting worse and blood was pooling in my eye, I was finally allowed to go to the doctor. I told the doctor I got hit in the eye playing baseball.

Private Affair

As the years passed and the abuse intensified, it became more difficult to hide. In fact, I was beaten in public enough for people to know. Even if they did not know, they could easily hear my screams. I missed more days of school than should be allowed, but because Tom was a teacher in St. Louis, he was able to get my school changed easily. This explains why I went to so many schools between third and sixth grade, and why school officials were never made aware of my suffering. When I went to school with marks on my face, no one ever asked any questions. I was never looked at by the school nurse, and it did not seem to matter what I was going through at home.

Millie was present for some of the physical abuse, so she obviously knew to some extent the suffering going on in that house. In fact, sometimes she was even the instigator. She would point out to Tom when

71

we didn't do the dishes properly; if we forgot to make our bed; if we didn't make her lunch the way she liked it; or if we didn't have her beer already cool when she got home from work. And like clockwork, Tom would fly into a violent rage.

Once he was worked up, Millie would try to tell him to calm down before his blood pressure got worse and to take his medicine. She would also yell at me for making him mad knowing he was sick. He had high blood pressure! This was the same woman who just told him what we had done, helped get him angry about some trivial oversight. But it was my fault.

However, there was a limit to his rage. Tom only put his hands on Millie one time that I remember. He was in one of his rages, beating us with any and everything. I guess he was being unusually hard on Jennifer so Millie stepped in to calm him down. He responded by pushing her away. She fell over an ottoman and landed on her butt. It sounded like World War III was coming. She lost control. How dare he lay a hand on her! She was yelling and screaming at him, attacking him with abandon. She immediately ran upstairs and began to pack. She was NOT going to live in a house where a man would ever lay a hand on her in anger.

Tom calmed down immediately and began to placate her, groveling and apologizing. He never touched her again. I resented her so much by this point that I wished she was dead. She could control Tom. I knew she could make him mad at us, but she could also stop his anger dead in its tracks, and she never lifted a finger to stop him from abusing me. She only stepped in when he was being too hard on Jennifer.

This is not to say that Jennifer did not receive her share of abuse. We were about the same age and usually together when we lived in St. Louis. Of course, Tom was not nearly as violent with her as he was with me. She was never beaten until she fell to the ground. She was never kicked in the stomach until she curled up into a ball. She was never choked until she blacked out. Nevertheless, she was pummeled and abused. There were times when Jennifer even took the blame for something I had done. She knew my beatings were much worse and I guess felt sorry for me a few times. I am forever grateful for those acts of kindness.

My other sister, Mary, on the other hand, was having none of that. She was a teenager when I was adopted. I guess there was not much physical abuse going on before I got there. I do remember Tom losing his temper with her one time while she was in her room. I heard him cursing and yelling, and then I heard a crash. The next thing I saw was Tom running down the stairs with Mary right behind him. She was beating the hell out of him with a large wine bottle. She got him good too. She moved out shortly after that and married her high school sweetheart.

Road Trip

We had a neighbor named Ritchie. He was a strapping boy who was the same age as Mary. He was a football player and very popular around the neighborhood. This boy was built like a professional wrestler and was a family friend. He was also very kind to me. He always tried to include me in the neighborhood events. When Ritchie was around, Tom would never lose it and beat us. He was like my big brother or guardian angel.

One year the family took a trip to Canada or New York, some place north. We drove the red van and Ritchie came along. This was the greatest thing for me, since I could finally let my guard down. I assumed Tom would never become violent with witnesses around. This assumption proved to be untrue. I remember the trip started off fine. We were singing songs and telling stories. Jennifer and I took turns reading from books. I was reading a Peanuts book to everyone, laughing at the jokes. I came upon the name Marcia and I pronounced it as it was spelled "Marseeya." Tom was driving at the time with Ritchie in the passenger seat of the van. Tom told me to read that again and get it right.

The mood in the van changed immediately. I really did not know how to pronounce the name correctly. Each time I would mess up Tom would make me reread the page even though I had no idea how to pronounce the name. Tom just lost it and began punching and hitting me while driving. I was trying to dodge the blows while Millie was yelling at Tom to watch the road. He just kept blindly punching as he drove until he was able to locate where I was cowering and then I was beaten pretty badly.

I looked up in time to see Ritchie looking out the window, purposely looking away from the violence. That was a crushing blow. I thought Ritchie was the one person in the world that would save me. Of course, I never wanted to test that theory, but it was good to have hope. He just let Tom brutalize me. In Ritchie's defense, he was probably only 17 or 18. I am sure he was in shock at what he saw.

The entire trip turned out to be a nightmare. We would spend the nights at camp sites along the way, mostly KOA's. There were two tents, one for the boys and one for the girls. To my chagrin, Ritchie chose to sleep in the van. This left Tom and me to share a tent. I remember getting into my sleeping bag and lying as far away from Tom as the tent would allow. He asked me what the hell I was doing, why was I laying like that? I started to answer when he told me that he did not forget what I had done that day. He told me to never get into my sleeping bag until he said so. That night was another horrible night for me. I cannot believe Tom was so brazen to molest me with his wife in a tent right next to mine, but he had been doing it for so long in a room right next to where she was sleeping that I guess he didn't care.

The Worst Day

Gradually the violence began in earnest, and his sexual advances toward me were no longer masked in parenting or caring, just abuse. There was no more shaving or showering, no need for enemas or suppositories; no peeing together…just his attacks. These had been some of the very toughest days of my life and I didn't believe things could get any worse.

By this time, his attacks were a constant part of my life. I don't remember individual events because there were so many and they merged together. This was a horrible time in my life and I was ashamed of what I was forced to do. I was also becoming ashamed of what was happening to me physically. I was getting older, and my body was reacting more and more. I wish I could say my penis did not get erect when he forced himself on me. I didn't enjoy the feeling at all, but I would still become aroused. I could not understand it. It was so humiliating and demeaning, and to know that he was getting me erect was maddening!

I still remember the day it happened. It was on his bed, during the day. I had gotten into trouble for something and the rest of the family was out of the house. I knew it was coming and dreaded them leaving. He stormed into my room and asked me why I made him so angry and if I liked being beaten. I was weeping by then, but it did not matter.

I tried to make a break for it, to run to his room or lock myself in the bathroom, but he caught me. He threw me on the bed, beat me, beat me hard until I was barely conscious and began his regular routine. However, this time something was different. This time, if felt different. He was very forceful but, the feeling was different. My body was reacting differently. I was suddenly aware of my surroundings and what was happening to me. I mean, I always knew what he was doing to me, but suddenly it was all so different.

I tried so hard to push him off of me, to make him stop, but he forced me to endure the horrible feelings that were mounting. I struggled and fought but I was too weak to get him off of me, I was too weak to stop him. This time I was almost in a panic, I didn't know why, but I had to get him off of me, I had to stop him…but I couldn't. Then all of the sudden, it happened. I had my first orgasm. It was so powerful and uncomfortable; it was almost painful. I didn't want it to feel good. All the other times I just tolerated it, although I was erect, it was never a good feeling. That all changed that day.

Aftermath

This really changed the way Tom treated me from that point on. The physical and sexual abuse was non-stop. From his perspective I became a willing sex toy he had to play with. I dreaded him coming into my room at night, or any time really. Until then, I was just a victim. I did not want, desire or enjoy anything he did to me. Even him forcing me to perform oral sex on him was not as unnerving because I cried the whole time, never a willing participant. Now, he had broken me, made me ejaculate in the most painful and debilitating way. Now in his eyes, I wanted it, he just had to beat me into asking for it.

Tom robbed me of something so valuable and important that day. Everything else he had done to me up to that point, everything he had forced me to do was still something involuntary, something I could honestly say I didn't want. These were all things I didn't like, and there was never a question in my mind, or in his, that I had no interest in what he was doing to me. Now that was gone, now he had his proof that I was a willing participant, that I had gotten something out of it, that it was a mutual interaction. So there was never any more gentleness or coaxing, there was only force and abuse.

Not only did this change the way I was treated, this changed the way I viewed myself. I never had an orgasm before. I was already somewhat sexually curios, but there was never any desire, interest, or curiosity for a man, or a boy, just curiosity for women. My curiosity was always for the opposite sex. There was never any exploration with another boy, never any trying to figure out another boy's body. I had heard of boys who were curious about other boys in the foster homes or group facilities, but that wasn't me. Now my first true sexual experience was with a man. It's hard to tell yourself that you didn't want it when you were able to have an orgasm. Something that felt good, no matter how much I didn't want it to. Even more than that, I wanted to feel that again.

I was so devastated, I believed I was worthless. How could I even look at myself as a normal boy anymore? I was no longer just a victim being forced to commit acts unwillingly. Another MAN made me have an orgasm! And it was not the last orgasm he made me have. There was nothing I could do to stop them from coming after the first one was dragged out of me. From that point on, I always had orgasms from his molestation.

I hated myself for what I felt, for what he made me feel. Although, I wanted to feel that feeling again. I wanted it so badly, but I didn't want it from him! I was too young to understand the value of that feeling and the emotional bond this wonderful feeling could bring about. Instead, I just had a desire to have that feeling, yet hated to have that feeling again. It seemed as if it was happening daily, something that felt good, yet I hated to have pulled from me.

It was only a physical feeling, instead of the love or the bond that should have been associated with it. In fact, not only was there no kind of emotion attached, there was a great deal of shame. What should have been one of the single most wonderful and important events was forever tarnished, forever a negative and shameful memory. This shame did not go away and never got any better.

Church

Eventually Tom grew tired of the Catholic Church. He was never a big fan of it anyway, and come to think of it, neither was I. I just could not understand how we could go to a mass at the old cathedral, where the entire mass was in Latin, and still be expected to get something out of it. So we joined a Methodist church. Tom immediately got involved in the church to the point of teaching Sunday school, and because I was his boy, I went to church with him while Millie and Jennifer continued to attend mass.

I remember messing up real bad one Sunday morning. I fell asleep instead of getting up when I was told. When Tom came upstairs, ready to leave for church, I was still asleep on the bed. He snatched me out of bed and began yelling and cursing at me until I was dressed. We made it on time. I went to Sunday school and then church service. We even stayed for the luncheon. I had completely forgotten about my infraction.

As the church cleared out we walked down to one of the lower floors of the church. Once we were out of sight of the few stragglers, Tom pulled me into a closet. "Did you think I'd forgotten about this morning?" He pushed me down onto my knees and pulled his penis out. I guess even God could not protect me from Tom Wilson. I started to really believe I deserved this treatment.

Time to Move

The house in St. Louis was falling further and further into disrepair. The roof was collapsing and leaking. The basement was still flooding and had standing water, constantly. A pipe burst in the yard and now the basement flooded even without the rain. Roaches were becoming more and more aggressive; they didn't even run when the lights came on anymore.

At this point, we started to go trailer shopping. Yes, that's right. Tom and Millie were contemplating moving from a stand-alone house into a trailer. The trailer they found was a new double-wide with two bathrooms and three bedrooms. My room was going to be on the other side of the house. I no longer had to worry about waking Tom and Millie with my coughing. There would be no leaky basements. Hey, things were looking up.

We were leaving Missouri and going across the river to a town called Freeburg, Illinois. This would be a new beginning. Tom told me that we were all making a fresh start in a new town. At this point things could only get better. (Wrong again!)

4. Freeburg - Home Life

New Life

I was getting ready to enter the seventh grade. We were moving for our health, our education, our peace of mind, and a fresh start. The schools were getting worse, the foundation and roof of our house had eroded past the point of saving. It made no sense to invest more money into a house that was going to eventually collapse on itself. It was time for change, to invest into something new. This was our chance to leave the old life behind; the old problems and the old sins were going to be left in St. Louis.

This was my chance to start life anew – a new school, new friends, and new location. I was going to remake myself. Tom kept letting me know that this was our chance to do away with all of the old problems. He would tell me this almost as a reassurance that things were going to get better. As the time for the move drew nearer things really began to look up. While he did not completely change his ways, he seemed too focused on the move to be as angry and lustful as he usually was. When I did get my "punishment," he seemed honestly remorseful once he was done. He would even weep and apologize! He would tell me that this move was going to change everything. He was going to take his medication and keep his temper in check. I believed him. At this point in my life, I needed some hope, anything positive to grasp onto, and this new move was it.

Town

I have read many books written by African-Americans that used words like drug infested, crack addicted, gun shots during the night, and violence when describing their traumatic childhood. This was the complete opposite. The new location Tom and Millie selected as our new home was a little town called Freeburg, Illinois. Freeburg had a bustling population of 2,500, was a mere 30 minutes from St. Louis, and about two decades away from the 1980's. Complete with two gas stations, one in town and one outside the town proper, this was a quaint little town. There was one stoplight in the center of town and two churches, one catholic and one protestant. We only had one grocery store - Sanders. There were no fast food restaurants, but we did have Hucks, similar to a 7-Eleven. Surprisingly enough, this small town had its own education system, with an elementary school and a high school. The small town mentality of Freeburg was best exemplified by the high school mascot - the "Mighty Midgets." And yes, they are still called the mighty midgets, even though midget is now considered a derogatory term.

On paper, Freeburg appeared to be the perfect little town. Just far enough away from St. Louis to avoid the influx of crime and the crack epidemic of the 80's, but close enough to still get to work with a limited amount of driving. The town was so small that you didn't even have to dial the full telephone number, just the last four digits to call a house inside the town. While there was one main highway running through town, there was limited traffic. You could actually see the stars at night, because we were surrounded by farmland and cornfields. This was definitely a suburb, not a rural area. The town had just enough retail to be self-sufficient, as long as you didn't need groceries after 8:00 p.m. There were only two police officers in the police department, the Sherriff and his deputy. It was quiet and it was peaceful.

New Home

My family bought a brand new double-wide trailer. While not as large as the home in the city, it was much better. Everything was new. The bathrooms did not leak. The toilets worked. The electrical system did not rely on fuses (or a penny, if you are old enough) and had a breaker box. There was a new washer and a dryer, no more laundromat. The greatest amenity for me was that Tom and Millie had a master bedroom at one end, and my room and Jennifer's room was at the complete opposite end of the trailer. I no longer had to worry about being beaten for coughing, because I would be too far away to disturb them. I figured he wouldn't dare try to come into my room at night because the walls were hollow and Jennifer's room was right beside mine. There was also nowhere to sneak me, unlike the house in St. Lois with its two floors along with the basement. Now we were all on the same floor, almost always in direct line of sight of each other.

This prefabricated construction was going to be a good thing, since we were leaving a house in which I could be beaten mercilessly without fear of detection because of brick walls. These new lots were so small that we could hear the neighbors' televisions at night, and the sound traveled right through the thin walls. I was going to be safe, merely by this new design. (I never really took into account that we were going to live in a trailer right in the middle of "tornado alley"). My prayers were finally being answered. I was going to be safe without having to lose my home and family.

The trailer park we moved into was also quite nice and upscale, if that makes any sense? There were street lights and semi-paved roads. It was right off the main highway and had plenty of double-wide and triple-wide trailers. Some of the people in the neighborhood even had Lincoln's and Cadillac's. One lady even had a Porsche. All in all, Deerfield Court was actually a pretty nice place to live.

Great Location

It seemed Tom and Millie had really made a good choice. The schools were some of the best in the state and it was a peaceful community.

I would have been proud to raise my family in this town, without a second thought…except for one thing. This town had never had a black family, or even a black child living within its borders. There had never been an African-American ever to attend either the elementary or the high school in the town's history.

Now, I know many people who went to school with only a few other minorities. But there is a big difference from being one of a few and being the only one. There is a huge difference between being the only black family and the only black person, especially when you are the only black child in a white family that has no idea how to understand what it is like to be black in the U.S. in the 1980's. Little did I know, I had an entirely new battle to face, and like always, I was going to be facing it alone.

Festival

The first weekend after we moved into the new home, Freeburg had a festival in its park. This was my first real interaction with the town's residents. We didn't know anyone, but Tom and Millie wanted to experience this new town. This seemed like the perfect opportunity. As I walked around, I realized the kids my own age seemed very excited to see me. There was a storm of activity around me as children started to realize I was going to be attending school with them. I was an anomaly, since most of these children had never interacted with a black person before. Now, they were going have a black kid in their class. I found out that for most of these children, the only frame of reference they had for black people was the Huxtable's from the Cosby Show and athletes they saw on television.

I soon realized that these children were excited to have a black boy coming to their school, dunking a basketball, running like a gazelle at a track meet, big afro with the pick in the back. They were excited to have the stereotypical African-American boy coming to their school dominating all athletic events, breakdancing in the locker rooms, beat boxing like Dougie Fresh… but that was NOT me. Being raised by white people my whole life meant that was never going to be me.

I did not speak slang, I spoke like they did. I could not moon walk, I did not breakdance, or even know any rap songs beyond "rappers delight." I didn't own any parachute pants and didn't dress like Run or DMC. I grew up listening to country music and classic rock. I did listen to some pop music, but kept my mind open to all music. I had no idea what the black culture meant or how to represent it. I was just a child, who happened to have a dark complexion. This was a let down to my classmates.

Small Town Justice

I got my first taste of the small town mindset that summer before school started. I also received my first taste of racial profiling. One afternoon, a Freeburg police car showed up in front of our trailer and the officer tried to arrest me. Apparently it was reported that a black kid was seen throwing bricks at a Corvette near the middle of the town. Two children had seen the assailant and provided the police officer with a description. Since I was the only black child in town, I was naturally the first and only suspect. As soon as he saw me, I could tell that cop just knew I was guilty. He was already filling out his initial arrest paperwork.

As fortune would have it, I had gone to work with Tom that day where he taught summer school. Usually I stayed at home with Jennifer, but on that day he wanted me to come with him. After some explaining, the police accepted my alibi. It was later found that the two kids that provided the identification were actually the ones who threw the bricks. Had I not gone into work with Tom, I am pretty sure I would have been held responsible for their actions all because, "I fit the description."

Abuse

Even with some of the early problems I had adjusting, I really believed this new house and new town was going to change my life. I believed the physical and sexual abuse was going to stop. Everything was shiny and new, with no blemishes or dirt. Our family seemed to be operating as a unit. Since we were all new, we were finally working together, trying to adjust to our new surroundings, and putting our collective best foot forward. There were few outbursts. Tom was keeping his temper in check. I interpreted his lack of sexual contact with me as a good sign that I was making him happy, since I wasn't really getting into trouble. Tom and Millie were adjusting to their new driving schedule and trying to make friends with the neighbors. It really seemed like this new and improved house was making us a new and improved family.

However, within a few months, the problems we had with the house in St. Louis followed us. While the new structure was still sound, we had brought the roaches and the mice with us. Since we did not keep a clean house, these critters began to thrive. As anyone who has ever had roaches can attest, once you are infested, it is virtually impossible to get rid of them, especially in a trailer. However, from the outside it still looked good and modern. To outsiders, it looked like the Wilson's were doing quite well. But from the inside, thing were quickly falling apart, filthy and dirty. Changing our location did not change who we were or how we lived.

Our family life soon deteriorated as well. Since Tom and Millie still worked in St. Louis, it took them longer to get home every day. Being surrounded by families with children, Jennifer and I became easily distracted and rushed through our chores and homework. We wanted to hurry so we could hang out with the neighborhood kids. Something was always left undone or forgotten; sometimes it was dinner, dishes or laundry. This meant there was always a reason to be angry.

Tom was quickly falling back into his old routine. Weekly he was becoming more violent, more abusive and back into his old ways. He was also finding more and more reasons to target his anger towards me. I fell back into my fear driven existence. The angrier he became, the more I messed up. While there was no basement to pull me into late at night, there were plenty of places to drive me where no one would see what he was doing to me. Just as we had brought the roaches and dirty living, we brought all of the family's dirty secrets, too. We had carried with us all of the evils and grime that infested our old life. I was fooled into believing things would be better, but I was wrong again.

Grade School

I started seventh grade at Freeburg Elementary School as the first and only black child ever to attend that school. I wasn't the typical black kid, so instead of being enamored, the children were just cynical. I was not a gifted athlete. I could jump, but there were other kids in my school that could jump higher. I could run pretty fast, but there were plenty of white kids that would blow by me on the track. I just wasn't that special or talented black kid. As such, I was just that black kid. I remember one kid asking me to come to school with my hair picked out like one of the basketball players he had seen on the Chicago Bulls. I had no idea what he was talking about. He asked me why I did not grow a natural, I told him that it was natural. He just walked away shaking his head. So instead of being the fascinating black kid, I was just the new kid who wasn't meeting anyone's expectations.

Education

The schools in town were amazing. The classes were small and much was expected of the students. Not that I did what I was told or what was assigned but I still managed to learn a great deal even if I wasn't doing all the work I should have. The teachers were also very skilled and very tough. You had to get a 94 to have an A. For the most part, I was not made to feel out of place by the teaching staff. I even met my favorite teacher, Mr. Brewer, at that school. He was our reading and English teacher. His afro was larger than mine could ever be and his wife was an opera singer. He was loud and kind of outlandish. Sometimes, he would have us listen to a moody blues record or ELO, an entire side, and then write down how it made us feel.

Other times we would read the classics like Hemmingway or Steinbeck and then switch to Doonesbury and Bloom County comic strip books. If you were not paying attention you may get hit in the head with a flying chalk board eraser. He inspired us not only to read, but to enjoy learning. He showed me that reading was important and it could be fun. You just had to sprinkle in subjects you enjoyed amongst the required reading. Even with all my internal troubles, he helped create an environment that had me feeling I had value and that I was important in this world. He did this for every person in the class.

Bullying

As the school year progressed I started to notice signs of trouble. I would get out of class to find that my locker was trashed. We didn't have locks in elementary school, but we did have lockers. Only my locker would be trashed, with my books and papers all over the hallway. Of course this was upsetting, but I would just pick them up and shove them back into my locker. I began to notice this happened more and more frequently as the year progressed, and it only happened to me.

I also became the target of aggression for the overweight kids in the eighth grade. The word "Nigger" would be overheard at recess and every now and then someone would push me into a fight. It seemed like the chunkiest kids were always the toughest only because they were the biggest. They were starting to come at me more and more on the playground at recess. Sometimes I would fight, sometimes I wouldn't. It just depended upon the circumstance. I tried to stay to myself and not draw any attention. I just tried to avoid the bullying. I didn't really attribute these attacks to racism, as much as bullying. It happened to other kids to, even if it wasn't as much. While I was the target of these kids, bullies will pick on any victim they can find, so it wasn't just me…it was just mainly me.

In eighth grade I noticed even more trouble. The year started off okay. Since I was one of the older kids in my school, there were still a few kids that wanted to fight me, but I could handle them easy enough. However, I started to run into high school kids at the bus stop that would try to pick fights with me, too. These kids were quite a bit older than I, but would still find their way over to where I was just to mess with me. They would warn me that I was going to be in trouble when I got into high school, their school.

Poverty

Going to school and getting to know the other students, I also began to realize we were still kind of poor, even by trailer park standards. Now, don't get me wrong, we did have a shiny new double-wide to be proud of. However, we were still driving the same old red van that would not start when you needed it to. Most of our neighbors had nice cars that still ran good. The neighborhood children were also pretty well off. Many of them had Nintendo's and Cable TV, while some even had televisions in their rooms. They also had nice clothes, name brand shoes, and good school supplies.

I never owned a video game console until I joined the Army. My clothes still came from the Salvation Army or maybe K-Mart. The Wilson's were still using rabbit ears for television reception when I graduated from high school and when I went off to the Army. It wasn't that we didn't have the glitz and things that would spoil a child, we simply didn't have much period.

A good example of our thrifty lifestyle was my bike. Like everyone else in my trailer park, I had a dirt bike. I know I should have been grateful just to have that bike. I was reminded of that quite often as a child. However, unlike everyone else, my bike was a hodgepodge mix of other bikes. It was a tragedy on wheels. That chain would slip off for no reason at all. The seat was not secure and would rotate if I wasn't careful. The front wheel wouldn't always stay aligned with the handle bars. This meant that if I did a wheelie or a jump, there was no guarantee my front wheel would be straight when I hit the ground. Ever the hard-headed child, I still chose to keep up with the neighborhood boys when we took to BMX trick riding. Leaving a dirt ramp and seeing your front wheel turn sideways, even though your handlebars are straight, still causes me to wince in hindsight. I ate more dirt than a little bit because of that cheap bike.

This is not a "poor-me" story, this bike almost killed me! I usually had to ride home from scouts with this raggedy bike. I had repeatedly asked my parents for a light or at least some reflectors. This was an investment they chose not to make. One Thursday after scouts I found myself riding home in the dark, with no lights and no reflectors. I was coming around a corner on the street when I heard a vehicle approaching. I quickly turned the handlebars to get out of the way and nothing happened. The handlebars turned but the front wheel stayed the course…and that van hit me, knocking me up and over the vehicle as it tried to stop. That cheap dirt bike almost got me killed.

Tom and Millie rushed to the hospital after they were informed of the accident. Tom seemed genuinely concerned for my welfare, but Millie's response was classic - *she* was so embarrassed. Why did I embarrass the family by doing this? What if the driver decided to sue for the damage I may have caused to his vehicle? We could lose the trailer! They made me go to scouts, because I sure as hell no longer wanted to. They made me ride my raggedy bike into town and knew that I would have to ride back in the dark! She never asked if I was okay! Thank God for a young body. I suffered nothing more than a twisted knee and swollen wrist and was back in school within two days. Ironically, I was actually grounded for getting hit by a car.

A Twist

Surprisingly, the beatings became a little different than they were in

St. Louis. While the violence was still unpredictable and painful, Tom was now pushing me towards something. He began to tell me during the physical abuse, "You know how to make this stop," while punching, slapping, and kicking me. Of course, I thought he meant by doing the right thing. But, that didn't make him stop. Telling him to take his medicine didn't work either. These beatings also lasted longer. He was now breaking my discipline up into two parts. He still found his way into my room at night; he still deviated down a dirt road on rides back to the house; He still forced himself on me, but it was different. He was no longer making his sexual abuse a part of my discipline.

The first few occasions of these new punishments were excruciating because they were long and he made me feel that I knew how to make it all stop. But he would not tell me, he wanted me to tell him. Each wrong answer drove him further and further into his rage until he said "you know what I want" and I finally understood. He wanted me to ask him for sex or to make him feel good. As soon as I did, the beating immediately stopped. He wanted a willing participant.

When I first arrived in Freeburg, the sexual contact was mild and Tom was treating it more like some innocent exploration, just something that fathers and sons do together. He tried to coerce me into being a willing participant who could learn to like or at least accept this sick type of affection. I never took to or enjoyed that treatment. It then became a type of punishment as a means of furthering his desires once he found his little night time or early morning touches did not stimulate my curiosity. But now, instead of the usual physical and sexual means of punishment, being psychologically molested became a way out of punishment. I guess he could justify his deeds by saying that I was asking for it. This had become the normal outcome of my punishment.

Now he had elevated it to something that I had to ask for. He made me articulate that I wanted to engage in sexual activity in order not to have further pain. In his sick mind I was slowly becoming this little play toy that was really performing sexual acts with him of my own accord. I also noticed that unlike before, he had to wait to complete his abuse. He could still beat me in the common areas as long as the beating continued in my room. Then he would wait for the right response from me before he stopped. He could no longer drag me into the basement or out of sight because we were in a trailer. So he would actually bide his time and wait until his opening was there. This meant he would drive me to band practice, or he would come into my room at night and wake me up. He would tell me to stop faking like I was asleep and say "you know what you asked me to do."

Hearing that door creak open in the middle of the night was horrible. Knowing it was coming, waiting to hear the door open, was even worse. Each time, I would hope he would forget about me being a "bad child," but deep down I knew he wouldn't, especially since I asked for it, literally. If I resisted, he would immediately begin choking or punching me while asking me with what seemed genuine curiosity – "what are you doing?" He would sincerely ask me why I was trying to not suck his penis or let him suck mine. He really seemed amazed and offended as if I had reneged on a deal!

I cannot remember how many times this happened. To me it seemed like a daily occurrence, which probably is not possible. However, it did happen often and became the only way out of the abuse and pain. He would just beat and beat me until I said those magic words. It could go on for hours. Then he would calm down and I would find myself on a drive in that van or alone with him in the house. He no longer had to keep beating me during the drive because I had asked him for it. It was like he was doing this for me, like he was doing a favor for me. He had no concern that he was going to get caught.

Trouble at School

This all happened before I was out of the eighth grade. I was still trying to hold on, trying to be a normal boy, but my home life really began to have a cumulative effect on me. I started doing worse in school, I wasn't turning in assignments, or doing my school work. I was fighting more and more and even getting detention. Being in a small town meant that everyone knew everyone's business. They even put the names of the children who had detention or a suspension in the town paper, the *Freeburg Tribune.* So the very violence and abuse that was causing me to lose control of my school life was being exacerbated by the fact that I was getting into more trouble - and the whole town knew!

I know parents out there are silently applauding this idea of publishing the names of children who get into trouble at school. Heck, as a parent, the idea even sounds good to me. However, as a Wilson, it caused me no end of misery. It is one thing to get into trouble, but to have my name in our paper meant that now Millie had skin in the game. I was embarrassing her! When she was mad, Tom was able to do just about anything to punish me. We lived in a trailer park for God's sake. What was she so worried about? Of course, she just thought he was taking me for a drive in that red van so that the neighbors would not hear me screaming from my beatings. Well, she was half right.

It was just a poisonous environment. Everything was my fault. Since Tom and Millie had no understanding of the racial problems I was facing, they thought I was just bad. The school didn't understand what I was going through at home each night, so the teachers just thought I was lazy and a troublemaker. I was just a bad child to everyone. Friends were becoming more and more scarce, tired of me mooching school supplies or money for lunch. Many of their parents did not like them playing with me anyway. I could not win.

New Scouts

I still had to do my scouting and joined a local troop. These were the same racist little kids I went to school with. I went to scouts with boys that called me a "nigger" on a regular basis. I had to sit with them, meet their parents, and still look to the next day when they would pick on me and fight me at school. I even tried out for the basketball team, but Tom came up to the school and pulled me out because it conflicted with scouts. I was so close to having my Eagle Scout that nothing would stand in the way, not even me. Finally, I got my Eagle Scout while I was in eighth grade, right after my thirteenth birthday. While this should have been an exciting moment for me, it was just pathetic. I was standing there with a sash full of merit badges and all of my "accomplishments" and felt no pride at all. It wasn't even really about me. It was Tom and Millie's day. It was one of the few times in my life that Millie actually seemed proud of me.

For me, the best thing about scouting was when Tom and Millie would send me to a few camps during the summer months. This was an opportunity to be away from the Wilson's. I could walk in the woods alone, thinking of what my life had become. I could perform tasks without that nervousness and fear that disrupted my thinking. I could fall asleep without worrying if someone was going to force themselves upon me. I was able to escape my stressful life and relax.

As always, Tom found a way to even make these peaceful excursions a bad memory. When I was a cub scout, Tom used to ask me about circle jerks during my camping trips and I never even knew what he was talking about. Now that I was older and his sexual deviancies were in full swing, the tone of those conversations had changed dramatically. I guess he hoped my experiences at home would drive me to homosexual activities. Maybe that is how he got his need screwed up. Whatever the reason, now he would debrief me as soon as I got home from these camps.

The most memorable event was my two week trip to the National Jamboree in Fort A. P. Hill. This was the longest I had been away at one time. As he picked me up, he again started talking about me sharing a tent with older boys. That I was showering with these boys. That he knew seeing these naked boys turned me on. He demanded to know what I was doing during this camp out and would not take "nothing" for an answer. He then became agitated and accusatory.

He could not believe that I just went to camp. He demanded that I admit that I was messing with these other boys. When I denied it he got mad. Yet he seemed to grow angry at the thought of me engaging in sexual activity with these other boys. He refused to believe that I never messed with anyone. I was so confused, but answered honestly. In the end, I was getting beaten for messing around with other boys when I clearly did not. I could not understand what he was trying to do or what he was trying to get me to say.

He was in some kind of jealous rage, punching and hitting me as he pulled over on the side of the road. Then he pulled out his penis and forced me to suck it saying he knew this was not the only penis I had been sucking on, asking me if the other boys were bigger than him. Did I let them cum in my mouth? Did I let them suck me off? Did I have anal sex with any of the younger boys? All the while he would get more and more excited as he accused me of these sick acts. It wasn't enough for him to be having his way with me; he wanted me to be like him. He wanted me to be gay.

So, my memories of the scouts were forever tarnished by the violence and sick abuse I had to deal with and because of Tom's demands to know how I interacted with other boys. I went through so much pain and misery just to complete something I really didn't want to do. My reward for getting my Eagle Scout was just more abuse and pain. In my mind the greatest benefit for achieving my Eagle Scout badge was that I got to quit the scouts.

Snuffing out the Light

As I matured, Tom's sexual abuse increased in intensity and frequency. I noticed that it also became more aggressive and demanding. What started out as almost a game or some demented sort of exploration quickly turned into Tom fulfilling his every sick fantasy. It was like I was just some sex toy or blow up doll for his pleasure. At this point, he was very aggressive. The beatings were extraordinarily violent with little or no precursor. It did not matter where I was or what I was doing, I was punched and kicked with a quickness. As such, I was physically disciplined for the most minor nonsense, just so Tom could began his sexual domination over me. Always telling me, I asked for it.

In the deepest recesses of my memory I can still vividly recall the beginning of what was to be the worst chapter of my young life. The abuse had been going on for years. I was about 13 years old. On this particular day, I cannot remember why no one was with us in the trailer, but it was just Tom and me. Of course I had gotten into trouble for something I did at school. I think it was my grades or forging their signature on my report card. I guess that was not so minor, but it did not warrant the discipline meted out.

I had already been beaten, one of the most severe beating I ever received. Tom was angry and I had done something really wrong. I remember Tom was standing over me while I was on my knees. He was angry and forceful. He was grabbing my hair and forcing me to perform oral sex. I was choking and gagging. All the while I was crying and begging him to stop. The amount of violence he showed was simply terrifying. He kept on forcing me to suck on him until I threw up all over him. He flew into a rage, punching me in the face and daring me to choke again. He kept telling me that I better not choke again. I could not help it, the smell and the taste was so bad and he had a hold of my head, forcing himself into my mouth. I tried so hard to keep it down, but I could not. Because of my position and the fact that he was holding my head, I threw up again. He finally let me go, yelling and cussing as he walked into the hall bathroom.

I really thought he was grossed out and was going in there to wipe the vomit off himself. However, he came right back in with a jar of Vaseline. I still didn't get it; I didn't know what it could possibly be for but I had learned not to move until I was told I could move, lest I rekindle his anger and get beaten again. He dropped the Vaseline onto the rug beside me and walked behind where I was kneeling. I knew I was not finished, until he was finished. I turned around, expecting him to be standing there, but instead of standing, he was kneeling behind be. He stopped me from turning around and pushed me down on all fours. I still did not know what was going on or more likely my mind would not let me comprehend what was going to happen next.

As soon as my hands hit the floor he pushed his penis inside of me. I went from crying and whimpering to screaming in absolute terror. I struggled and tried to get away from him, anything to get the pain to stop. All fear of making him angry was gone; I just did not want this to happen. I just remember screaming "Why? Why?" I felt like I was getting ready to pass out from the shock and pain. He responded to all of my struggling by just falling on top of me while putting his hand over my mouth. This drove him deeper inside of me. God it hurt so much, so much.

While my screams were muffled by his hand, the only thing I remember hearing is his moans and groans. His face was right beside mine, beard scrapping my face, his hot breath on my neck and hair. He did not try to say anything to me, he just did it. Beyond the pain, was the shock. I was just lying there still struggling in vain to get him to stop. I was screaming and yelling, but his hand was over my face. I could barely breathe and I was panicking.

I was so very scared because I did not know what else was going to happen. I could not breathe and he was crushing my chest so I couldn't even draw in air. I had used all of my air screaming. In my head I thought he was going to kill me right there. In my heart, I really wanted him to kill me.

I cannot say how long it lasted. While it could not have been more than a few minutes, it was an eternity for me. As things began to get really hazy and my body began to feel numb, he released his grip on my face, he was finished. I just lay there on the carpet as he got off me and walked into the bathroom. When he came back out he asked me why I was still lying there. He told me to get up and go to the bathroom to clean myself up. I could not move. I felt paralyzed. I was in such shock at what had occurred that I just could not assert any control over my body. Seeing that I did not respond, Tom repeated his question, and this time yelled the order to go clean myself up. With this, I finally got up and stumbled into the bathroom.

Once I closed the door, I just sat on the toilet and quietly cried. Everything hurt so much, even sitting on the toilet hurt. It hurt to wipe myself, it hurt to even move. I was scared to even be heard crying. My body was trembling, and I was so scared. I tried to clean myself up with toilet paper but the pain was so intense that I had to stop. I wanted to take a shower and let the warm water clean me off. Tom came to the door and told me to hurry up because Millie and Jennifer would be home soon. So I had to hurry up and finish. As much as I wiped, it seemed that more blood and slime came away each time.

I finally just put some toilet paper in my underwear in hopes that the bleeding would stop. I wiped my face off and went to flush the toilet. I remember looking inside the bowl and seeing the water. It was beet red, like I had been shot. I just remember how red the water was as I flushed it down. It was so much that I had to flush it again, since the water was still pink after the first flush.

When I walked out Tom told me to stop faking it for attention because I was limping when I walked out. He also told me that it only hurt because I did not relax. He treated this like it was all my fault, and that I could have avoided this pain if I had done the right thing. He also told me that it would not hurt as much next time and that I would get used to it! While that was not said in a threatening way, I heard the threat. This was going to happen again!

That night I did not sleep. I just lay there. There was no anger or even self-pity. I was just in shock about what happened. My body just shut down. As I lay in bed looking up at the ceiling I was just completely overwhelmed. Just when I thought I had experienced all of the pain that life had to offer, I really did not think I could have sunk any lower, or that things could get any worse. Now I saw my life for the bleak reality it was. Things would always get worse. Tom would find new and surprising ways to destroy my trust and eviscerate my spirit. I just lay there in that bed until morning. All I could do was pray, but the words sounded hollow after what I had experienced. I could not see any hope for my life.

That night was more terrifying than anything that had been done to me to that point. I knew he was violent, but this horror was overwhelming and all-consuming. It elevated my fear of Tom to new heights. I didn't know anything could hurt so much. I am not only speaking of the enormous physical pain, but the emotional trauma as well. I had trouble getting up out of bed the next morning and I had to sit out of gym class that day as well. In fact, I was so scared that I did not have a bowel movement for almost a week. When it did come out I started bleeding all over again. The pain of going to the bathroom was so intense that I almost bit through my tongue trying not to scream. Yet, that wasn't the worst of it.

More than all of the physical pain was the humiliation and the stark reminder of how I was violated. The next day I had to deal with the fact that semen and blood kept running down my leg. My jeans were wet, even with toilet paper in my crotch. There was no way I could tell myself it didn't happen, that it was just a dream. While I might have been able to dismiss the pain, pretending it was a larger than normal bowel movement, I could not dismiss what was leaking out of me. I thought everybody knew. I tried not to walk funny, but could not help it! Even though I had dark jeans on, there was a wet spot in the rear! How could they not know? I was leaking blood from my butt.

It may seem like this would be less shameful than being forced to perform oral sex on a man, but that was not the case for me. I felt there was some part of me that was safe, that I wasn't gay as long as I did not let that happen to me. Maybe it was because that was the only thing left that Tom had not taken from me, it was all I had left. Then, he took that from me too. All of my struggling and fighting meant nothing. I couldn't even defend myself from being anally raped. I couldn't even look at myself in the mirror. What kind of boy lets this happen to him?

I never imagined he would have done that to me. I knew it happened to other people, but I never thought Tom would have done that to me. For some reason, I thought his love for me would stop him from 'going all the way.' He may have continuously hurt me, but I never thought he would ever do anything to ruin me. I never thought I would ever experience something like that. Not after everything else I had gone through. But, I was wrong again!

His attack that night made it clear that Tom had complete control over me; that he could hurt me in any way he chose and in ways I could never imagine. From that night on and for years to come, I was utterly terrified of Tom. I never wanted to feel that kind of pain again. The beatings still came, and of course he still molested me when he felt the desire. I wish I could say that was the only time Tom actually raped me.
Because of my mental blocks, I don't remember, but I know the other dark spots are in my recollection. I know that if I put forth the effort, I could recall each time in detail. However, I choose not to do that for fear that the

stress of all of those repressed memories will move to eclipse the life I have fought so very hard to achieve. However, it is safe to say that it happened on more than one occasion. It is also safe to say that I was able to completely block out these debased and horrid events of my life…eventually.

The effects of those violations had a traumatic impact on my childhood and my young adult life. There is nothing more helpless than being forcibly taken in such a way. Oh, after a while Tom seemed remorseful. He even got me my own tube of Preparation H. He told me that I would feel better and it helps heal the rips and tears. That is not true, and it hurt like hell when I put it on. Of course he apologized about 'losing control' and promised it would never happen again. By that time, we both knew it was just his little game. Eventually it would happen again, maybe not as bad, or maybe even worse. He knew what he intended each time he made that promise.

The shame of feeling the greasy leakage going down your legs never completely goes away. A little boy having to wipe semen from his body leaves a scar. Knowing you have committed every homosexual act deemed as a sin in the Bible affects the makeup of your very being. It is much, much more than the physical impact. After all, the rips heal; the bleeding stops; eventually you can have a pain-free healthy bowel movement. But, you can never undo what was done, even if no one ever knows about it but you.

Just to know you would do anything to avoid the pain becomes a shame all on its own. Even if it means learning how to perform fellatio without gagging, or allowing a man to ejaculate down your throat without throwing up. Knowing you will do anything to appease a man who is supposed to love you, supposed to be your father, and that you will ask to perform oral sex, and will even try to do a good job just to avoid having him force his penis inside your butt is so humiliating. It is all the more humiliating when deep down inside you know there is nothing you can do to stop him from doing it again, and the debilitating pain of knowing that he will do it again and again. That no one will stop him, certainly not you! How do you survive that?

The Knife's Edge

I remember one night about a year later, I was still trying to deal with my humiliation and misery. While I tried to have faith in God, I could not even have faith that things would ever get better. Tom's sexual assaults had progressed to the point where anything was possible. I never got used to what he was doing to me, but I could not stop him. He took me down that horrible path again and again stripping me of my humanity, violating me, and making me clean up the mess. I could not wipe away what he did to me; I could not even have normal bowel movements anymore. Everything hurt: mentally, emotionally and physically.

Once again, I had to succumb to another vicious beating from Tom. After this particular beating I just lay on my bed resigned to what I knew was going to happen next. I eventually grasped the understanding that the more vicious the beating, the more aggressive his sexual assault would be. I had just taken a pretty bad beating and I dreaded the knowledge that I was going to wind up quietly shaking and sobbing on my mattress with Tom's hand over my mouth and his body pressing me down. I knew it was coming and I was scared.

Tom was sleeping on the couch, which meant he was definitely planning on visiting my room. I cannot remember when or exactly why, but I started keeping a kitchen knife between my mattress and box spring sometime before that night. This was not something I only did out of anger. Of course I was angry for what that man was doing to me, but it was really out of fear. Tom's physical attacks had become more and more vicious. I no longer trusted him; I no longer believed he had boundaries he would not cross. I knew now he was capable of doing anything to me. I really believed he was going to kill me one day.

That night, instead of waiting for him to come into my room I decided to go to him. However, I was not going alone; I was bringing the knife with me. I didn't know how that night was going to end, but something told me I had to do this. Once I heard him snoring, I quietly entered the living room and placed the razor edge of that wooden-handled silver kitchen knife to his throat. The light through the window reflected off the blade as I placed it on his neck. All I had to do was draw back and the abuse would be over. The beatings would stop. I would be free.

Something stayed my hand. I cannot tell you why I didn't go through with it. There was no reason not to. It was quiet; the knife was serrated, so it would have done a great deal of damage, even with a single swipe. He had just finished beating me severely. I knew that the beating was just a gauge to the sexual assault that was to come, but I could not do it. I could not kill the only man who ever wanted to be my father. I just stood there looking at the way the light played on the edges of that blade, trying to get up the nerve to end this horrible existence. But I could not. I went back into my room and put the knife under my pillow. While I could not kill Tom in his sleep, I knew if he came into my room that night to assault me, I would kill him. I knew I would.

I stayed awake the whole night, but he never visited me. The next day, I took the knife out of my room. Of course he came other nights and the beatings continued for some time, but I never took that knife out again. I was so sick with myself for being so weak, for not being able to stop Tom from abusing me. I was even more sickened by my desire to be part of a family, at any cost apparently. I continued to let myself down and demonstrated just how weak and needy I was.

How would the world have viewed me if I had killed him? Of course, after reading this, most would have considered it justifiable.

Although, to the world at that time, it would have been a little troubled black youth murdering the only man who took him in. Claiming that he was being abused? I would have spent the rest of my life in jail for a situation I was thrown into and for an action that was totally reasonable under the circumstances.

Escape

To get away from the pain and suffering in my life, I began to run away during the end of my 8th grade year. It was never planned or orchestrated. It was always just me running from Tom. Sometimes it was at night, other times it was during the day. Sometimes it was from an especially severe beating or from the violent and painful sexual assault that followed. Oftentimes, it was during the break between the physical abuse and the sexual abuse, after I was made to ask for it. I would just run before I had to do it.

Sometimes I would stay out overnight. I would just run and run. No plan, no idea where I was going. One time I just hid in a church, another time I slept in an empty van, and another at my friend's house. Sometimes I just slept in the abandoned shack down the street. I was finally beginning to realize there were worse things than being alone; there were worse things than being without a family. I was living those worse things every day.

I always returned home, not because I wanted to, but because I could not survive on my own at 12 or 13 years of age. I had nowhere else to go. Sometimes the police brought me back, most of the time I showed up on my own accord. When I arrived home it was pure Hell. I owed him now and he had every right to do whatever he wanted to me. It was always a hell of a physical beating until I begged to please him, not asked, but begged. By coming home, I was admitting defeat, admitting I was weak and he was in control. He would make those times I returned home especially degrading and painful.

Of course, he would want to know the juicy details of my night out. He would want me to tell him salacious and sick stories about my sexual exploits while I was gone all night. "How many penises did you suck?" "I know you went to the truck stop." "I know you sold your body for a place to sleep." "I know you were in the back of those trucks with several truckers." "I know those truckers were all over you when you walked up to ask for help." "Did you let any of them fuck you in the ass?" "You didn't even make them wear a condom, did you?"

When I would deny or shake my head no he would slap me across the face or punch me on the side of my head. It still wasn't enough that I was being sexually assaulted and he was having his way with me. He always wanted to reduce me to nothing. I ended up having to make up and agree with stories about me willingly engaging in homosexual acts with complete strangers.

This is what my life had been reduced to. I was coming back to a man that knew he was going to be in for a treat and felt I owed him something special. I was coming back to a woman that had no maternal feelings for me whatsoever; to her I was just in the way, just an embarrassment. I truly had nothing. I had nowhere else to go.

On to High School

By the time I was ready to enter high school, I was mentally in shambles. I had to give up any thought of my life being or getting any better. I had to relinquish all thoughts of family and what it meant to have loving parents. I had nothing and no one. My life meant nothing and I was of no value to anyone. I had tried to be strong my whole life, but I was starting to unravel and lose all hope. At this point, I believed that somehow I must have deserved this. That I had done something wrong and God was punishing me. I was trying to keep it together, but I really had nothing to grasp onto, no foundation to stand on.

10,000 Hills

5. High School & Moving Backwards

The Basics

Most children who leave 8th grade have well founded fears of their first year of high school, and mine were just as legitimate. In 8th grade you are one of the biggest and oldest kids. In fact, you proverbially run the school. In a word, you have comfort. You are familiar with your surroundings and confident in the processes involved in your school life. There is still homeroom, small lunch facilities, and even recess. You know all the kids in your class and most of the children in school know you. Since you have spent so much time there, you even have a relationship with the teachers and administration.

In high school you have to change classes, oftentimes being required to go from one end of the school to the other. Now we have new lockers and have to remember not only where our lockers are, but we must also remember a combination! I still have nightmares where I am late for class and cannot remember my high school locker combination. We no longer bring our gym clothes; we now have lockers in the gymnasium. This was a new building that seemed so much bigger than the little area we occupied in junior high.

There were new people. No longer was I one of the biggest kids in school, now I was one of the smallest. There were students that looked like full-fledged adults, complete with beards and mustaches. The wispy little hairs on my lip were barely noticeable. Kids even drove themselves to school in their own cars! And of course, these older students all had this air of confidence that no new student could possess. The teachers were new, the administration was new, and no one even knew who you were as a mere freshman. As with any grouping of people, there is a hierarchy that is unfamiliar. Instead of having a reputation to fall back onto, I was again just a number and a new face. I was starting from the bottom again.

In my freshmen class, most of us were just trying to keep a low profile and avoid any attention until we could get the lay of the land. All I wanted to do was find out how to get from class to class and not rock the boat or draw any attention from the older kids. As with any school, that was attention nobody wanted. Accidentally bumping into a senior or sitting at the wrong table at lunch were automatic ways to draw the wrath of older students. Let's face it; there were plenty of older kids who did not mind some good-natured hazing. It is the same in high school, as it is in college, sports teams, band, and even the armed forces. Most folks that were hazed just cannot wait to return the favor to the new incoming class, and my school was no exception.

The negative effect on kids of hazing or bullying may not have a significant impact itself unless the child is different. As such, most people may even have fond memories of the hazing during their high school and college days. The light hazing for being the new kid, the silly things they were forced to do, or the crazy menial tasks they had to do to be accepted. But if you were different, there may never be acceptance, only trouble.

Being Different

Because of the demographics of Freeburg Community High School, there was no way I could go unnoticed. Again, I was the first black child ever to go to that high school. While many kids from the town of Freeburg knew me or knew of me, there were now elementary school graduates from other towns that went to Freeburg High. So I was automatically the target for harassment from the older kids, as well as the kids in my own grade.

My color meant that I stood out everywhere I went: the hallway, classes, and the lunch room. Because I stood out, I became the target for any and every kid who needed an outlet. If someone wanted to be funny, they could just start telling "nigger" jokes while I was walking around. If someone wanted to be tough, they would try to get me to fight them in the hallway. If someone was bored they would just slap my books out of my hand as I went from class to class. I became the butt of every joke and target of every bully. When I would kneel down to take something out of my locker, someone would step on my back foot and cause me to fall. When I walked down the hall, someone would kick my back leg, causing me to trip on my own feet. I heard the word "nigger," porch monkey, spear chucker, or coon each time I changed classes. These things happened to me every day!

While I was not a violent person by nature, I had no problem defending myself. I had been doing it all my life, but High School was very different. To begin with, many of the kids that were pushing and tripping me were also substantially older than me. I was skinny for my age and most of them were good sized boys. It is kind of hard to try to fight a boy that outweighs you by 100 pounds. Although I tried to defend myself, I was no match for these kids. Most of the time, I was just pushed up against the lockers or punched in the stomach for not backing down.

The fights began on the first day of school and just kept happening. It was always the same, the larger and slightly overweight kids looking for someone to pick on. It was common hearing "nigger" from different directions when class let out, and being rammed against the wall every day after math class when the shop kids got out. I was just trying to remain inconspicuous in the hallway at lunch time, trying to avoid any attention. But that never worked.

There were times when I would be challenged right in the middle of the hallway, in front of everyone. The aggressors were usually much bigger than me, and were surrounded by friends, egging them on. Most of the time, I would just walk away, or try to. Every now and then, I would be surrounded and forced into a confrontation. I would usually just submit to being shoved or punched in the chest a few times.

I would try not to seem weak, but still not be threatening. Bullies like weakness and attention. It's hard to find that line and still be safe. I never struck first, never tried to hurt anyone, and tried to never exacerbate a situation. Usually, I would simply stand there and take whatever was coming. Even this was not enough to keep me out of trouble. There were simply too many bullies and I was 100 pounds soaking wet.

Occasionally, I would actually get into a full-fledged fight in the hallway. Even if I had to square off against a bigger opponent, I would try. Even if I managed to get a few licks in, others would join in and make it impossible for me to do anything but take a butt whooping. It was always a lose–lose situation, with no right way to deal with or handle the situation.

"Where were the teachers," you ask? That was the same question I asked. There was no way the teachers or administration could not predict this was going to happen. There was no way they didn't see what was happening to me. I could hear "nigger" in every class and in the hallways; the teachers were also in those classes and hallways. When I was getting soundly beaten by a larger opponent, I would look for a teacher to break up the fight, yet that rarely happened. It seemed as if the administration was willfully ignorant to what I was going through.

Defending myself did not result in a more favorable outcome either. Walking down the hall one day, I was confronted by a group of upperclassmen. One of the smaller ones stepped to the front, apparently trying to prove his worth. He was not overly aggressive, but was being encouraged into the confrontation. I was surrounded and he threw a punch at me. He missed and I stepped aside and grabbed his other arm. As it turns out, his arm was broken. And I got suspended.

Another time I was walking home from school, when a boy confronted me near the park. I was tired and had a bad day, so I did not back down. We fought for a few minutes. I didn't throw a punch, but managed to beat the boy by throwing him around a bit. However, our principal was driving by at the time and there I was, suspended again. All in all, I was suspended many times during my freshmen year, all for defending myself.

Others just got detention for fighting, I got suspended for fighting; or as I like to call it, defending myself and taking a butt whooping. Not only did I come out on the losing end of most of those fights, I would get into trouble as well. Granted the aggressor would also get detention, but I would get punished for defending myself. I would have to sit in detention after school and be made fun of and called names by the very person who started the fight.

I was roughed up in gym class constantly. Whenever we had a sport with any sort of contact involved, it was basically a pile on. I got elbowed and jabbed, pushed in the back; any way to get a cheap shot in. The gym teacher saw this and never interceded. The teachers heard them call me a "nigger" every day and did nothing.

The only time a teacher ever got involved was when I was winning a fight. If I was surrounded and being punched, there was no teacher in sight. I slowly started to get the picture - not only were the students after me, but the administration was indifferent to my plight. Every time I tried to defend myself, I found myself in trouble. This conspiracy was starting to wear me down, and I found I could not win.

This harassment was like clockwork and by the end of my freshmen year I knew exactly where I was going to get pushed and tripped. I knew what group of boys was going to start making racial jokes or using racial epitaphs as I approached. I knew who was going to try to fight me in the hallways. If I walked away, I knew I would be humiliated. This also empowered that kid and all the other kids who saw me. If I continued to fight, I knew I would just take a beating or get into trouble; usually both.

Stage

Being the target of daily harassment was difficult enough, but the social impact of always being constantly harassed was even more damaging. Again, none of these events happened in a vacuum, they happened in public. This happened in plain sight of my classmates and the halls were always crowded. In fact, a joke is not funny if no one hears it. So many times, these kids would wait until there was a crowd around to tell their newest "nigger" joke. They would wait until the hallway was full before they smashed me against the lockers and slapped my books out of my hands. Every time, I would hear everyone laughing at me.

The kids did not want to share in my misery. Friends I had in 8th grade would still say hi or smile at me, but didn't want to engage me in conversation for too long or to be seen with me. In hindsight, it's hard to blame a 14-year-old freshman for not wanting to be around me once they saw I was becoming the butt of every joke, or the punching bag for every overweight or overly-developed kid with something to prove. There was no one on my side. No one saying "kick his ass, C.T.!" There were always crowds of people cheering for the other kid, cheering for the bigger kid who started the fight and cheering for the school bully. And there I was, fighting my battles alone. No one wanted to stand up and defend me, even if I was outnumbered or overmatched, lest they too incur the wrath of the older kids. They just wanted to survive, too.

Girls

When I was in junior high, I had a few girlfriends. I knew plenty of girls and talked to them. They may not have been interested in me, but they were always nice to me. Now that we were in high school, things were different. These girls were now blossoming and becoming young ladies. They were now grading boys on more than just personality; they were looking for those who were popular, athletic, and smart. You can imagine the effect my harassment had on the girls in my school. My color now solely defined me in the most pejorative way possible. No girl wanted to be known as a "mud shark" or "nigger lover." Therefore, I wasn't on the radar of any girls anymore. There were girls I had known and been friends with since moving to town that wouldn't even acknowledge me in the hallways.

Football

I played football my first year, and to everyone's disappointment I was not the star athlete I was expected to be. This experience also turned out to be a nightmare. Practices were grueling, not because of what the coach made us do, but because of the actions of my classmates when the coaches weren't looking. The practice field was just another chance for these kids to attack me. In fact, they could hit me and be congratulated for it. Even in half pass I was getting tackled as if we were playing full speed. I took many cheap shots during practice - knees to the stomach and kidney punches in the tackles.

There were countless times when I was on the bottom of the dog pile even though I didn't have the ball. I was spit on repeatedly by my own teammates; coming out of a pile up with my facemask covered in someone else's spit. Kids from the varsity squad would even urinate on the stuff in my locker. I had to wear a piss soaked uniform onto the field. And these were *MY* teammates!

My performance on the field was abysmal. I couldn't focus or get into the rhythm. During games, the hole I was supposed to go through would close up before I got there, turning every play I ran into an outside run. I sucked that year. My confidence was broken the first day of practice for that school. In the end, I couldn't clear my head enough to perform. The funny thing was, excluding my high school experience, I was actually a pretty good football player. I played tackle with many of these same boys outside of school and could not be touched. I wasn't a fast runner, but I was quick and could read the field. I played full contact organized football in the Army for years, with only one year of organized football under my belt. Confidence made all of the difference.

Hopelessness

Between my home life and my troubles at school I was a complete wreck by the end of my freshman year. My grades were failing and I didn't know if it was because I was stupid or because the teachers were also racist. I sucked in sports and didn't have teammates that would support me. I had no friends that would publicly acknowledge me. I also had a hole in my heart where my need for family had been. I had given up on family or anyone having value in me.

I had no place to go to escape my life. Everywhere I went I was alone and suffering. I was barely hanging on. I still attended church but was having a difficult time believing that God had a plan for me. As I began my sophomore year, I became more and more withdrawn. I felt an inescapable hopelessness that my life would always be this way. My thoughts often turned to suicide. This wasn't because "nobody liked me" or "I was so alone," it was because I knew I had no place in this world and my life was worthless. I never really tried to commit suicide simply because I didn't have enough faith that I would make it into heaven. If my life was this bad, I surely didn't want to go to hell.

No Celebration

The end of my freshmen year brought another change in my life. Tom and I had started going to church more often now. We were also involved in the Salvation Army. I actually found a way to find some peace. I found a group that would accept me for who I was and seemed to love me all the same. Tom was also heavily involved with the church and it seemed that he was trying to become a better person and exercise his demons.

Or maybe I was just getting older. I was getting into fights practically every day at school. After my freshman year I realized the boys that were fighting me were much bigger than me, which meant they were also bigger than Tom. Many of them were athletes and in great physical condition. Tom, on the other hand, was a squat man of 5 feet 7 inches. He was pudgy and kind of nerdy. For the first time in my life, I was fighting people much larger than Tom...and I was surviving. Tom was losing his hold over me, because I no longer had the same fear for him I had before.

My body was also maturing and I was able to duck and dodge most of his blows now. When he did connect, I noticed that it didn't really hurt as much as I remembered. The fact was, I was now bigger than he was by quite a few inches. I realized that Tom didn't have the power to physically hurt me anymore. I wasn't scared anymore. I wasn't fearful of him anymore. I didn't have to beg him to stop beating me because he really couldn't do a lot of damage anymore.

Unfortunately, this was no Hero's story. There was no final battle. His temper no longer frightened me, and I think he knew it. When he would get mad, I would not flinch. His outbursts became less frequent and less violent. He no longer had an easy target. Oftentimes, I would see his anger rising and just walk away or go into the other room. All that yelling and threatening no longer had an impact, and without that fear I saw that he was just a pathetic little man.

However, I never had the heart to hit him back, to teach him a lesson, even though I had all of the reason in the world to do it. I owed him and I was angry for being the constant victim at school, but something would not allow me to strike him, ever, because I still loved him with a child's heart.

This didn't mean he gave up on trying to have sex with me. I would wake up with his mouth on my penis or his hand going under the covers. I would just push him off of me, I never got overly angry, but I would let him know that I did not want him to touch me. Of course we never discussed it, but he eventually realized that I was not going to let him do anything with me or to me anymore. I was not going to be a willing participant, or a participant of any sort. His hold over me was finally broken. This end of my sexual assaults should have been a great thing to celebrate, but there was nothing to be happy about, no victory that was won. It was just the end. And the damage was already done.

I had performed so many despicable acts that I found it hard to look at myself in the mirror. While I was not gay, I could not deny the fact that I had committed many homosexual acts. I had even asked to perform those acts. I allowed myself to become the victim of a sick man's every deviant and poisonous desire. And I still loved that man. I didn't even have the heart to hate him for all the things he did to me.

Back to High School
I went back to school as a sophomore and a beaten man. I was withdrawn and had no confidence. I quit football after only two days of practice. It was the same crap, the same ignorant comments. I was walking into the same school with the same racism, and the same hatred. I didn't want to be there anymore. Whereas I began my freshman year with some sense of self-worth or confidence, now I had nothing. I was out of gas. I stopped trying to fight back and just took the attacks now. I didn't have a reason to defend myself. You have to find value in something before you will use the energy to defend it. I was worthless and I knew it.

I was not able to find my niche, a place where I belonged. There wasn't a group in that school that accepted me. I was not an athlete. They were some of the most aggressive and racist people at my school. I was not a stoner, I did not do drugs to that extent, and that group was also not welcoming to a black kid. I didn't fit in with the nerdy smart people; I was barely scoring high enough to stay in class. I wasn't popular and I wasn't even a bad boy. I was not accepted by anyone. I was alone.

Although I was not being molested anymore, I couldn't find solace in that either. After all, it's not like Tom saw me in some new light. I was still a little sex object for him to play with and he started trying to find other ways to play with me. His forays into my room at night attempting to have sexual contact with me in my sleep reminded me that he had not changed. He was still trying to turn me into a homosexual. I even watched him hide *Forum* magazines in my room that had stories about bisexual encounters.

Tom never stopped because he found value in me or realized the damage he was doing. He stopped because he just couldn't do it anymore. And there was also a difference in me. I saw the world for what it was and understood that I could not find a way to be happy. This is also around the time I finally stepped away from my faith and religious values. What good had they done for me? What difference did it make if I followed God or just did my own thing? I was damned either way. Life was going to suck no matter what I did. At least I didn't have to worry about unanswered prayers. I stopped praying.

Quitting School

I finally dropped out of school. I just couldn't take it anymore. I just stopped going to school. I just sat in my room trying figure a way out of this life; a way out of life in general. I couldn't run away because there was no way I could outrun my past or the things I had done. I sat in my room with no direction and no answers. I thought of taking my life every day. The residuals of my religious beliefs were the only thing staying my hand. I didn't have the energy to take another punch, another kick, or hear another name insulting my race. There was no one I could talk to that understood, no one I could tell what I had been going through at home. Although there was nothing stopping me, I never thought that I could tell someone about my abuse. I had been keeping this secret so long that it didn't even seem like an option.

All I kept thinking was "what was I doing wrong?" My life just kept getting worse. The one exception was my time with the Apsher's and it was clear they didn't want anything to do with me. I hadn't heard from them since I left. No letters or phone calls. Everything else in my life was just a series of tragedies that left me hollow.

I tried going to a school in St. Louis and found that didn't work either. This was an inner city school and I had no idea how to make it work. While I was black in color and wore that mantle every day in Freeburg, in actuality I knew next to nothing about being black. I didn't know how to dress, talk, or act in a way that would not have made me stand out. I had a mullet for God's sake (later I found out that it would have been a 'blow-out' with a little hair gel). The good thing is that I didn't consider this new school to be an opportunity to make things better. I had long since given up on things getting better. So I left that school after only three days.

After 50 days of being absent, I returned to Freeburg High School. They had a new principal now and I spoke to him. He gave me his personal guarantee that I would be treated fairly. I had little hope for any great change, but I took him at his word that at least he would treat me decent. He kept his word.

Eventually things got somewhat better in school. I was able to make up some of the work I missed so I could graduate on time. Some of my friends became a little more forward and were there for me. I ended up running track that year and going to state as a pole vaulter. I set the school record that year as well, even though I never really tried. While I never found a girlfriend in Freeburg high school, I did get a job at the mall and found an Asian girlfriend from a few towns over.

I still lived at home and had to sleep in the same bed I was molested in for years. I had to see the same man that molested me. I had to rely on that man as a parent, but had lost any faith for what family really meant. I didn't care what happened to me or them. I had emotionally checked out. I had some anger in my heart, but it was always quenched by a lack of faith in anything. I stopped expecting it to get better and just tolerated my life. I was numb. Drugs nor alcohol could fill the void or stop the anguish I felt. The self-loathing was inscribed into my very being. I had lowered my expectations for life and the people around me. I was not going to be disappointed again.

I bided my time and finished high school with a low C/high D average. Of course, there were fights and racism, and I still fought from time to time in school. I was never invited to parties or had a date for the prom. I started drinking on a regular basis and experimenting with drugs of all kinds. I had a few friends in school, but that was it. I was arrested several times near the end of my high school career for fighting and assaulting police officers. College was not an option for a kid from a trailer park with those grades. I had multiple police contacts and a small conviction record, so I couldn't even join the air force.

At this time, there was a war going on. Iraq had invaded Kuwait while we were graduating. I decided to join the U. S. Army. I didn't join because I was a patriot (although I sure as hell left as one). I joined because I was out of options. I was 130 pounds with no self-esteem, no family that mattered, and no one that cared if I lived or died. I knew this was the only opportunity to recreate myself or die in the process. I was leaving the family that adopted me, the families that sent me away, and a town that called me a "nigger." I was going to try to escape from all of them, but mostly I was going to escape from myself. I knew the war had started and the Army was going to be deployed. Even if I died, at least it would be at the hands of the enemy as a hero, instead of taking my own life as a coward. I had already been through 18 years of hell and disappointment, how could serving my country during a war be any worse?

For the first time in my life, I was finally right.

PART II

10,000 Hills

6. The Long Road

The impact of my childhood has extended far into my adult life. I have come far from that teenage boy that was willing to go to a warzone just to escape and find some meaning in life. Today, I have a great family, a successful law practice, and a powerful voice in state and local government. I've come so far from that helpless and despondent teen who had nothing to tether his existence to; no family, no outlook, and no one to even care what he thought.

My life today, with all of its happiness and achievements, is still not without pain and struggle. I am not able to simply wash away everything I went through in my childhood and escape unscathed. Years and years of abuse and mistreatment took a toll. All of the pain my body and mind experienced left deep scars and dents in my soul. The effect of this lingering damage seemed to grow as I matured. The emotional distance between myself and loved ones increased with age, along with an absence of confidence in, and general distrust, of others. The memories of what I had done and was forced to do against my will were a humiliation that I could not escape. Time only made me feel worse about myself and the role I played in my own suffering.

Imagine my horror and disappointment when I began to realize at about the age of 20, that no matter how much distance I put between myself and my childhood, I might never be normal. I would have to deal not only with my horrible childhood, but also the aftereffects of the abuse and neglect for the rest of my life! The ghosts of my past were very real, not only haunting my nights, but affecting my daily life and everything I hoped to accomplish.

What started out as mere pain and confusion, over time, graduated to hatred, mistrust, and self-depreciation. As I learned more about the world around me, I began to understand how children were supposed to be treated; so different from my childhood. Maturity awakened disturbing psychological and emotional demons that had been crafted through years of suffering at the hands of trusted loved ones. It was not only the pain and low sense of self that grew as I got older, it was also a sense that I may become worse, and that my thoughts and mistrust would eventually ruin my life. The irony of it all was that the very defenses I had used to survive were starting to impede my growth and success. Knowing that I was still a victim after all of those years filled me with deep shame.

The following chapters are written to communicate what I and many others go through once the abuse stops; to show how my abusive childhood impacted my adult life, and still impacts my life to this very day. As I grew older I became aware of the pitfalls that I could have avoided with some warning, as well as possible solutions and remedies that could have worked to get me through my issues. To some, these ideas and thoughts may sound preachy, but they are meant to provide some insight into how my life continues to be impacted by my childhood, what I went through, what I am still going through, and how I deal with it.

No More Turning Away

The fact that I was physically abused, neglected, hurt, and humiliated as a child should not be a badge of shame. However, even in writing this book I have had to deal with deep feelings of shame. I have been warned that some people may doubt my experiences or want actual proof of my abuse, that I need to be careful or I could get sued. This is what I have been told as a grown man who is trying to tell his story of abuse to help others. Why in the HELL would I make this stuff up? What possible benefit could I gain from the emasculation and dehumanization that I have related? Even years later, I have to worry about someone believing me…and I am a licensed attorney! It is no wonder why children still don't come forward about their abuse.

It happens in our society, more frequently than we would care to know. The impact on the life of a victim, even from a single instance of abuse, is devastating and long lasting. Yet, too many people continue to ignore this dirty secret. By keeping the abuse hidden, it affects our society and its victims like a cancerous tumor, invading and corrupting anything and everything. We must confront the effect this abuse and suffering has on a person. We cannot pretend that once it stops the damage ends, no more than we can allow the victims to pretend there is no continuing impact on their lives. We would only be lying to ourselves.

I know now that I may have avoided many of the problems in my adult life had I been more forthcoming about my childhood. But, because I treated my abuse as this dark and dirty secret, hidden away from everyone, the pain just sat inside and festered. It is one thing to feel bad about what you went through, what you were forced to do, what you lived through; but it is quite another thing to be ashamed because you feel that you allowed it to happen.

This may sound like semantics, but to me there is a difference. There is a difference between acknowledging I had a tough childhood, that I allowed myself to be abused; that I allowed those horrible things to happen to me; that I let someone force me to perform acts I knew were wrong. But I made it my fault, owning it as an active participant. Child abuse is so shameful and secretive. I had no one to turn to, no one who would believe me, no one to help me stop it.

I internalized my suffering. I felt I was at least partly responsible for my abuse. With no one to turn to, I just buried the suffering deep inside and treated it as my shameful secret. Meanwhile, the effects of what I experienced continued to bloom - the bad habits, the pessimistic outlook on life, the lack of faith and trust in those around me, and a general emotional disconnection to everyone and everything. These things became my scars and I didn't try to improve upon them because I didn't see them as problems. In fact, I viewed many of my reactions as survival techniques.

I wish I could tell others that they need to immediately tear away the falsehoods that surround the pain of their abuse, but it took me so long to come to grips with my childhood that it seems hypocritical to preach openness at this point. So, all I will say is that writing this has forced me to look deep within myself and uncover events and issues I have tightly held and kept hidden for so long. In revealing them, I have learned a great deal about myself. It has been cathartic, to say the least. But even more than that, it has been an emotional release. I have finally begun to put my self-hatred and shame to rest...at least to a small degree. I still feel a great deal of shame, but it is much less of a burden than it has ever been.

But these revelations do not come cheap. Ripping the scabs away is painful, so very painful. In order to memorialize the abuse of my childhood, I am forced to actually relive parts of it - the sounds, the smells, the pain, the shock, the horror, the feeling of betrayal, the sense of helplessness and loneliness. However, in doing so, I can actually view myself in a better light. When I go back and read some of the things I went through, I am amazed that I made it.

Revealing my most shameful and humiliating moments has somehow, and in some way, instilled a sense of pride I have never experienced before. Hiding the specific events of my childhood did not cover the detrimental feelings my suffering created, it only covered the cause of those feelings. For years I had just been walking around, living with this sense of self-loathing without even knowing why. Now I know why, now I remember.

Introspection and accepting the reality of my childhood has revealed more about my life. Of course, now I realize why I have such a violent temper, why I have such a low sense of self-esteem. I understand why I find it hard to trust women, or develop true friendships; why I am more sexually motivated; why I never expect good things to happen to me; why I never really believe people can like me without ulterior motives. These are not things I ever wanted to feel, but they were created by my troubled childhood. This is not the basis of an excuse, but it does reveal a causal connection. As such, I can now work on the learned reactions and attempt to better myself. I do not have to continue on with habits that make my life worse or cause me to miss out on the great things life now has to offer. Each victim deserves this opportunity.

A Scar's Impression

The scars on my face are but a minor reflection of what lies beneath. Most people will never even notice the imperfections that are the constant reminders of my pain. But these marks on my face are so much more than physical marks; they are a reflection of the deeper damage that lies within. Each time I see them, I am reminded of my victimization and humiliation. As I grow older, many of these scars fade and diminish, yet the emotional toll remains. The cessation of the abuse did not end the torment within; a reminder of so much which I have yet to let go of, or leave behind.

When I am in a rush or running late, I can get dressed, shave and run out of the house without even noticing the scars. Some mornings there is no reminder of my past, because my present is too demanding and consuming. My good friend Ronald Townsend cannot say the same. The physical damage left by his abuser runs too deep. Although his abuse was short lived, the damage he suffered will last a life-time. Each time he has to change his colostomy bag, each time he is unable to get an erection, each time he has to visit the doctor to find out what else in his body is failing - he is reminded of his abuse.

Of course he still wakes up screaming at night. Of course he doesn't like sleeping alone, but cannot trust himself to sleep in his girlfriend's room due to his night terrors. Not a week goes by where he doesn't speak to me about being held down by his relatives while they shoved an air hose in his anus, destroying his gall bladder and damaging several other internal organs. The physical damage he suffered is not just scaring; it has left him disabled and unable to enjoy the complete function of his body.

Ron, and many others, have had their entire lives altered from their abuse. The damage is permanent. He was not able to walk away from his abuser and try to forget about his ordeal. As you read this book he is still suffering from his childhood abuse. How can I tell him to 'just let it go and move on? How can I tell him that things will get better over time? They won't. He is 47 years old now and his abuse occurred when he was 15 years old! He doesn't just have hidden emotional scars; he will be dealing with the physical damage of his abuse for the rest of his life.

I consider myself lucky when I think of Ron. Yes, my scars are still there and they serve as a reminder of horrible times, but they are just scars. They have healed, even if the emotional damage is still open and raw. Yet, I know there are many people just like Ron who cannot let go of their abusive childhood, even if they tried. When the memories of my pain surface, I can decide how much time I spend reliving my past, or splash cold water on my face and try to put that past behind me. Over time, I hope that those emotional scars continue to fade, just as the physical ones do.

7. Loving Your Abuser

For years, I would get into a sour and negative mood around the second week of August. Unfortunately, this coincided with my middle daughter's birthday. During these difficult times, I wanted to just ride out the depression alone, until it passed. However, this was always the time when my wife would have her entire family over for my daughter's birthday celebration. It was not that I was not happy about the birth of my daughter; I just could not help myself. This never went over very well with my wife or her family. Of course this was one more time for me to be perceived as just being anti-social and distant. I tried to get into better spirits, but it seemed the more of my wife's family I was around, the more dour and depressed I got.

I had gotten so used to these mood swings, I forgot the reason why. Truth of the matter was that my daughter was born days after the anniversary of Tom's death. And his death hit me pretty hard. I can vividly recall the days before he passed. He was so weak, so skinny, he could not even speak loud enough to be heard...it was just a little squeak. Cancer was quickly destroying him. I was out of town for work when Millie called me. I knew it was the end. There I was standing in front of his casket, with Jennifer, Millie, and Mary. This was the last time we would all ever be together again. Then, I was at the grave site waiting for his casket to be lowered into the ground. These days they have stopped doing that in front of the family, but I had to see for myself.

To some, it may be unreasonable to hold such affection for a man who caused me so much pain, but I just could not help it. You would think I would have been relieved by him dying, but his death hurt. And it hurt for years. He was really the only dad I ever knew. While I had other men in my life, no other person let me call him 'Dad.' Even though he had many faults, and that is putting it mildly, I thought he loved me! When he wasn't beating and abusing me, he tried to be an affectionate and loving father. Yet, he caused me so much pain and misery, more than everyone else in my life combined. My feelings were not only of grief, but of anger and disbelief that I could be so hurt that he was gone. Years later, why did I still feel sadness around that time of year? Why was this man's death affecting the celebration of my daughter's birth? I could not find peace even after his demise.

I believed I was truly the lonely and lost little boy that Tom wanted. I was desperate for love and affection and he was there to cherish me and victimize me in equal measure. It wasn't that I was just any old punching bag or a little boy to play with. I was HIS punching bag, HIS little boy to play with. He took pride in that. Early on in the adoption process, he baited me in and lavished me with affection. As the years passed, Tom continued to fulfill the role of a father in my life. My relationship with Tom was never all out evil and hate, he was never the full-time villain. He always said he loved me. This is why it was hard to hate him, especially when I didn't fully realize just how wrong my life was and how much damage he was doing to me.

My Captive Mindset

So, there I was a grown man with children, still dealing with the effects of my years of abuse, and suffering from the emotional turmoil of Tom's death. I just could not understand what was wrong with me. Why was I still feeling sadness for the loss of a man that caused me such pain? Then it hit me, I still held on to the notion that Tom loved me as a son! No matter how perverted and misguided that love may have been, I truly believed he loved me. Reflecting back on my childhood, it is easy to understand how I could confuse his actions for love. I was a foster child who came upon someone who showed what appeared to be an honest interest in my well-being. Tom wanted to get to know me, what made me tick. He wanted to spend time with me, showered me with attention and affection. I had never really been the center of anyone's attention before and it seemed a wonderful notion that I was finally going to have someone care about me enough to keep me.

Tom was not some drooling pervert that was all over me the first night I spent in the Wilson household. Tom lured me to his side with the promise of the love and attention I thought I would never have. There was the back-handed slap, and an apology or warning that I brought it on myself, and the peeing in the same toilet or showering together, because "that is the way men do things." As a child, I could not understand those things were wrong, even after they became horribly wrong. I was always able to overlook the humiliating things Tom had done to me when balanced against the positive things he had done for me. In my mind, he rescued me. He clothed and fed me. He gave me a family to call my own and put a roof over my head. It is only now that I realize what Tom did for me was no great feat. It was just the bare minimum. But, at that time it was everything!

Even during the initial writing of this book, I constantly referred to Tom as "Father" or "Dad." During earlier renditions there was gratitude for all he had done for me. I was just grateful for someone to call me son. This was indicative of the low standards I held of what I felt I deserved or my value as a person. I even wrote during the earlier chapters that the abuse I suffered, the humiliation and the indignity, was better than being left in the foster care system. However, the more I uncovered, and the more I wrote, I discovered that even my description of love and parenting was skewed. I was still making excuses for Tom's abuse, still minimizing his actions and the impact it had on my life. I had thoroughly confused Tom's mistreatment for LOVE. It was only when looking at my entire childhood and understanding its impact, did I realize that I was uplifting Tom because I had been brainwashed into believing he was the good guy. I carried that misguided logic into my adulthood.

Stockholm Syndrome

Some people reading this book may question why I continued to allow these vile things to happen to me as a child? Why didn't I run away and tell someone? Or, why did I still choose to even communicate with Tom after I joined the Army? The more victims of abuse I spoke with, the more I learned that each of them was plagued by these same questions. Not only questioning why, but also questioning how they were able to be manipulated so easily.

It was only after reading a news article about a kidnapping victim and the Stockholm syndrome that I began to understand what I was missing, why I was taking the blame. In 2009, Jaycee Dugard, was finally freed from 18 years of being a sex slave to a husband and wife in California. She had even given birth to two children who were 11 and 15 years of age when she was set free. She had been held captive in the backyard of that couple's house during most of that time, living in a series of tents and shacks. Many people just could not comprehend how she had gotten so brainwashed that she was able to accept her captivity as normal.

The article showed how captives could actually develop affection for their captors. As much as I often scoffed at psychoanalysis and therapy as a solution to my problems, this article included a psychological analysis of captives that allowed me to understand my confused feelings about Tom and my situation. I could finally see how I had been fooled into believing that my treatment was love; that even an adult could confuse abuse as acceptable treatment.

Inability to Escape

In many cases, the victim believes there is no escape from the abuser even if the door is left wide open. The situation is created so a victim would not dare run away or try to gain their freedom. Many people questioned why the 29-year-old Dugard didn't just walk away. It was explained that in her mind, she couldn't. She had been made to believe that even if she left, she would be found and brought back. The simple fact that she was imprisoned in plain view was daunting enough to keep her from fleeing. The fact that for many years no one had stopped her abuse, demonstrated her captor's power and control.

As a foster child, I was sure I was never going to have a family of my own. Once I was taken away from the Apsher's, I realized the Wilson's were my last hope. I was desperate for a home, desperate for a family, desperate for love. While the outright abuse didn't start until after I was adopted, the inappropriate touching and loss of temper began before it was all finalized. Tom was already laying the groundwork by establishing that he had the power to do what he wanted. After my adoption, the abuse increased exponentially in a short period of time in full view of the family and neighbors. Still, no one interceded on my behalf; no one stopped him.

I was convinced that no one else would ever want me as their child. I felt he had rescued me from a life of loneliness. I knew I had nowhere else to go. The Apsher's never called, Martha from social services never came by anymore, and I had been portrayed as a troubled child. I even portrayed myself as a troublemaker to cover Tom's violence and sexual abuse. I believed that I was this bad child, which added to the knowledge that I would never find another family to take me in. And running away didn't help. Neighbors saw a troubled child. Ironically, running away also made the Wilson's look even better for continuing to try to work with that troubled little black boy. I had nowhere to go and no one to take me in. Tom knew this! So I would always come back into the abuse and humiliation, no matter how bad it got.

Helping the Abuser

The Stockholm article further explained that when your kidnapper is the only person to treat you kindly, you end up protecting them. You will even participate in your captivity by keeping your situation a secret. When you are let into a family and provided a home, you feel this is all you have and you can't lose that home. When you feel the abuser is still taking care of you and that no one else will, you end up feeling that you owe that abuser. This is what I experienced.

I was the one who made up the lies and covered for Tom when he was molesting me. I did this partly out of fear, but also out of a need for love and a deep rooted fear that things could get even worse. Tom and social services made it clear that I was not going to find another home and that I was on my last chance. I had been sent away from many homes before and knew that it could happen again if things got too bad, if the rest of the family knew my dirty secret. I was so intent on finally having a family that I would lie to protect Tom, at my own expense, even if it made me look worse.

I was the one who told Millie or Jennifer that I had done something wrong when we came home very late. That I had walked off and Tom had to search for me. That I had run away and Tom had to come find me. Or, that I had fallen asleep in a back room and didn't tell Tom where I was. All the while, Tom was taking me to a park or a parking lot; dragging me crying into the back of the van where I was beaten; and forced to perform sexual acts with him. Then, I would have to go to a gas station and clean myself, just to go home and tell everyone it was my fault we were late. Tom never had to cover for himself because he knew I would have an excuse, just in case a family member questioned me about where we were. I was lying to protect him and helping him continue his abuse.

The Abusers Perspective

I also learned that captives often begin to view the world through the eyes of the captor. They end up using the same reasoning the abuser is using to rationalize their suffering. I rationalized that parents could discipline their children when they wanted to and how they wanted to. While I thought the beatings I received were harsher than the spankings my friends got, I was convinced it was just because I was a very bad child. I told myself that I deserved my abuse because my actions were just that belligerent. While the beatings I received were much more harsh and violent than my sister's, I knew I deserved them because I misbehaved more.

I learned to tolerate the physical abuse. Not that I easily learned to endure the beatings, but I began to accept them. Tom would always tell me I brought it on myself and that I made him mad. I knew he had high blood pressure, and yet I still failed to do all of my chores. I still didn't know my multiplication tables. I still couldn't see the can or bottle right in front of my eyes. If I could only learn to act right, then Tom would not lose his temper and he would not need to beat me.

I accepted a different rationale for my sexual abuse. Tom often told me that he could tell that other men wanted to have sex with me. He worked to convince me that it was natural for an older man to have an interest in a young boy. I remember watching a movie called Jason and the Argonauts, an old Greek mythology flick. In the movie Hercules had a young boy servant named Hylas, and they were always together. At some point I think a giant creature was destroyed and crashed to the ground killing Hylas. Hercules refused to leave the island and continue his journey, staying to mourn the loss of his servant. Tom took the time to explain to me that the two were lovers and that it was quite normal in many cultures for those types of relationships.

Imagine a boy of 10 years old being told that Hercules was not only gay, but that he liked small teen boys. Tom continued to find these examples in movies such as Batman and Robin, and things around the neighborhood like the coach across the alley and his players. It was always the same theme of an older man having a younger boy as a companion. He would even jealously question me, insinuating that I was somehow flirting with these other men or teenage boys that he would see talking to me. Because I had experienced sexual deviancy with my birth mother and her friends, I started to believe that it was me; that I was doing something to cause adults to treat me this way. Over time, I began to believe that older males only talked to me because of a sexual desire not out of kindness. While I never wanted something like that for my life, I began to accept men were attracted to boys; that it happened all the time; and that I caused men to be attracted to me.

Appeasing the Abuser

In another article, I read that captives quickly begin to see the pattern of their captivity. Once that pattern is understood, the trapped person begins to find a way to minimize the violence and pain by trying to keep their captors happy. Captives will often try to find ways to manipulate the abuser into being less dangerous, at least for a little while.

Unfortunately, there was little I could do to pacify Tom. Laying out his clothes in the mornings; making breakfast and lunch for him to take to work; washing the clothes; draining the water out of the basement; cleaning the house. Even when I did everything I was supposed to do, it was never enough. I tried so hard to "help" him not lose his temper. It just never worked because he wanted to be angry, he wanted to continue hurting me in every way possible; and he wanted me to ask for it, even beg for what would stop my physical abuse.

As the beatings became more and more violent, they were often followed by bouts of sexual abuse as an extra form of punishment. Then it got to a point where the sexual abuse became a way to stop the beatings. As the beating and punching would get more and more violent, Tom would tell me I knew how to make it stop. Sometimes he would only whisper it in my ear, so I alone could hear him. Even though it took some time, he finally had me trained to beg for sexual abuse, just to stop the violent attacks. Asking him to go somewhere or take a drive so he could calm down would then stop the physical attacks. This became his little game, and I was so mentally distraught that I could only play my part. It was something that would distract him and calm him down almost immediately.

I was only a little boy. I wasn't even a preteen at this point. The sexual abuse was going to happen anyway. I knew it was just going to follow a prolonged physical beating. I could not stop the sexual assault, but I could reduce the physical abuse by trying to appease Tom. It was going to happen, whether I asked for it or not. The only choice I had was how long I was going to be beaten.

Unfortunately, I found a way to minimize my physical abuse. I was guided by self-preservation. In the end though, it didn't really minimize my suffering, it merely traded one form of abuse for a less violent but no less painful and a much more humiliating form. I knew how the abuse would play out and just what Tom wanted me to do to make him stop.

Eliciting Pity

Another method for the captor to have control over the captive and to form a bond is to share personal information with the victim to promote pity. Tom never showed any remorse for the physical abuse he inflicted. But his sexual misdeeds often led to remorse. This remorse did not show itself until Tom began to find ways to fully satisfy his urges. He never really stated it was wrong or that he had done something he shouldn't have, but he showed sorrow. He would tell me this did not have to happen again. That WE could make sure that it didn't happen again. I just needed to do right and remind him to take his blood pressure medicine.

To see a man you love and fear more than anything else on the planet weeping had an effect. Watching a man who is powerful enough to beat you unconscious cry, a man who controls every aspect of your life, a man so dominating that he can make you do whatever he wants you to, will cause you to feel pity. It totally distorted my view of his role in my abuse.

I felt pity for Tom until I started writing this book. I felt more pity for him than I did for myself. I thought, how horrible it must be to be a good man at heart, but still be cursed with the desire to have sex with little boys. I believed Tom showed remorse because he hurt someone he loved, because his curse caused him to do something he did not want to do. And he wept for his actions. For most of my adult life I pitied Tom for what he had done to me. His tears and crying affected me so deeply that I saw us both as victims.

I had forgotten that those tears would dry up very quickly and he would beat me and sneak into my room within a day or two. That crying and weeping never stopped him from causing me pain. When I cried and wept, he had no pity for me. He just continued to beat me and have his way with me. However, the pity I had for him allowed me to never hold Tom accountable for his actions.

Small Gestures

Often, kidnappers will provide small gifts or treats to their abducted victims after periods of abuse to show that they are not all bad. As the abuse and sexual molestation hit its stride, on random occasions I sometimes would receive special treatment. Once Tom was done with his sexual attacks, he would oftentimes take me to get an ice cream cone or a few white castle burgers on the way back home. My face would be puffy and bruised, my eyes swollen from crying, and I would get a little food for my troubles. No, it didn't do anything to lessen the pain and humiliation, but it did make me feel he thought I was special, that he had some value in me.

If you ask my sister, she might even say that Tom loved me more

138

than her. That Tom treated me better than he treated his own daughter. It may have appeared that way to everyone since they didn't know what I was going through. He would never take Jennifer for a drive after we were disciplined for whatever nonsensical reason. He would never spend extra time in Jennifer's room explaining to her what she had done wrong. He would only want to spend that extra time with me. That extra time exacted a heavy toll.

It made no sense that I would have an ice cream cone in my hand, nursing a busted lip that I got for misbehaving so badly that Tom had to take me on a ride to get me to act right. The rest of the family may have believed I was causing trouble and forced Tom to spend extra time talking to me. They may have believed it made no sense for me to get a reward for bad behavior and that Tom was just being soft on me. But that wasn't the case. It was just a treat to keep me believing that he loved me and to keep me confused about just what love was. And it worked.

Unlearning Behaviors

While not kidnapped, I was no less a captive in that home. Tom had assumed the role of the captor and established his control and dominance over my whole life. My time in foster care had taught me how to adapt to a new situation, so I just tried to learn to adapt and keep my new home. So, there was no constant desire to escape, to free myself from this nightmare. Oh, I wanted it to stop, prayed that the pain and abuse would end. But, I had been made to feel as though I was powerless to do anything. I felt that no one would believe me, that no one else would want me and that I brought these things on myself. I believed I was getting the best parental love I was going to get.

So I just accepted my life as it was. Instead of expecting things to get better, I learned to lower my expectations for myself. I learned to make excuses for Tom's actions like his blood pressure and my bad actions. I started to share responsibility for all of my abuse, even the sexual abuse. I just figured that little boys were going to have to constantly avoid older men, lest they become sexual objects. I learned to be grateful for the little things, and the little gifts I received since I could not stop the bad things Tom was going to do.

After reading the article regarding Ms. Dugard, I understood that I had not unlearned the lessons my life with Tom had taught me. I was old enough to understand that no child should have been treated like I had been, but I could never let go of how I learned to view my relationship with Tom. I never faced the fact that it wasn't love. I It wasn't even close to love. I didn't realize that I still viewed Tom as my father, my dad, and still made excuses for Tom. I was still emotionally distraught when the anniversary of his death came around and ashamed for still feeling such a loss because of his demise. Even as an adult, there is a lot of emotional cleanup to do. I have just as much to unlearn as I had to learn!

It is a long hard road of recovery for a victim of child abuse. The feelings of helplessness linger. Although physically free of the abuse and humiliation, the mental captivity often remains. Once you have become accustomed to having no control over your life, no ability to make things better, it is hard to exercise the new found power to make things different. Unfortunately, it becomes second nature to just go with the tides of fate. You get used to expecting only the worst out of life and grateful for pain free days. You become happy to simply exist in this world, instead of trying to take control of your life and decide your own fate.

Unfortunately, this can become its own prison of malaise and apathy. Life may improve very little even after the abuse subsides. Some victims even prefer the comfort of mistreatment and abuse. They may even seek out other reprobates to fill the void of abuse, pain and humiliation. Others may become so anti-social that they never have the courage to love or trust anyone again. If love caused them so much pain as a child, then love is nothing to pursue. If anything, love will be viewed as a weakness; a mere symptom of dependency and the precursor to misery.

Love should never justify weakness. I realize now what Tom had for me was not the love of a parent. I am a parent now, and understand how all-encompassing the love of a parent truly is. It is important to be able to differentiate the "love" you received from your abuser, from true love. Love is not having to make excuses for someone else's behavior. It is not covering up for someone who mistreats you. It is not lowering your standards of how you are to be treated. It is not allowing someone to harm you because you may have deserved it.

A Definition of Love from a Parent

When I consider the relationship I have with my own children, I realize that I knew what love was all along. My children's love for me is unconditional, and my love for my children is unyielding and unending. Parental love is when you give of yourself without hesitation, without thinking twice. A parent realizes that the life and future of the child is much more important than the life of the parent. A loving parent demonstrates a willingness to engage in constant self-sacrifice for their children.

Even in something as simple as dinner. I cannot begin to count the times when I sat down late to a meal, only to have my children ask me "Are you going to eat all of that?" If it was something particularly good or their appetites were not satiated, they would begin eyeballing my plate, before I was even allowed to take the first bite! Heck, I weigh more than all of my children combined. I would bark at them to let me at least taste the food before they begin to pick off my plate.

Yet, as always, I let them eat off my plate until they were full. I have eaten many bologna sandwiches for supper just to make sure my babies were fulfilled. They are my babies, and although asking for food off someone else's plate is rude, I would never think of eating until they got their fill. That is just an example of giving all for my children. I don't even want to get into how old my shoes are, or the fact that most of my casual clothing are older than my kids. I love them and they are worthy of my sacrifices.

Now don't get me wrong, my love for them also means that they will not always like my decisions. My job is not to make them happy children, but happy, productive, and independent adults. So, yes they eat their peas and carrots, yes they do their homework, yes they have a bed time, and NO they do not have a Facebook or any online social networking account! It is not enough that they do what they want to do, but that they do what they *need* to do. If they don't like what they need to do, they still need to do it well, or they will do it again until it is done satisfactorily. This means sometimes being the bad guy, instead of taking the easy way out or the path of least resistance. As a loving parent, I don't always get to do whatever I want for my children. Their welfare comes first. That's my love for them.

And that is what I deserved as a child. Once I realized that, I could begin the journey to overcome my abusive childhood. I know now that I did not create the reason for ANY of my abuse. Tom chose to put me through hell. Tom was not a victim. He was not a Dad. He was just an abuser. It just took many years for me to understand that.

Understanding

It is no wonder that my daughter's birthday parties caused me misery. Watching my wife surrounded by her loving family, I felt I was always on the outside looking in seeing a loving family embracing this woman. Watching my children grow, I knew deep down that my love for them was never the kind of love I received from Tom. I had not acknowledged that it was never love, only abuse. My misguided conceptions of love could not coexist with the reality I was witnessing. With all of these discordant feelings, I would annually just sink down into depression and shame.

It took me a long time to come to the realization that, although I was finally free from my abusive household, I remained an emotional prisoner. I was thinking like a captive, trapped by the excuses I had created so long ago. After all of these years I was holding on to my distorted views of reality. These misconceptions were now blatantly obvious, nothing more than malformed half-truths and a bastardized view of love. The anniversary of Tom's death caused me such heartache because I was never able to reconcile my abuse and victimization with the love I had convinced myself I received. It is impossible to call that love. While writing this book, I took the first step in my healing and freed myself by accepting the truth, never making excuses for Tom again. It wasn't the end of all my troubles, but at least it was the beginning of a solution. I realized I still had work to do.

10,000 Hills

8. Effects of Abuse on Sexuality

I remember learning in college that erections are common occurrences in male infants. At such a young age, that response is not remotely based on any sexual desire or even stimulation, it is merely nature. However, as a child matures, he can become aroused by physical stimulation as well. This too tends to be a natural response and has nothing to do with that child's sexuality or sexual desires. Under normal circumstances, little boys have very little physical drive to perform sexual acts prior to puberty. It is common to have to some mild curiosity about the body and even the similarities between boys or the differences between boys and girls. This is considered normal childlike behavior and curiosity. There is nothing sexual about this curiosity. But what happens when unnatural elements are introduced into a child's sexual development? What are the effects of introducing a child to sexual acts too early? How does repeated and forced sexual contact of a prepubescent boy interfere with his sexuality and development? Can these disruptions to that development distort a child's view of sex and sexuality?

My introduction to sexual activity occurred while I was still in diapers, before I was placed into the foster care system. I know I was too young to understand what was happening, but my curiosity was stimulated nonetheless. Why would a group of adults be naked and all over each other in the living room or the back yard? Why did they make those sounds, those noises? Why did the adults make such a big deal out of this? What is so entertaining about me lying naked on top of my sister? That was the

145

extent of my reasoning at that tender age. There was no real desire, just a genuine wonderment. While I was innocent, what I experienced predicated a lifetime's worth of struggle and confusion.

Pandora's Box - Time with Mom

I never thought of my time with my birth mother as bad, when compared with the rest of my childhood. I romanticized my time with her, remembering our time together as more of an adventure than a struggle. Of course I remember being hungry and alone, but that was still worth the time we shared together. The reality of course was much different and dangerous. Another thing I minimized was the impact she had on my sexuality.

I believe children possess a natural curiosity about their bodies and the bodies of others. I cannot tell you the number of times I have had to use a men's public bathroom with one of my young daughters! Trying to find a way to keep them safe, by bringing them into the stall, while still blocking their view of me urinating. Of course I spent half of the time looking back at them to make sure they were not looking and the other half peeing all over the floor and toilet as I moved and changed my position to block their inquisitive eyes. All the while I had to try to explain how I was able to pee standing up. Going to pee in a public toilet was like a mental and physical battle with each of my girls, trying not to let them see anything inappropriate while attempting to minimize what I was doing. I knew if I made too much of a deal about what I was doing, that would just drive them to be even more curious. I certainly did not want them to see what I was doing. They were too young for me to explain our differences, and that is a conversation my wife is much better equipped to handle anyway.

However, growing up with my birth mother, there were no such barriers. Looking back, it seemed like illicit sexual exposure was a constant in my life. I saw my mother and many other adults naked. I also saw her and other adults doing things while they were naked. I also experienced other adults engaging in sexual behavior with me. All of these things just drove my curiosity. When she allowed me to satisfy my curiosity by touching her, I just accepted these things as normal. As such, I began to equate that sexual contact with love and affection. Not the desire you have for a compatible mate, but that innocent love and acceptance you are looking for from a family member. So I had no idea that the deviant actions of her friends were really a bad thing. I accepted it as them just having fun and showing me love. Of course, some of these things were uncomfortable and weird, but no one ever tried to hurt me or cause me pain. So I never really made a big deal out of what I witnessed. It was just part of my life.

As a little boy I knew my mother loved me. In fact, I never had any doubt. I can also remember those moments when she was intoxicated, high, or just out of it. It was at those times that her affection would cross over to things that a little boy should not experience. It didn't happen often, but it happened enough to form an impression on me. Only as an adult do I see that I was the subject of inappropriate contact by my mother and exposed to sexual behavior that no child should witness or be a party to. While I do not remember any force or malice, even this painless exposure was something that never should have happened. Although I dismissed it, this early exposure to sex was very damning and invasive, causing my sexual curiosity to take hold before my mind was mature enough to understand my desires. This is where I learned to equate sex with love, and I was not her only child to suffer because of her sexual predilections.

My poor sister Heather was just one year younger than I and the recipient of plenty of sexual attention from my mother's friends. Therefore, as she matured she also equated this sexual attention as love. When she found out this "love" was not fulfilling, she would search for more attention as a means of gratification. By the time she was 15-years-old, she was forced to move back in with Grandma because her adoptive home could not control her. The older she got, the more sexually active and driven she became. It came to the point where she even tried to sleep with one of my mother's brothers. This misguided need for sexual attention was part of the reason she ended up in state prison. She was angry with the man who said he loved her and then wanted to leave.

So prior to being in any foster facility or home, I was emotionally damaged. My curiosity for sexual activity predated any contact with my adoptive father. Because things had gotten so much worse for me with Tom, I never realized the time with mom would have such a devastating impact. In hindsight, I understand the unhealthy sexual interest that was created during that time in Rolla with my mother. While that time seemed so short, it was long enough to start both Heather and me down a bad road. Luckily, Holly and Candy were too young to remember.

Foster Care

As such, I entered the foster care system with quite a bit of emotional and psychological baggage. My early exposure to sexuality set the wheels of my curiosity into motion before I was even old enough to communicate in complete sentences. My curiosity was innocent enough, with no real desire to do anything other than explore. Early on this curiosity would manifest itself in ways such as playing doctor or hide-and-go-get-it with the girls in the homes I was placed. It was more fun and games than any desire or need to fulfill some sexual desire.

When you are that young, there is nothing much more to gain from playing house than feeling grown up. Like all children, I emulated the adults I had come into contact with. Every child wants to be grown up, or at least act like the grown-ups. There was nothing devious or bad natured, just a curiosity to explore and see what the adults found so fun.

But what I thought was fun exploration was surely disruptive in the lives of the girls I was playing with. Just as I was introduced to sexual activity, my actions may have also brought their sexual curiosity to the forefront before they were able to understand it. While it was all fun and games, I am sure that little girls can be started off down the wrong path just as quickly as I was. I know that while there was never any force or mean spirited attacks, innocent exploration could still cause trouble.

And, as the father of three daughters, I know I would lose my mind if any little boy attempted to engage in any sort of inappropriate sexual activity with my daughters. Innocent or not, that little boy would be lucky to escape unharmed. So I can just imagine what my foster parents would have thought if they had gotten wind that I was playing hide-and-go-get-it with their daughters. I am sure they would be more than just a little troubled. Heck, for all I know, that may have been a reason for some of the hasty and unforeseen changes in foster home placements.

Adopted

I have always wondered just how it was that a child who was already sexually curious could be placed in the home of a pedophile. Was it mere coincidence or did Tom just know how to pick his victims. Either way, my entire life was going to be distorted and turned around by this man, and I was already confused and going down the wrong path. By the time I moved into the Wilson residence, my curiosity for the opposite sex was in high gear. What I brought into the adoption was a misguided curiosity for the opposite sex, but came away with more damage and distortion than I could ever imagine.

Tom's initial inappropriate behavior was barely recognizable to me. Even the enemas and constant checks for hernia were disguised as caring for my health and well-being. But once my adoption was finalized, his intentions became pretty clear. While I may have believed the physical abuse was warranted, I never thought his sexual desire for me was based on love. In fact, I had no idea what was going on or how it got so bad. As a prepubescent boy, I could only believe it had something to do with me. My sexual identity was soon thrown into complete confusion by Tom's sexual deviancy.

Even before puberty, my sexual knowledge and desire was already well in advance of many other children my age. I wanted to have a woman to have this feeling with, but I was too young to have any kind of relationship with a girl. And then, in comes Tom, forcing me to engage in sexual activity with him; forcing me to allow other men to look at my bare body; forcing me to create stories about wanting to please other men; forcing me to tell him made up tales about my sexual exploits with other boys and men. I was worried about how I was going to end up. Tom's advances and attacks made me wonder about my sexuality.

He would tell me about different men that made passes at me in public. I never saw any of them, but he would tell me "you see the way that man was opening and closing his legs, that's a sign that he wants you." "You see the way that waiter keeps looking at you? He wants you." Every time I was near a male it seemed that Tom would tell me that the man wanted to have sex with me. His comments and attention were wearing me down so much that I began to think that I may BE gay. All of these men were trying to come onto me! All of these men wanted me! Therefore, it must be something about me.

And there were never any women that looked at me that way. What woman would show any sexual interest in an 11-year old child? Only men, to hear Tom tell it. Tom wasn't just sexually violating me; he was trying to guide me down a path that being gay was my only alternative. Although I had never been attracted to men, I had no idea how to avoid being gay. It never dawned on me that you needed to be attracted to men to be gay; I thought it was just the actions themselves. Since I did not understand homosexuality, I thought I was becoming a homosexual. I was thoroughly confused by this point.

The truth is, through all of my abuse and my sexual awakening, I never wanted to be with a man...any man. The sexual abuse never got better, it never got easier. Although I was weak at times and may have even avoided most of the beatings by giving in early, I never wanted it. Tom tried to make me want it. He always tried to kiss me on the mouth, to force me to kiss him. To have someone hold you down and kiss your bloodied lips, to force his tongue inside of your mouth while you cried and resisted, is humiliating. To feel the unshaved rough beard on your face, instead of the soft skin of a woman is too painful, even now to fully bring back up. With these feelings, how could I be gay? But, by these actions, how could I not be gay? I prayed this wasn't the way my life was going to be.

I would be a liar if I said that I did not hate the homosexual lifestyle I was forced to live. Even after I was no longer being molested, I was still forced to deal with the memories of all I had been through. And that made me hate all homosexuals. I was a male, and homosexuals had sex with other men; Therefore, I internalized all of my abuse and blamed it on the homosexual community. I thought all homosexuals were like Tom, and would have involuntary sex with a boy just as easy as they would have voluntary sex with a man. No, I was never violent or outwardly hostile towards gay men, but I did despise all homosexuals as a teen. I didn't know any, but deep down I hated them for what I went through.

Luckily, once I entered the Army I realized things were not simply as black or white as I thought they were. I realized Tom was just a pedophile. He was a pervert that liked having sex with little boys. That wasn't gay, that was just sick. In the end, I had to let go of my hate. When given the choice of attacking or defending the down trodden, I would never attack those that were being persecuted, including homosexuals, even after what happened to me. I could not hold all homosexuals responsible for the actions of a deplorable man.

Hyper-Sexuality – Maturity and More Problems

My sexuality may be the greatest determent that I have inherited from my childhood. I know anyone that goes through sexual abuse, especially at the hands of a loved one, experiences damage and emotional scaring. I realize that my sexuality was awakened too early with my birth mom and my view of sex and relationships was skewed. Here you have a little boy, whose curiosity was aroused before his mind could begin to understand the emotions that come with those feelings. This also caused what can only be explained as an addiction to that feeling.

Now, couple this heightened sexual desire with being sexually abused and humiliated by another man. While I was never attracted to a man, because of the acts I had to perform I was determined to prove that I was a man at any cost. And, what is considered the most masculine thing in our society? Sexual conquests. Proving you're a good lover who can please women became my overwhelming need. So I found a way to please both my need for sexual pleasure and still prove to myself that I was not gay. I could prove myself and fulfill my need by having as much sex as I could.

As a teen, I was already thoroughly confused and pained about my sexual identity. In addition to being in an all-white town, I was definitely not desired by any girls I knew. I was skinny, not a great athlete, and a below average student. I was a normal kid in horrifyingly bad circumstances. I had no way to balance the horrors of what was happening at home with a feeling of being desired by a female. Girls weren't looking at me anyway, especially not in a sexual way.

When the opportunity came, my only goal was to be a good and learned lover. This is how I measured masculinity. Not as merely having sex, but being great at it. I am not talking about an emotional exchange or a quality relationship, but just the physical act of sex. It was never enough to have just one woman at a time. Real men had multiple partners, plenty of women on the side. Not in a masochistic or dominating way, but I definitely focused on my needs by fulfilling theirs. I had regulated myself as a sexual object, to be used for a woman's sexual pleasure. Now I was a young adult who was finally gaining weight and maturing, I was finally viewed with interest by women. I was developing muscles. I was around women that found me attractive, and I was now able to satisfy my urges and self-doubts.

However, because of the abuse I suffered at the hands of Tom, I no longer equated sex with love. In fact, I completely divorced sexual pleasure from any emotional bonding. I knew the pain and shame of an orgasm, but wanted that physical release nonetheless. This childhood physical need for affection bled over into my adult life, with no emotional understanding of what sex really meant. Instead of looking for that innocent bonding, I was just looking for sex. I was searching for that feeling without the shame attached to my childhood orgasms.

I was also searching for something to fill that void. I knew there had to be something more than a release, that an orgasm could not be the end all. I was searching for that lost innocence, to recapture that first time, but to experience it with a woman, and to have that powerful feeling with somebody of the opposite sex. I didn't have the tools to tie love and sex together. As such, I matured into someone who merely used women to get that feeling and prove I wasn't gay. No, not just to prove I wasn't gay, to prove that I was a man! One that was capable of pleasing a woman.

That's not to say that I never fell in love. Oh, I was also searching for that unconditional love and acceptance I had never experienced, but I felt that sex and love were mutually exclusive. Sex was that lusty desire that was shameful and embarrassing. Love had little to do with sex, to the point where I couldn't find an emotional attachment to anyone I slept with. The world told you that love and sex should be joined, and that you couldn't have one without the other. So I just kept on entering into relationships, meaning I became a serial dater or a womanizer.

I found myself always searching for that next accomplishment, that next conquest. Instead of focusing on sex as an expression of myself and love for another, I was merely looking for validation. As such, it was never enough, no matter how pretty the women or how many women I had, I was still left empty and unsatisfied. I still felt the need to prove something to myself and the world around me. It was a never ending cycle. And because I did not value sex, I was unintentionally hurting girls who deserved better.

My sexual confusion became a destructive force in many relationships and even a marriage. This self-doubt and weakness was a predicating factor in my inability to focus on one woman and exercise any self-control. Beyond my inability to maintain a healthy and loving relationship based upon trust, I used sex as a way to satisfy myself and my need to be masculine. It was not merely the physical feeling I desired, it was the need to show myself that I was no longer a victim, that I was a man. I allowed my shame and humiliation to take such control that a monogamous relationship was all but impossible. Having other women find me attractive or sexually interesting became a salve for the pain and suffering I had been through. No matter how many women I was with, I could not undo the pain inside for what I had done as a child.

Wrong Answers

Other victims of sexual abuse by a loved one react in the opposite manner, much like my sister Heather's response. They equate sexual attention with love. Since the person who violated them loved them, anyone that they have sex with must also love them. Since most victims are looking for love, they end up using sex as a tool to get someone to "love" them. This creates its own set of problems. In the end, these individuals do not feel valued unless they are sexually involved. They do not see any value in themselves other than their sexual ability. In the end, they are unable to have a normal relationship that allows them to offer more than their bodies.

In either case, sex is still a powerful focus in the lives of childhood sexual abuse victims. Whether it is a need to satisfy the sexual desire without emotion or the desire to satisfy an emotional need with sex, sex is the main drive. This distorted view of human sexual interaction makes it all but impossible to maintain a healthy adult relationship. Instead of monogamy, many childhood victims keep searching for the love/sexual relationship that will fill the void left by their abuser.

I finally realized that I was trying to fill a void in my own heart, trying to find self-worth and define my sexuality. I was looking for something that simply did not exist. No one can fit that description, fill that emptiness, and be that loving yet distant sexual partner. Those needs can only be filled by the person suffering the most. I had to come to terms with what I went through and how I was affected by my childhood experiences. I had to realize that sexual ability alone could never define masculinity. I had to understand that I would fail at any attempt at a loving relationship if I could not exercise self-control over my desires.

When I looked back, all I saw was a path of destruction in the lives of the women I had dated. I was not a positive memory to them and my legacy was going to be nothing more than an emotionally stunted person who could never be happy. I knew I was worth more than my sexual desire and deserved to be loved. I let go of the self-loathing and realized that I was not gay; I was never gay. There was no need to prove something I already knew.

Until we come to terms with what we suffered and realize it has made us different, our lives will continue to be disrupted. Our marriages will fail, our relationships will remain hollow, and our lives will feel unfulfilling. The truth can be as painful as the lies we live. It's not others that can release us from this pain. The answer lies in our own hearts and self-worth.

10,000 Hills

9. Race and Racism

Sign Waving

While standing on a highway during my campaign, I got a blast from the past. I was on a main road leading out of my district doing some sign waving. I had several young high school volunteers with me on the side of the road. We were a mixed group that day with both black and white people holding signs. We were doing the political thing by standing there and waving at cars that were driving by. At some point early that morning a man in an old pickup truck sped by and yelled "nigger" as he passed our little group.

Now, I reside in a district roughly 20 minutes south of Washington D.C. My county borders the most affluent African-American majority county in the country. The year is 2010 and we even have a black president. However, while my county is almost 50% minority, an African-American has never been elected to state office in 350+ years. I was campaigning to be the first.

After a small pause, because we were all taken a little off guard, the kids that heard this were immediately outraged. Some yelled and screamed back at the man as he drove down the highway. One kid even tried to run down the road in a vain attempt to catch the speeding vehicle. They eventually all looked back at me to see what my reaction was. I was almost completely balled over with laughter.

As the teenagers gathered themselves, they came back to where I was standing, still laughing and chuckling. One of the young men asked me what was so funny. He wanted to know why I was laughing so hard. I responded by saying, "I cannot believe that you guys let him call you a nigger!" I explained that he obviously was not talking to me. "I live in a nice house. I drive a very nice car. I am a successful lawyer and have a great life!" There was no way that he was talking to me. So I jokingly exclaimed that it must have been one of these young men that he was yelling at. They looked at me as if I was crazy. But they got the idea.

Each one of us knew that this man was actually calling me a nigger. It was my black face that was on each of the signs we were holding. It was me that was running to be the first African-American to ever represent my county. And most of the kids were white. However, I had come so far in my life and achieved so much that "nigger" had lost its meaning. It didn't really strike a chord with me anymore. Besides, if you would have seen the condition of that old beat up truck, it was clear that this man was no threat to me. I am not trying to minimize racial aggression, but suggesting that you take the source into account.

This is not a disclaimer that racism does not exist. Of course, there is still plenty of overt and covert racism, and it can still be very painful. Although, there are plenty of ways to fight it, being happy and successful is a clear way to combat racism. The ignorant comment of a passing motorist could not do me any harm...unless I let it.

There are many people now who see me wearing a buttoned down shirt, suit and tie, arguing to toughen criminal sanctions for violent criminals that will assume that I am not a real black man. That I have never suffered or had to deal with what it is really like to be black. Since I am light-skinned with curly hair, they assume that I have never been ashamed of my looks; that I never suffered from low self-confidence; that I always had women wanting me. They would be wrong. Before I came to grips with who I am, that word, "nigger," caused me a great deal of self-doubt.

Growing Up

As a parent, I realize a lot of what I went through in school was just bullying. Of course there were racial overtones, but it is something our children now have to deal with every day. I was just the easiest target. If not me, then it would have been some overweight boy, a child with a speech impediment, or someone who was small for his age. But at the time, it was one of the most important oppressive struggles I was going through.

I got used to many of the negative things surrounding my childhood, but the racial taunting I received as a student was something I could not find a way to deal with. I wasn't just singled out and insulted a few days at the beginning of each year - my color caused me to be isolated during most of my high school years. Who would want to be a friend of someone who is being made fun of? Who was going to stick up for me and risk getting harassed and beat up, too? What girl wanted to be called a "nigger lover?" And, during my school years there were NO other black students at that school or in that town. I was never more alone than during those times. I felt like everyone despised me because of my color, and I mean everyone.

As a teen I could never seem to ever escape my racial identity. I remember walking home one day from track practice during my freshman year. Of course, it had been a long day of harassment and physical contact at school. Then, it was off to practice where I would hear "nigger" this or "nigger" that during practice and in the locker room. I wasn't the fast runner everyone expected me to be, so I took up pole vaulting and distance hurdles. This resulted in even more harassment since I couldn't be the stereotypical black athlete that would benefit the team. So I continued to be the target for everyone. There was always a group of jocks pushing me around and calling me names, but there were too many to fight back. They were much bigger and older than I was so I just took it, instead of getting into an outright fight. After showering, I had to walk home.

I had learned early on that even walking home had its share of problems. I had gotten into many fights and even suspended for just trying to walk through town to get to my trailer park. If some of the older kids saw me walking down the side of the road, they would yell out racial slurs or throw things as they passed. So I learned to take the back way home by following the railroad tracks. This was a longer way home, but I would not be on main streets to be harassed.

I remember walking behind one neighborhood where I saw a little boy in his backyard. He couldn't have been any older than four or five years. As I got closer to his property, he started walking toward me. When I was directly behind his house, I looked at him and smiled. He responded by bending down, picking up some rocks and throwing them at me. All while he was yelling at me to "leave my house alone" and "You don't belong here!" He kept yelling until I walked out of earshot. Although he did not hit me with his stones, I was simply crushed.

I had always thought that once people got to know me, then they would see that I was just like them. I tried to listen to the music they liked, tried to speak like them, I even liked the same girls they liked. Sadly, this child showed me that I was wrong; it was not going to get any better. The parents of that child taught him to hate people that looked like me, even if he had never seen one in person. I was devastated because new generations of people were being taught to hate on sight just because of color. I had tears rolling down my face the rest of the way home. I had no hope that I could be ever be happy to be black.

Self-Loathing

My skin color always made me different, but now it was making me miserable. The older I got, the more miserable it was to be black. My color became the bane of my existence. I began to pray to God to change my skin color to white. This was not some childish whim. I would pray until tears would roll down my cheeks, fervently begging God for this one request. I did not even want to be called black. I would tell people I was Indian or Italian, anything but black. I avoided anything that was stereotypical black. I refused to break dance or to listen to any of the new black music like Fat Boys or Run-DMC (sorry, DMC). Instead, I listened to classic rock and roll like Pink Floyd and Aerosmith. I dressed as preppy as I could in knockoff polo shirts and cheap blue jeans. It wasn't that I was just trying to fit in with my surroundings and show these white kids that I was just like them, I really began to despise being black. Growing up in that community I was exposed to the same stereotypes my classmates were. It caused me to look down on black people, too!

I could not find beauty in my own race. As a teen, I rarely saw black girls and never interacted with one until I was a junior in high school. I liked the exact same type of woman my friends and classmates liked. I adopted their definition of beauty. When black girls would approach me at track meets or in the mall, I would rudely and quickly avoid them just in case a cute white girl was watching. I even found their round butts and kinky hair unattractive (my, how times have changed). Long, straight hair was alright. Skinny legs and small frames were sexy. There were very few black sex symbols on television to alter what my view of beauty was in the 80's.

So you can imagine the culture shock I faced when I joined the Army. There was very little doubt to anyone that I was not white, no matter how I talked or acted. The problem was, I was just being myself. I was raised by white people, around white people, and attended an all-white school. I was not even exposed to R&B, Jazz, or even much Rap as a youngster. But to everyone around me, I was just trying to be a white boy. I soon found out that trying to be white can be offensive to black people. By claiming to be something else, some other race that I obviously wasn't, I was also sending a signal that I was too good to be African-American.

Having posters of only Marilyn Monroe all over my side of the barracks only showed that I didn't see that black women were as beautiful as white women. Not hanging out with the black soldiers was taken as a sign that I was too good to hang out with the black guys. While I was only gravitating to what I was comfortable with, I was called an "Uncle Tom." Since I still believed at that time that being black was a bad thing, I guess they were correct.

This was just one more vestige of my confused and troubled childhood to deal with; one more superfluous hurdle; one more hill to climb. The culmination of my life experiences did not prepare me to be a black man in this country. Even if I wanted to learn about my cultural heritage, where would I have learned it? Who would have been able to teach me? I was never in a position in my life to appreciate my ethnicity or what it meant to be black. All the racism and harassment I received because of my race was never balanced with any pride. Contrary to what we may want to believe, there is a difference. There was no easy way to escape being black by calling myself "brown" or "mullatto" or "mixed." While all of those things may be an accurate description of me, I had to realize that I was a black man, even if I did not want to be. I needed to embrace my culture and be proud, lest I live my life in shame for the color of my skin.

Not Black Enough

I eventually learned to embrace the fact that I was black. During the first few years of my military career, I slowly discovered some of my culture. Of course, I researched black history and the experiences of those that came before me. I couldn't help but be proud of so many men and women who suffered just so I could enjoy a desegregated military, voting, equal access to employment, and education; all of the things African-Americans fought so hard to attain. I was finally exposed to black people on a regular basis. The more people I met, the more I realized there were not so many differences between blacks and whites, or other races.

We all want the same things - to be accepted as equals and to be happy. We all endeavor for some modicum of success. Yet, I was able to truly appreciate the differences my culture offered. I finally saw that being different did not mean second class or less than average, it was just different. My view of beauty was broadened and I was able to see black women as the beautiful creatures they always were. I no longer avoided being around black people because I was finally proud to be one myself. Yet, I still found myself not fitting in AGAIN!

During my time in the military, I cannot tell you the number of times I had white people say that even they were blacker than me. Or, when another black man told me I spoke like a white boy. I never learned how to dance or listened to music that you could really dance to. I could not grow an afro. My skin was a little lighter than most. While I broadened my musical taste, I still listened to classic rock, in addition to R&B and Rap (sorry, but I was never cultured enough to get into jazz). Growing up in a trailer park did not leave room for the appreciation of fashion. So, I still bought regular tennis shoes and jeans that I could afford. Although I had learned some slang, I still defaulted to the Midwestern dialect I learned as a child. So I went from being called "nigger" on a regular basis, to be referred to as "white boy." Of course, black men never beat me up for this, and black women did not totally avoid me because I wasn't black enough. However, I still did not feel I fit in as a black man either! I knew I was not white, but was told that I did not look or act like a black man. It was still another damn hill to climb on the road to having a normal life.

It is ironic that there is still a stereotype that even the most liberal white person and many black people hold on to about what it is to be black. I hear all of the time that President Obama isn't black. Or that some black athlete who speaks well and marries a white girl is not really black. I hear some of the most liberal white people I know saying these things, too! There is this pervading ignorance that "real" black men have to retain some of that street thug mentality. That no matter what they do for a living, a real brother has no problem getting into a physical altercation, even if it means jeopardizing their freedom, family and livelihood. Never mind what struggles that man had to face because of his skin color, what jobs he was denied because of his race, or what crimes he was wrongfully accused of because of his features. While there is a glamorized fringe element in the black community that will easily resort to violence and womanizing while shunning education and self-improvement, they do not represent the entire range of the black experience. We need to teach our children we are so much more.

Race and Parents

I always jokingly tell people that the one lesson I learned about race growing up was to never order fried chicken at lunch time if you are the only black person in the school. Even though that was minimizing my issues, the truth of the matter was, I was never taught how to deal with racism as a child. I assume the reason I was never prepared to fight racial insults was that I was only placed with white families. None of these families ever talked to me about race or my differences. While I was young, I did notice that I was different, but no one prepared me for the battles that lay ahead.

I was never taught how to recognize racial epithets or jokes. I remember the pizza man down the street used to always ask me if I wanted a watermelon and chicken pizza when I came to pick up our order. He did this right in front of Tom on several occasions, and I was nonplussed the entire time this old man was making fun of a nine-year-old child. The Wilson's had no clue that adopting a black boy was going to be different than having a white child. Telling me that I was not "full black" or that I was "mulatto" was really just denying the obvious. They had no idea that hair spray or mousse would not work for my hair; that my hair needed some grease! (As such, my hair stayed extremely dry for years on end.)

It is pretty obvious that the Wilson's did not think I was black or they did not understand that being black made me different. No one ever prepared them to raise me as a black child. This was made all the more obvious since they picked up and moved to an all-white town and placed me in an all-white school. At no time did they even tell me that I may have some difficulties because of my color or that people would hate me because of how I looked. These were lessons I had to learn on my own. When I got into fights at school and tried to tell them, the Wilson's just dismissed me as a bad child. They said I had a chip on my shoulder. To be fair, I guess if you have never experienced racism then you could not really imagine just how tough it could be. So I could not even talk to them about being called names or that some of the teachers just stood by. They thought I was just making things up.

There was no one in my life to balance out what I was going through. No adult who had experienced racism, or at least understood it, to advise me on how to handle things that were coming my way. I had no family members who looked like me or shared my skin color to show me how to stand strong. The Wilson's didn't even try to bring me around other black children so I could finally be accepted. There was never any sense of pride developed in my spirit, just dejection and shame about the way I looked. They never told me I was a good looking kid or that one day girls would find me attractive, so I just figured my skin color made me ugly. So, I had to fight my battles at school alone, and then had to come home to other struggles. My self-esteem suffered to the point that I regularly prayed for God to change my skin color. No child should feel that bad about themselves.

Reason

I am not writing this to make you feel sorry for me or to show that I suffered from racism, in addition to all of the other things I had to deal with. In hindsight, racism was definitely not the worst thing on my plate as a child. I am not writing this to complain about interracial adoption. Far from it! I realize that in many states, African-American children are overly abundant in the foster care system, but that there are few black parents to adopt them. As a matter of fact, I believe that any safe and loving home is a good place for any child, regardless of the color of the parents or child.

I am conveying my struggles with race for a reason. A great deal of what I went through could have been avoided if Tom and Millie were actually prepared to adopt a black child and understood that there was a difference. Based upon what I went through, I believe it is important for any prospective parent who plans on an interracial adoption to be prepared to deal with the racial implications. Racism still exists! We cannot ignore our racial differences. This country is not as advanced as we want to believe, no matter how liberal your neighborhood is.

If you adopt a black child, please understand that you must be willing to raise your black child as a black child. He/she is not a mulatto, not mixed. They are black. Their hair is different, their skin is different, and they will be treated differently. Their hair may not comb straight and their hips and legs will be a little thicker. Ignoring these differences will not change them and, they should not be made to feel ashamed.

If the parents do not open the child's mind to reality, they will be unprepared for the hard lessons life has to offer. They must be raised to be proud of who they are and what they look like. There must be a way for the child to share in the black community, even if that means joining Jack and Jill or another black organization. As uncomfortable as race prejudice is, especially to those who are not racist, it is a fact of life. If they do not learn how to survive as black people, they will be ostracized by both races, confounded by situations they find themselves facing and spend valuable time and effort trying to find out where they fit in.

Getting their minds ready for these struggles will also arm them with the knowledge of how to deal with things they cannot change. They must be prepared for the upcoming struggle lest they be carried away by the opinions of others; weakened by the stereotypes that abound; unprepared for what roadblocks they are to face as an adult.

Like it or not, black men are oftentimes seen as a threat in this society. I cannot tell you the number of times I have been accosted at gun point by a police officer during a routine traffic stop, or told by law enforcement that I am being stopped because I fit the description...even though I am a delegate and a chief prosecutor! I have had white co-workers pass throngs of people just to ask me, and only me, if I have seen their purse or some other item of value, even when I am in an entirely different area. I have been denied jobs where I was the top qualified applicant. I have seen women switch their purses to the opposite side of me in an elevator. I have had judges ask me what delegate I work for when I request a legislative continuance instead of expecting me to be the elected official. I have been called "nigger" as I stood on the side of the road during an election season. Racism still exists.

The difficult thing about most of these experiences was that I was never sure if it was racism or just coincidence. If you are not prepared, it can drive you crazy and have you jumping at shadows. Once you are used to dealing with subtle racism, then you are not as bothered or surprised. If you know there is a possibility you are going to have to deal with racist ideology, then you may be able to avoid it, or at least learn to deal with it.

For a child not prepared and not fitting a racial identity, this can be the least of his problems. If a child is taught to avoid any racial identity then he will be influenced by what his surroundings show him. In most parts of this country, the African-American culture is still portrayed as a mere caricature of what being black truly means. Only the most negative aspects of the black race are portrayed and glorified. Black men are only seen to be of value only if they are thugs, musicians, or athletes. If your child is not exposed to any other black influences, then he will believe what he sees on television, and will shun it. If this is all he sees, and he is never around any positive black role models, what would he have to be proud of? Why would he want to be black? Unless he has something to prove, he will just end up emulating these horrifyingly negative stereotypes.

As he comes to experience racism first hand, he will be caught off guard by the unfairness of being profiled and dismissed if he is caught unprepared. As many black people know, the weight of this prejudice can be crushing. If there is no counter-balance to what he will face, despair can easily set in. If no one is there to warn him of what he may face in the real world, or at least explain the ignorant mindset some people have and the things he cannot change, how can he be expected to keep trying? It is so much easier to stop trying to succeed when you feel everyone is trying to hold you back. It is easier to go ahead and be the ignorant and uneducated criminal ("nigger") he is constantly accused of being.

Reality is not always pretty, but some things have to be acknowledged and taught. I know many parents do not want to ruin a child's view of the world and only wish the best for their child. However, race and racism need to be confronted early enough for a black child to get a proper understanding of what he has to face. Make no mistake; he will have to face it. How that child has been prepared to face this can make the difference. Giving a child pride in himself and the ability to fight the battles to come, will and can mean the difference between success and that cycle of poverty that many foster children are trying to escape.

While having to overcome so many other hurdles in my young life, it was unfortunate that racism took so much energy out of my life. Instead of learning how to overcome the abuse and neglect of my childhood, I was busy trying to fit in, trying to be white, and then learning what it meant to be black. Having some racial identity and pride was important, but the time and energy I spent dealing with racial issues could have been better used learning to deal with the abuse and neglect I had suffered. This trade-off is the reality of the world we live in. Little foster children need to be armed and prepared to deal with this reality.

As for me, I have embraced my culture and my race. I am highly educated and a master of my craft. I am a trained litigator and trial attorney. There is nothing to be ashamed of, and everything to be proud of. I am proud of my race and proud of what I have accomplished. While I can find beauty in all races of women, I found it important to marry a black woman. Although my little girls are each different hues of light brown, they all know that they are black. They are proud of their culture, heritage, their shape, and their hair texture.

Some days I may be driving from the gym dressed in a tank top and sweat pants, bumping some vintage Public Enemy, or Lupe Fiasco, or even some Bruno Mars over my speakers. All while conspicuously displaying my somewhat muscular physique (my wife says I look like a chunky retired linebacker) and many tattoos that cover it, just enjoying the sun through the sunroof. Other times you may see me walking around the courthouse in a three piece suit carrying a brief case, listening to some old Supertramp, or Willie Nelson, or Maroon 5 on my iPod. Stopping to compare notes with other defense attorneys or reliving old trials, just enjoying the freedom of owning my own firm. I love my black culture, but do not feel bound by it. I do not need to fill a stereotype or convince others just how black I am. I know just who I am.

I also realize that not all of the people I went to school with were bad, even those that ignored me, called me names, or picked on me every day. They were just kids, growing up and responding to peer pressure, just like I was. As damaging as my high school life was, I hold no grudges against anyone. Some were just products of their surroundings. I am sure there are some who still hold onto racist ideology. I am sure there are those that still throw around the word "nigger" and judge folks by their color. I don't begrudge them either. Some ignorance cannot be helped or changed. Some people never interact with anyone outside their race and fall for the stereotypes and the media's portrayal of black America. Some of these same people will never lose their prejudices, even though we have a black president. It's up to them to change. It's not my place to judge them, or allow them to make me angry.

Anger will not end racism, revenge will not teach a bully. What my life has taught me is that the best way to overcome racism is coincidentally also the best revenge on those who have caused you harm in your past - success. Accomplishing in spite of the anger and hatred you received is ultimately the solution to racial animosity. Giving in to anger, demonstrating outward hostility, or capitulating to worthless feelings is the only way I could ever be damaged by racial slurs. In order for words to have an effect they must be believed, otherwise they are just words. To me "nigger" has become just another word.

The great thing about succeeding is that it causes you to evolve. The more successful you become, the less need you will have for revenge. Now I push toward success, not to prove something to those who have harmed me, but to help those who are still suffering. I am even now arming my children for the battle that lies ahead. My wife and I are preparing our girls to deal with racism head on by instilling pride in their appearance and culture and keeping them focused on their future. They may not have to face many of the same issues I faced as a child, but at least they will be ready for them. They will not go through them alone. I will teach them how to overcome their racial struggles.

10. Religion

Throughout my entire childhood, I had always had contact with the church in some form or another. When I was with my birth mother, I remember church ladies dropping bags of groceries on the porch or bringing us to church for Sunday school and a meal. Each foster home I can remember required a focus on religion. The Bombers were avid Christians who began teaching me bible verses and how to pray on my own. The Apsher's were strong Baptists that believed the Lord's Day was for church, and we spent the entire day in worship and fellowship. I was baptized more than a few times, by each family I was with. I was drenched in religious doctrine before I was old enough to even read.

I truly believe that my strong spiritual foundation was important at that time in my life. I needed something to believe in while navigating the foster care system. I needed something solid to hold onto as my life continued to change. I was constantly placed in situations where I had no control, moving from one family to the next without any input or understanding. My mother turned her back on me and left me to my fate. My sisters were taken from me and I didn't even know where they were. Home after home seemed to reject me and send me packing. I felt continually let down by everyone around me and alone. I had to accept that there was someone looking out for me, that there was more than meets the eye. I was taught to accept things that I may not understand, learn to move on from things that seem unfair or unjust, love my fellow man, and believe in things without proof. So I held onto the belief that Jesus loved me no matter where I was or what was happening to me.

Once I was adopted, I still held onto my faith. Of course I had to switch to attending mass instead of church since the Wilson's were Catholic. But soon enough, Tom and I were able to attend other Baptist or Methodist churches, while Millie and her daughters attended mass. When my life began to take a horrible turn for the worse and Tom began to become more violent and more sexually interested in me, I turned to the one thing I learned to hold onto. I fell back on my religious beliefs. Following a higher power at least gave me comfort that I wasn't really alone. Although I had no idea why I was going through these things, I tried to have faith that God would watch over me. I would read the book of Job for inspiration, pray every night, and try to member that Jesus still loved me. I did not relinquish my faith, which was something Tom could not take from me, even if he took everything else.

As a child I had the faith to move a mountain. I would believe without a reason. Even when I was being beaten senseless, I used to want to try to walk the straight and narrow path. Although I was being violated in the worse way imaginable, there was a fire in my heart and a passion in my soul. I believed in the Lord even as I was forced to my knees to do and perform things much worse than prayer. With everything else that was happening, I had no choice but to believe that Jesus loved me…because I was sure that no one else did.

However, things were taking their toll on my spirit and my faith. I know individuals that have suffered a great deal can find it increasingly more difficult to believe in God. Children who have had their innocence taken are even more susceptible to this loss of faith. To be clear, this doesn't mean that I didn't believe in God, but I started to wonder if God had forgotten about me. How can you expect a child to believe that God cares about them when they are suffering so horribly? But if I lost my faith in God, then I would have nothing. So I held on. But, day by day, I was losing that little soft-hearted boy.

Looking Back

As a child I was taught to follow God and Godly men. When these same Godly men, whether they be your preacher, priest, deacon, or your own father, perform such evil and depraved acts like sexually abusing a child, that child's faith in God is diminished. You end up submitting to men that have been blessed by God to lead a church, that have standing and title in a church, that have the influence and reputation of good men. Some of these men use their power and influence to intimidate children into these acts and into covering up these acts. When these Godly men continue to commit these evil actions while praising God, even using the church to lure or molest children, how can these little ones believe that God loves them? I know my faith was sorely tested.

It is easy for people who have not suffered through these experiences to dismiss the doubt caused by saying the abusers were not Christians. How do you explain that to an eight-year old? To a 10-year old? When the abuser is their preacher, their priest, their father? A child cannot understand that "this" person is not a Christian when he is in the church; when he leads the church; when he is held to a high esteem and higher standard by the church; when the abuse happens inside the Lord's temple.

In the Church

Tom did not refrain from abusing me; his anger knew no bounds and his lust seemed never to be satiated. I faced many abusive nights on church outings, church camping trips, and was even molested in the church proper. He would not hesitate to beat me or force me into the back room of a church to perform some sexual act when I deserved it. I was shocked to see that I wasn't even safe in God's house. I guess Tom figured God was looking the other way?

But it wasn't only Tom's actions that chipped away at my faith. One of Tom's good friends was the head of a church in Missouri. This preacher was big and burly. He had a great sense of humor and was able to grow the youth ministry by leaps and bounds. I met him many times at church retreats and youth camps. He was always the star of the events. This was around the time when the public began to hear reports of priests and preachers molesting boys. I was surprised when the news came out that this man, Tom's friend, was accused of molesting young boys in his church.

This man played a role during the formative years of my Christian walk. He was a big man, gregarious and larger than life. He inspired young men to step out on faith and go against the grain. He led us to believe that it could be cool to be a Christian, that we could be the change in our schools and neighborhoods. We didn't have to be like everyone else, we could make everyone else want to be like us. He even introduced me to Christian rock as an alternative to rock and roll. He said it was just rock with a message. These were the years when I gladly looked for leadership, looking to follow any person who knew God and could teach me to be a better disciple.

And then he was indicted for having sex with a number of young boys in his church. Even though no one talked about his actions, I was crushed. I believed in this man, that this man was Godly, and all the while he was destroying the minds and bodies of these young men. He was no better than Tom. He was preaching love and accountability while toying with these young men. His only explanation was that it was consensual.

I respected this man. He was everything I thought Tom wasn't. He was still cool, still relevant. To me he was like Sampson, big and tough, unafraid to take on the devil himself. I believed that I could be that type of Christian. As the story came out, it wasn't just one boy; it was a large group of them. Each with the same story - that it was all consensual. Even those that knew it was wrong did not immediately step forward because they figured no one would believe them. The stature and status of this preacher was immense. He had the respect of the church and the entire community. Each of these boys thought they were the only one. Each thought they were the lone victim that no one would believe. It was his status that allowed him to have a string of victims. It was his position that ensured his victims would never tell. After all, who would believe them? More likely, who would WANT to believe them?

And through all of this, I tried hard to be a good Christian.

Turning to the Preacher

Later that same year while I was entering seventh grade, I remember running away after a severe beating and long Saturday night of 'punishment.' For whatever reason, Millie called out to Tom in the middle of the night and he was interrupted, forced to go back into his own bedroom. Interruptions such as this always meant I 'owed him one,' and he always kept track. I just couldn't face another day of chores and beatings just so I could be touched and forced to perform acts on him later that night. As usual, we still went to church that Sunday morning. I was so tired of being beaten and hurt. I was angry that I was so weak, that I had given in to the abuse and sexual attack again. I felt like I just couldn't take it anymore. I needed to get out of this situation, I wanted to be safe. I knew Tom was going to beat me again because he was unable to 'finish' the night before. I knew he was going to get what he wanted, as always.

I did not have a plan, but knew I had to do something. I knew that if I went home, I would be subjected to the worst abuse this man had to offer. As we sat through Sunday school and the church service, I realized Tom was still agitated and angry. He was very short and clipped when he spoke to me. When he put his hand on my shoulder to walk with me, his grasp was painful. I just knew I was in trouble. Although I didn't know what excuse he would use, I knew he was just biding his time, looking for any reason to be angry with me. At this point in my life, the abuse seemed a part of my daily life and Tom's methods were predictable.

As we exited the church, Tom went to the van and yelled for me to hurry up. That is when I made good on my escape. Instead of walking to the car, I sprinted away from the parking lot toward the main road. Due to traffic, Tom couldn't immediately follow me in his van. Instead of continuing on my course down the main road, I jumped into a ditch and hid. Once I saw the van drive past, I doubled back to the church. Since I was already in my church clothes, I just walked back in. Once inside, I made it to the back offices and kitchen area. While I was hungry, I dared not try to find food and instead found a cupboard near the pantry. I just stayed there, waiting until it was dark. I had no plan; I just wanted to be safe.

I could hear voices down the hall, there were still people in the church. I tried my best not to make a sound, but I knocked the broom down when I leaned back. Several minutes later I heard someone call out. It was our pastor. He said he knew someone was in there and they better come out before he called the police. I immediately opened the cupboard door and came out. He was very angry and asked me what I was doing in there? I immediately began to cry, telling him that I was running away from home. I begged him to please not call Tom. I told him that Tom beat me and I was scared to go back home.

As I started explaining myself, I could see that he didn't believe me. He told me that I should be happy just to have a home; that it was a sin to lie. There was no compassion as I pled with him. I didn't tell him about the sexual abuse, I just begged him not to send me back. He didn't call Tom, instead he called the police. I was detained and the cops called my father to pick me up. Because Tom was such an upstanding member of the church, the preacher agreed not to press charges and I was given back to my family. He never told the police what I told him.

When your own pastor refuses to protect you, then what? I could not help but be crushed by his lack of compassion. I was always taught not to have faith in any man because he will fail you, and only to have faith in the Lord. So I still held on.

Cherokee Street Boy

My faith had survived the abuse and violations that were now a regular part of my life, in fact in many ways I was more of a believer than I had ever been. Things were so bad that I had to have something to hold onto, so I held onto the Lord. As the old saying goes, when you fall flat on your back, the only way to look is up. And I was looking up, to God. The abuse was still occurring and I was still praying for it to stop. As mentioned before, I figured that if my life was this bad, I never want to find out how miserable Hell is.

I was a counselor at a church camp that I attended during the summer. Not only did I get to learn about God and be around other Christians, but it was for the whole summer! This was time I could escape from my horrible home life, the isolation and hate of school, and my own failing sense of self-worth. I was not some zealot, but I made sure to keep God in my life and kindness and prayer in my heart.

I was also involved in a great church and its youth ministry. I even planned on going into ministry after high school to be a preacher. My goal was to become a minister and save the world, one soul at a time. So on some Saturday's, we would go minister to the teens, the partiers, and the lost souls in the streets. This was our missionary work. Trying to show people another path to happiness. I recall ministering to a homeless man about the gospel. He was devastated that his wife died recently and he had no direction. I gave him my new coat and talked him into coming to church with me. This was the type of mission work we would do, not to be judgmental, but to just invite. To provide a path to happiness that could only be gained from a relationship with Jesus our Lord.

On this particular day we came upon a loose group of teens standing on the corner of Cherokee Street. This was considered the "head" district. Where all the hippies hung out, with shops and stores that sold bongs and other drug paraphernalia. As I approached the group, I saw a boy I recognized. I don't know how, but his face and hair struck a chord in my memory. I immediately selected him as the person I was going to minister to, while the rest of my group picked out other young men on that corner.

We exchanged introductions and pleasantries for a while and then I asked him a little about himself. I always found it odd that some church folks would try to speak to people about the Lord without ever taking an interest in who they were talking to. As it turns out, my memory had served me correctly. He was also a ward of the state and we had crossed paths in the system. While neither of us could put our finger on it, we knew one another. We knew the location of boy's homes, the names of counselors, and roundabout dates of our whereabouts. The note of surprise was telling in his voice. He was a nobody, out there in the streets, how could somebody know him?

At some point, I asked him what he was doing out here in the streets. Was he between homes? Did he run away, or just age out of the system? He told me he was working. I could see that he was somewhat embarrassed to tell me this. Being 15-years-old, I was still not quite getting it. I asked him "What kind of work do you get paid for out here on the corner?" He then blurted out "I'm a prostitute, I get paid for sex!" Still oblivious, I jokingly replied 'women, pay you to sleep with them? Sounds like you are doing OK!' Then he clarified it for me. "I don't get paid to sleep with women; I get paid to have sex with men."

I had no idea what to say, so I just kept talking to him as if he said nothing out of the ordinary. After all, sin was sin, and none greater than the other. After that loose and somewhat non-conclusive reminiscing or catching up, I got to the matter at hand. I began to minister to the boy about the power of the Lord and how he could change his life forever, no matter what sins he had committed in the past. I looked into his eyes to gauge a response, to see if something sunk in, to let him know that I was a kindred spirit and it was all right. Then I told him of how Jesus suffered and died for our sins so that we may be forgiven. He responded in a terse manner and dulcet tone, "AT LEAST JESUS GOT TO DIE." Then he walked away. I let him walk away.

I immediately understood just how his way of surviving was tied directly to a difficult life in the foster system. Bad things happen to kids with no voice. Bad things happen in foster homes, and in boys' homes. Many boys who have been subjected to sexual abuse quickly degenerate into young predators and victimize the smaller and younger boys, just as caregivers and foster parents sometimes violate the trust of their charges. When you are abused so often by those you trust, it is easy to feel that being abused by strangers isn't nearly as bad of a letdown. At least you can make money, or survive. This boy's lifestyle was merely his survival technique, and I am sure he would not have chosen to live like this if he had another option.

All at once I felt like a blind man who was suddenly able to see. All of my faith fell in that instant. Reading and re-reading the book of Job suddenly meant nothing. Heck I was ministering to these people about a God that didn't even see fit to stop my abuse, to pull me out of my personal hell. I had lived much of my young life as Tom's unwilling sexual toy. Now I had my own demons to deal with, lust and desire with no outlet that would allow me to feel fulfilled. Lust was a sin, and although I wanted to be with a woman, that was a sin. If I chose to have sex with a woman, I was a sinner, so I resisted because it was what a good Christian was supposed to do. But I was still left with all of this turmoil and self-loathing that my years of abuse had created. Although I was trying so hard to live right, I was still living a life of misery and humiliation. The inconsistencies of "Jesus Loves Me" and my entire childhood were laid bare. It seemed as if the blinders were torn away.

Doubts

I was able to hold fast to my religious beliefs through the years of hoping to see my mother and sisters again, only to be let down. I was still looking to God. Even being moved around from family to family and the insecurities I developed, I still wanted to be a good Christian. While I was beaten, battered and violated at the hands of someone who claimed to love me, someone I called dad, I held onto my beliefs that Jesus loved me. When I saw all of my pain and misery reflected in the eyes of that young man on Cherokee Street, the flood gates came undone.

Since I could remember, I had always believed in the power of prayer. The Apsher's prayed daily, with every meal and at night. I prayed with the Bombers and even during my time within the boys' homes. I have always prayed, this is how I was raised. Why did my mother just let me be taken, why did she not try to find me? I always wanted to know why I wasn't wanted by anyone. No one ever asked my opinion, where I wanted to go, or if I wanted to go. I was just tossed around. Where were the Apsher's during my suffering? I thought they loved me. Why would they let me go? I had always believed that God would provide these answers in time. It was then that I realized no matter how hard I prayed, God never answered my prayers. And he wasn't going to.

My young mind wondered why an all-mighty and all-controlling God would allow an innocent child to suffer so much. Why would he allow my abandonment, my loneliness, the destruction of my innocence? Why would he allow the demons of sexuality to be thrust upon me, on top of all of the other events in my life? And on top of that, allow me to be moved to an all-white town and an all-white school where the last vestiges of my self-worth and value would be eradicated by isolation and the word 'nigger'?

When that boy on Cherokee street said "at least Jesus got to die," my faith was finally broken. All the hope that God would eventually make my life better vanished. In its place appeared years and years of pent up doubt, anger, and misery. I realized at that moment that if I was suffering this much with God in my life then what was the point? The reason I didn't stop that young man from walking away from my witnessing about the word of God was because I was walking in the other direction. Away!

Missing Person

The older I got, the more I began to realize the lasting impacts of my childhood. I was trying so hard to become the opposite of the pathetic little boy that went through all of that pain and abuse. I was angry and filled with hate for everyone that let me down and hurt me. But, I felt the most hate for myself, that weak little child. Of course I was a victim; I was too small, too nice, and too loving. I saw my need for family, friends, relationships, love, and acceptance as a weakness. After all, it was that need that was constantly exploited. I hardened my heart to everyone around me and eschewed my religious values as a joke. What was the point of following Christ if it only caused pain?

I never completely turned my back on religion. I never doubted there was indeed a higher power or that God existed. But by the time I was a young teen, I just gave up on believing I was special enough for him to notice. I stopped reading my Bible and saying my prayers at night. Oh, I would still pray, but it was as a last resort; when I had nothing or nothing left to lose. I actually feared to pray because as a child, it seemed when I prayed, the opposite of what I actually asked for would occur. So my life began to gradually change. Faith was replaced by doubt, peace was replaced by turmoil, and love was replaced by anger. I figured if I was going to be alone, then I was going to fight alone. If no one was going to be there for me, then I would not ask for help from anyone, not even God.

This was not some vain confidence, just a resignation that my life was always going to be a losing battle. Oh, I would still strive for accomplishments, but there was never any hope of success. In fact, I always expected to fail, always prepared myself for the worst and never dared to hope for success. In that way I could avoid disappointment, but I also missed out on a great deal of joy. If I succeeded, it was by my own merits. If I failed, it was never going to be because someone let me down. I used anger as my shield against all incoming arrows and missiles. I didn't see myself as special or blessed. I had no expectations that I was going to rise to any great heights. I was merely surviving, unhappy, alone, and without hope or expectation.

I was living and getting by. As I matured, I was even successfully moving forward in life. I was educating myself by going to night school while on active duty and deployments. I was building my body each day, ensuring that I would never be made fun of for being too skinny again. I was learning different martial arts so that I would never have to capitulate to abuse and to always to be able to defend myself. I learned to avoid placing my faith in anyone or anything. I was trying to become the man I always thought I should be - independent and alone, tough and self-sufficient. Yet, each day began to drag more out of me. And inside I was left restless, hostile, negative, and so very empty.

From the day I walked away from that young man on Cherokee Street, and my spiritual faith, I refused to look back. I allowed my abuse to make me hard and grizzled, never appreciating anything I had. Instead I always saw what I didn't have. I now only saw life as a glass half empty. I never took the time to see what was right in front of me or the good life I had at the moment. I never took any pictures to memorialize my life. There are very few pictures to remind me of my military service, no keepsakes of my childhood, or the time spent in other countries. I have very little to remember in my life before 35 years of age. I spent that part of my life being angry and unhappy about my circumstances, no matter how nice they may have been.

Growing

It wasn't until I was 35-years-old that I began to realize that all of the strife of my childhood was merely robbing me of any sense of peace. I found myself missing the inner love and strength I had when I was young, even in the midst of all the turmoil and abuse. I wanted to find that little boy who had hope and could see the bright side of life and the best in people. I realized that honest love and faith was not a bad thing, and being a good person even when you were not being loved is something to be admired. I wanted to find that missing little boy.

I finally saw that surviving my childhood trauma was actually one of my greatest accomplishments. This surpassed my time in the military, passing the BAR, or becoming a chief prosecutor. I realized that it was my childhood that prepared me to stand and fight. It was that little boy that never surrendered or gave up, even when all he had was faith. I began to see that I was able to fight and achieve, that I was no longer going to be a victim again. Even with all of the accomplishments in my legal career and successful trials, I still wasn't happy. I still couldn't find inner peace and the innocence I once had as a child.

Then it hit me. The abuse I suffered as a child not only gave me strength to deal with life's challenges, but it also gave me compassion. I really never stopped trying to help others; I still tried to give as much of myself as I could to those less fortunate. My personal relationships may have been in shambles, I may have been distant to those closest to me, but I still tried to reach out to the children and adults most people never thought about. Those that suffered, those that were abused, those that allowed the abuse of others, or their own bad choices to beat them down. I always found time to help the less fortunate.

I finally realized that for whatever reason, God allowed me to go through that horrific and painful childhood so I could help others. The drive to never again be a victim had pushed me to succeed and attain higher goals. However, I never just sat back and enjoyed the fruits of my labor and success. I used my different positions to influence others, to let them see that they didn't have to be gifted to be successful, and to show them that they could survive, even if everyone else turned their back on them.

But I was still trying to figure out why God would allow me, or any child for that matter, to go through abuse and sexual depravity. I couldn't understand why a loving God would allow anyone to go through what I went through. If he protected children, then my story would be unnecessary. However, it was enough to renew my faith and see that maybe God did have a plan for me. Maybe I wasn't going to find all of life's answers. But, I could still be happy. I just needed to have faith. Faith is what I had as a little boy. Faith was what I was missing. So tentatively, I began to once again explore my faith and my Christianity. I just had to accept Gods word, even if I did not understand it.

I remember a conversation I had with a friend who heard me speak at a foster youth rally. He was an agnostic, or maybe even an atheist. He asked me how I could believe in God after all I had been put through. This was a question I dealt with time and again as a child and as a young adult. The abuse and neglect that had plagued my childhood haunted my beliefs in a loving God. I explained that I never doubted the existence of God, based solely on the unexplained miracles in my life, the wonders of creation, and the possibility that all of THIS happened by coincidence. Even the most learned scientists realize there was some design to the evolution of man on this earth, even if they didn't follow a Christian God.

I was able to understand more as I grew older. I saw that my suffering could have some meaning. My struggles were not so uncommon that I couldn't reach out and help others get through. My childhood taught me compassion and understanding. I do not look down on those that are still struggling, even if it seems by choice...you never know what that person has had to endure in their life. I related this view to my friend. I let him know that I had found peace in knowing that my struggles had prepared me to help others in need. He laughed at my reasoning. He said "your loving God put you through so much suffering, so that you can help others that he will put through that same suffering?" If that was my God's love, then he would just as well do without. In fact, he stated that he would do well to avoid any kind of love that involved intentionally harming anyone! He did not understand why I would ever worship a God that allowed such pain to exist.

I must admit, I was stymied by that remark. Since I am no theologian, I had no response to his doubtful remarks. I just dismissed his reasoning as my lack of knowledge of God's master plan. I fell back on the tried and true Christian answer when the questions came too close and raised self-doubt. It may have sounded good, but it did not quell the inner turmoil that this question brought. I had finally come to grips with my sufferings. I was finally able to put aside the anger and self-pity I felt because of my situation. I was helping people, I wanted to help people, and God put me in a position to do just that. My life softened my heart to those that suffer and helped me relate to them in a way which allowed me direct influence. I had been through their struggles and could guide them through the path I used to escape my mental anguish. But, his one question stayed in the back of my mind. If God is so loving, why does anyone have to suffer? If he stopped all pedophiles then my story would not be needed and my suffering would not have been necessary.

Then, while listening to the radio, I heard a letter from a 15-year-old girl written to a Christian artist. That letter spoke of her need to understand her suffering and pain. She had a tough childhood and was feeling that she was never going to experience God's grace. She ended her letter by saying that she finally understood why God puts us through such suffering. Without trials and tribulations there is NO triumph. The light clicked on full strength! If we were born with everything we ever needed, we would never aspire for anything else. If we never had to go through lean times, we would not be able to fully appreciate blessings. For there to be light, there must be darkness…and we need both to know the difference. Or, to put it another way, it was my old saying put in the context of faith. Success is not measured by where you are, but by how far you have traveled to get there. It is the immense and numerous hills that truly define my accomplishments, not the gifts I was born with…or the family I was born into.

I realized that I had mistakenly believed that being a Christian was a way to escape all pain and misery. That once we were saved, our lives would be changed forever, and we would no longer be tempted by sin nor would we have to suffer from bad things happening. If we just prayed about it, only good things would happen. And when bad things happened, I prayed.

As a child, I prayed for God to take care of me. I prayed for food and a loving family as a child. I prayed for the abuse to stop as I got older. I even prayed that I would wake up white. In many respects, God didn't answer any of these prayers (even though I became one of the whitest black men in the Midwest). I believed God simply didn't care to answer my prayers and just allowed things to happen to me, regardless of the damage that was done.

I failed to realize that God doesn't always change what is going to happen to you. But he does give you the power to deal with those problems. The inner spirit and strength I possess allowed me to survive under the most extreme circumstances. I could still try to be a good caretaker to my sisters when my mother was passed out on the couch. I could still wake up every morning and continue to go to school, even try to learn sometimes, after a night of abuse and degradation. I could keep my head up and sit in class even though I was alone and friendless at my school. When I was full of fire and love for God, I was able to take all of my life's struggles and still be positive. I never lost my sense of self.

My prayers were answered because my childhood did not destroy me. I was still allowed choices in my life, still allowed to make mistakes. Those mistakes did not destroy me. Even when I turned away from my faith, I still retained some of that determination and inner strength to make it out of the Wilson home. The time I spent looking for answers and trying to put my past behind me was so difficult because I had given up on my faith. More so, I had given up on the fact that I was special, but God did have a plan for me. Only when I realized there was a plan, did I move forward with purpose...and more importantly, with happiness.

Of course, this does not undo all the pain I still feel or the issues my childhood has forwarded into my adult life, but having some understanding of God's plan does help. I am still trying to regain that innocent and trusting outlook on life; that little boy that held onto hope when all hope seemed lost, who could still try to be positive in the face of violation and abuse; that little boy who stood alone with resolve and compassion when all those around him were letting him down; that simple, positive innocence, that missing person, is who I am still searching for. That loving and trusting little boy may be buried deep inside of me, but I WILL find him someday.

10,000 Hills

11. Relationships

Past Relationships

After joining the Army, I had a series of relationships as any maturing young man would. Some of them were flings, others rather serious, but all had one thing in common - they ended spectacularly bad. Now I know that most of these were destined for failure, due to our lack of maturity. Each relationship I tried to build seemed to implode as soon as they were established. This was a chronic problem for me. I could not seem to maintain a healthy relationship. I just could not figure out what I was doing wrong.

At this point in my life, I realized the damage I had experienced was still right on the surface, raw and festering. My emotions and grasp of reality were in disarray. I did what most men do: ignored the damage, ignored the pain, and pretended to live a normal life. This was a time in my life where I used alcohol and anger to mask my past. I had a very low confidence level and was trying to prove to the world, and myself, that I was man; that I wasn't a sissy; that I wasn't gay. I was trying to outrun my past by becoming someone who was never a victim, or at least would never be a victim again. As long as I kept people at a distance, then they would never see the weak and helpless boy I always saw.

With all of this hidden angst and burden, I did what any young knuckle head would do...I got married. Since I was an enlisted soldier in the Army at the time, it was not unheard of for young soldiers to take a wife as soon as possible. It was a sure way to increase your income and move out of the barracks. My new wife was young, smart, and very pretty. We rushed into marriage and I revealed only a limited amount of information about my troubled past. I assumed she would pity me, so I never gave her the chance. My defense mechanisms kicked in and I became impossible to deal with. Since I saw weakness, I assumed she did, too.

One of my most effective and debilitating defenses was this ability to shut my feelings off to those closest to me. I felt the best way to stop a loved one from hurting me was to maintain a safe distance while keeping them guessing as to my feelings for them. If they didn't have any confidence in my love for them, they wouldn't be able to take me for granted or be able to hurt me once they got close. I didn't want anyone else to hurt me. I didn't want to feel so much for someone that I would allow them to make me a victim again. I was unwilling to give of myself in my relationship with my first wife, and ensured that she knew she wasn't that important. I wanted her to feel that I would be just fine if she wasn't around, even if that was not true. No one was going to take me for granted again.

And then there was the womanizing. I am not proud of my actions, but I want to be truthful. At the time, having many women served multiple purposes. It served to keep some distance between me and whoever I was in a "committed" relationship with. I never had to put all my eggs in one basket. I knew that if one relationship failed, then I had several on the side to keep me occupied. I didn't fully commit to any one girl and no one girl could break my heart. In my eyes, it also went a long way to proving my manhood. Since I could bed many women, I had to be manly...right? This is what society taught me - that true men were ladies men; that real men had lots of women, and sex was just a sport. As long as I was pleasing all of these women I could consider myself a real man.

This is what I had been doing in every relationship so far. I wasn't cocky or mean; I was just always distant and non-committed. I would do anything to win an argument or keep a woman guessing. By any means necessary, I would make her feel insecure about her looks, her weight, or her sexual ability. I would let them find numbers in my wallet or leave some indication that they were not the only one. Some of this was the macho military mindset, but it was mostly a way to keep things unbalanced, so I could always have control. If I was in control, then I couldn't get hurt. If they were unsure of how I felt about them, they would put energy into making me love them, instead of taking my love for granted. I utterly refused to allow any woman to see my kindness as a weakness.

With these ignorant concepts, it was clear that my first marriage suffered the same fate as all of my previous relationships. I had not dealt with my childhood. My view of reality was so skewed that I had no idea how to love someone or even allow myself to be loved. I was suffering, and my first wife suffered, too. It ended in divorce.

Keeping Good Ones Away

It was always the people who were closest to me that betrayed my trust and hurt me in the most intimate ways. My lack of faith and trust in supposed "loved ones" became an interference in my life as I repeatedly pursued interpersonal relationships. It was difficult for me to trust enough to love someone. A child's love in unconditional; it is ever giving and it is one of the first emotions an individual experiences…love for their parents. When that trust is broken, where do you go? How do you trust others who are less familiar or more distant from you? I thought, "If I couldn't trust my parents, who could I trust?"

To me it was a clear fact: only the people closest to you could cause you real pain. Trusting someone with all of me, my weaknesses, goals, thoughts and dreams, was too much for me to do. As long as I didn't give all of myself, I had something to build upon if I had to start over when that

191

person turned on me. I had to save something for myself; something that no one could touch; those quintessential components that made me, ME. If there was no one that was close enough to destroy me, then I could survive. It would only be those closest to me who would have the ability to take everything I had. I would keep that healthy distance to ensure that I would not lose everything.

I was never a hateful guy that didn't value love. In fact, like most people with a past similar to mine, I craved love and acceptance. I just didn't trust that anyone would give it to me, or that I was worthy of such love. It's hard to have a strong loving relationship without the ability to trust. As I matured into adulthood, I continued to enter into intimate relationships only to see the ghost of my past interfere. Unconsciously, I was allowing that past to cause others misery. It was never my intention to cause these women pain, but the distance I created with my cold heart and womanizing only hurt them, just because I did not want them to hurt me.

While being distant and nonchalant to those closest to me worked to protect me from harm, it also pushed a lot of good people out of my life. No woman wants to be with a man that doesn't value her enough to show her love or concern, or who is emotionally distant. I pushed many women out of my life that may have honestly cared about me. Then it dawned on me that you don't have to be a foster child or abused child to get dumped, to get your heart broken, or to get cheated on. Many people go through those tribulations and grow from them. Avoiding an emotional bond cheated me from experiencing a normal part of life. So I passed from an abnormal childhood to an abnormal adulthood. I went through my childhood feeling alone and my own actions were making me a lonely adult. It was clear that while I would never feel the agony of disappointment and heartbreak, I was going to be alone. I decided that I did not want to miss out on the joy just to avoid the pain.

Women

After my failed marriage, I realized it was not general mistrust, it was my mistrust of women that truly impeded relationships. (I hope someone sees the irony in the fact that I am now in a household surrounded by women. God definitely has a sense of humor.) By now it was obvious that Tom's abuse caused so much mistrust and self-doubt in my life that it was a wonder I was able to form any relationships at all. I have several male friends that I have held onto for years. I trust them fully and always have. However, I have always had a difficulty connecting and trusting the women in my life.

When I entered the foster care system, I did not know it was going to be permanent. For the longest time I held onto the fact that I already had a mom. She was not the most educated or attentive woman but she was my mother and could not be replaced. She had my unconditional love that lasted years after I was taken from her. Whenever I entered a new home, I would have great difficulty dealing with a mother figure in the house. This doesn't mean I was rude or angry, just distant. It was hard for me to look at another woman as a mother and allow her to take mom's place. I felt they were trying to make me forget that I even had a mom! As such, I would resist their nurturing and maternal affections even more.

This is the same mindset I brought into each foster home, and kept even after I was adopted by the Wilson's. I still held onto the fact that Millie could never replace my mom. I am sure this was not a good start for our relationship. But, she was not like my other foster mothers, either. She was fairly cold and aloof from the beginning. As time went on, the distance merely increased. I have always wondered if she even really wanted to adopt a child or was I just a disappointment? Either way, we were never close.

However, once Tom's physical abuse began, I learned to resent her. She was present for many of the abusive sessions and never interceded. If she did try to stop the punching and kicking, it was only to protect Tom from having a heart attack; to remind him to take his blood pressure medicine. Sometimes, she would even be the cause of the beatings. Knowing what Tom's reaction would be, she would still tell him when I messed up and stand there while I was being attacked. Her actions showed me that she believed I deserved all of the punishment I received. Where was her maternal instinct when I was getting beaten with a wooden stick, being kicked in the stomach, or punched in the face? What mother can stand there and watch a child get beaten until they are bloodied? She never once came into my room to tend to my bloody face or bruised body.

She also never stopped Tom from regularly giving me enemas or being in the bathroom while I showered. She would never comment when Tom and I would disappear for hours after a beating. Tom started spending long parts of the night in my room, and she didn't intervene, even when she would see him asleep on the floor in my room the next morning. Tom even began sleeping out on the couch on a nightly basis, and she would never question him. She never asked me about the sounds coming from my room at night, or why I was crying when I had to use the bathroom. There were enough signs of my abuse if she cared to notice.

The one time I tried to tell her that Tom was molesting me, she refused to believe me. She lost it. She was yelling and telling me how much I was embarrassing the family. She began slapping me and calling me a liar. They sat me in a chair and Tom beat me until I admitted to Millie that I was lying to her and nothing ever happened; that he never touched me. Much later that night, Tom was in my room "finishing" the punishment he had delved out earlier that day. He was actually calling me a liar as he was molesting me. He said I was lying about something that he was actually doing to me at the time. That night Tom was extra abusive and loud. We lived in a trailer and Millie had to hear what was going on, but she never believed me, and she never came to help.

That was the straw that broke the camel's back. I had to accept that

I was going to suffer alone. That was the night I also finally let go of any notion that my mother was going to come back and rescue me. I began to hate my birth mom, hate her for having me, for giving me up, for sending me into this horrible life that I was forced to endure. I hated Millie for not loving me and for not saving me. So far, no woman in my life had found me important enough to fight for or protect. These two women had abandoned me in my darkest hours and left me to suffer.

By the time I was done with my disastrous high school years, having dealt with four years of being the only black boy, and never having a girl find me attractive, I was done. I was angry at these girls for not even giving me a chance or just having me as a friend. For never seeing me as worthy of affection, for allowing me to be alone in school. Once I joined the Army, learned to be African-American and gained some weight, my dating prospects soared. But, my view of women was already damaged. I did not hate women, but my childhood had revealed to me that deep down I knew I could never trust a woman.

It was only after my divorce that I realized how poor my view of women was. Even though I considered myself a good guy, I had left a trail of young ladies who thought I was an absolute ass...and they were right. My childhood pain and self-doubt had caused me to hurt these women who were only trying to get to know me and show me love. I returned those efforts by treating them lousy and trying to sleep with their friends. This was not the memory I wanted to leave behind, so I had to try to change. I had to find a way to open my heart and let a woman in. I had to try and trust the next lady enough to show her my true feelings. I had to give women a chance to treat me right, instead of assuming that they would just hurt me once I let my guard down.

Bad Love

Based on my self-diagnosis, I realized I had let my childhood experiences hurt others. I had hurt women who did not deserve to be hurt.

195

It seemed that by the time I was reaching my 30's, I finally recognized that I had to view women in a better light, and not be so defensive. So I decided to let my guard down. I would look deep inside and make sure that any relationship I began would have a chance to succeed. I would look for the best in any woman I dated from that point on! But, as I said earlier, God has a sense of humor.

I was not aware of it, but my ability to properly select a mate was damaged by my childhood sexual and physical abuse. I found myself gravitating toward the wrong women, looking for love in all the wrong places. I became willing to accept anything as love including lies, infidelity, and abuse. What I failed to realize was, if you were used to getting battered and abused by a parent who tells you they love you, your expectations for "loved ones" can be lowered dramatically. You may even have a problem differentiating love from abuse. If your mother told you she loved you, and she neglected you, if your father was the person that cared the most for you, but he also beat and molested you, then you would have a skewed view of what love was. They fed you, clothed you, and they abused you.

I believed Tom loved me although he had abused me in some of the most painful and harmful ways imaginable. Therefore, I had to believe that someone could love you and still be capable of hurting you repeatedly and intentionally. Now that I had let my guard down and was determined to do right by any woman I was with, there was an almost comical change in circumstances. I found myself pursuing women that had no intentions of treating me the way I deserved to be treated. I worked so hard to give each girl a chance and I dealt with all of the neurosis and disruptive behavior that each one could muster.

I had changed my outlook on women and relationships. I went from never trusting and being emotionally aloof to allowing myself to be treated like a doormat. My childhood abuse had caused me to lower my standards instead of just lowering my defenses. Now, I gave each lady the benefit of the doubt. I had gone through so much as a child that I just excused the mistreatment and bad behavior, the violent outbursts and the lies. Instead of holding them accountable, I worked even harder to show them that someone cared. Each time I thought we were kindred spirits. I believed that they had suffered just as much as I had, and that they just needed someone to love them for who they were. I thought if I just hang in there and didn't give up on them, they would change. After all, it wasn't the worse treatment I had received!

And there were quite a few of those bad relationships. Some were worse than others, from being taken advantage of and lied to, to being cheated on and physically attacked when things got heated. It seemed as if I was now seeking out those lost souls, chasing them down and trying to save them. Deep inside, I thought that maybe I deserved this treatment. Not merely as some cosmic karma or payback for the pain and womanizing I had done in the past, but because now I was in familiar territory. I was in relationship after relationship where love was defined by the excuses I made for their behavior, just as I had done with my birth mother and Tom, two people I believed loved me. There was a strange comfort in trying to change a woman who was just bad for me. I was attracted to these bi-polar, love-hate relationships, women who claimed to love me but mistreated me all the same.

Now, I know you may feel like I was getting what I deserved. At the time I thought the same thing. I was getting what I deserved and that I was not going to do any better. As long as they said they loved me, everything else could be forgiven or overlooked.

Although I had improved upon myself and the way I treated women, I failed to identify that I still did not know how to recognize a healthy relationship. In order to improve my decision making, I had to realize that I had a propensity to make bad choices when it came to choosing a mate. I also had to stop trying to rescue people and make them love me. In fact, I had to change my definition of love. In order to change my view of love, I had to change my view of myself. I had to realize I deserved better. Love is not made up of excuses, and the abuse I endured was not my fault. If I didn't deserve it as a child, I definitely didn't deserve it as an adult. Most importantly, I had to realize that pain, deceit, mistreatment, and lies was never love. I had to finally admit that I was not loved as a child. I was abused, neglected, and tortured and that could never be considered love.

I had to come to grips with my issues and poor judgment, so I took a break from dating. Thank goodness law school made it all but impossible to focus on anything besides studying. Since I had never witnessed a healthy and loving relationship, I had to start from scratch. First, I had to realize what love wasn't; I certainly had enough examples of that. Then, I created a standard of how I wanted someone to treat me. I could not tolerate or excuse everything. Some things had to be deal breakers. While I could not readily identify a healthy relationship, I knew how to recognize a red flag and a bad apple. Through this process, I had to constantly remind myself to keep my heart and mind open to intimacy and emotions. While this took some trial and error, I re-entered the dating scene with a better sense of self and confidence with the knowledge that I deserved to be happy.

Airing Dirty Laundry

You have to have faith in someone, other than yourself. It requires you to open yourself up for further disappointment. It means you have to communicate and commune to attain that healthy relationship. You are supposed to relinquish control and allow another person to help fulfill your personal needs. Someone who is to be closer than any friend. It means that you must trust someone that may cheat on you, may take all of your money, and may tell everyone they know about your deepest fears and secrets. But you should never excuse any intentional mistreatment. I was now mature enough to realize that relationships and marriage required you to have enough trust to rely on someone. Someone who was fallible and human with their own issues and idiosyncrasies.

But even that wasn't enough. Now that I was a good candidate for a serious relationship and I had a standard for the type of woman I wanted to settle down with, I was still forced to overcome another big hurdle that my childhood had set in my path. Honesty. Not just about the day to day things, sharing and an emotional exchange, but revealing the details of my past. Any potential partner also deserved to be able to make an informed choice to be with me considering all the baggage I was bringing into the relationship.

I know now that it is so important to share your suffering with your significant other before they become your spouse! Especially if you have experienced the suffering and abuse I had to deal with. They have a right to know about your physical and sexual abuse. As much as it pains me to say, it is a horrible cycle that seems to get passed down from generation to generation. This requires a lot of faith, but you must lay it all out there on the line, instead of holding it in like some dirty little secret. If you really love someone, they deserve to know what you have been through and what to look for if some deviant behavior is triggered.

It was extraordinarily difficult to tell my current wife about the suffering I endured as a child, prior to getting married and starting a family. Early on, I intimated that I had a difficult childhood, but with little specificity. I know she figured something was odd when I had no family show up at my law school graduation, but she didn't pry and I didn't offer. However, once the relationship became serious and we started discussing a family, I knew she had the right to know about the horrible past.

I remember the evening I told her everything. I told her about my mother abandoning me, the foster homes, and the let down when I left the Apsher's. I told her about my relationship with my adopted mother and about being the only black kid in my school. I told her about the physical abuse Tom delved out. And, I told her about the years of sexual abuse that went on during my childhood. Her response was utter and complete silence. In my wife's defense, I dropped a huge bombshell on her with little warning. She was not prepared to hear my story. Who would be?

Why would she ever expect that my childhood was so horrible? My outward persona is confident, even cocky. Some may even consider me arrogant. The man she knows works out every day, weighs 230 pounds, and was a bouncer in D.C. night clubs to help pay for law school. She sees me with all of my tattoos, my guns, and has heard all of my soldier's stories. I have always presented the image of a protector. Now, she was being shown a little boy, huddled up in a fetal position listening for the telltale heavy footsteps and the creaking of his bedroom door late in the middle of the night. Her future husband was being described to her as an introverted punching bag that no one wanted or valued.

The man my wife fell in love with could not have possibly been the boy I described to her that night. In her mind, I could tell that she was trying to discern what kind of baggage she would now be taking on. Who could blame her? Would I want any of my daughters to get into a relationship with a man with my past? Someone who most likely had any number of issues just below the surface. But, she had seen my heart and my potential. We still waited quite a few years before we got married, just to make sure that neither one of us was getting into a complete mess. But, to her credit, my wife knew that while my past was not her fault, it could have been her burden. Yet, she still chose to accept me as her spouse (or as I always say 'thank God for women with low standards').

I learned that the issues I brought into the relationship were not insurmountable, but they had be aired and dealt with. Anyone who has suffered from physical, sexual, or mental abuse should definitely inform their loved one of those sufferings, at least the gist of it. If you are with a person with some odd characteristics when it comes to trust or intimacy, there may be childhood events that are a precursor to these inhibitions or limitations. If you are the person with these issues, your spouse deserves to know enough of the truth, so they can at least understand you. Your past is not an excuse for your current actions, but it may clarify some of the hurdles or hindrances you are dealing with in your relationships. You owe it to your loved one to tell them enough to be able to make an informed decision whether to continue the relationship. Hiding your past is not a good start for a healthy relationship.

10,000 Hills

12. Family

A Family Bond

It seemed for once that I had finally gotten over a general mistrust of women and my total inability to maintain a healthy interpersonal or intimate relationship. I thought I had crossed a major milestone in my life. I was in love and was able to trust this lady with my heart and my future. So everything else should be fine. Of course, I knew there would be other hills to climb, but I figured my personal life would be much better. But, when I got married, I didn't just gain a wife, I gained an entire family. Uncles, aunts, mother-in-law, father-in-law, brother-in-law, cousins, and all of her other relatives. Cookouts, family trips, family reunions, complete strangers giving me hugs, and even staying at my house. I was not at all prepared for that. Since my first marriage was during my military service, there was never any real contact with my first wife's family, beyond introductions. Now this! This was too much!

After returning from my military service with a destroyed marriage and no real direction, I went back to Freeburg to visit my adopted family. Tom was sick and dying of cancer. I began to realize how deep the scaring was from his abuse. I began to recognize how my childhood had molded and confused my emotions and thoughts. Now, the one man who I thought loved me was dying. I cannot say that I was happy, that I hoped he got what he deserved, because that would be a lie. I was sad, I was devastated. Even with everything he had done to me, he was still the only person I thought of as a parent, the only family I had. The day of his funeral was the last day I saw anyone from my adopted family. Once he was buried in the ground, I divested myself of any ties to the Wilson family, beyond keeping my name.

It wasn't even hard. There was no feeling of regret or loss. In fact, I was unburdened. I did not have to ever see anyone who knew how bad I had been treated. I could close the book on the people that never lifted a hand to save me. I did not want to live out the remainder of my life in touch with people who had pretended that everything was alright. Not when I was still uncovering the lingering effects of my abuse. The word "family" had been a negative term for me most of my life. That word was never associated with any joy or happiness, always neglect, disappointment, and abuse. From my birth mother's family, the foster families, and my adopted family, there was nothing I desired to hold onto or emulate. I just wanted to be done. So I cut everyone off and moved on.

By the time I got engaged, (yes, for the second marriage if you're keeping count) I no longer had any use for a family. Of course, I was in a better place and wanted to be married, and I wanted to have children. I thought that was more than enough. I mistakenly thought that was all I was going to have. Then, I was introduced to my wife's close-knit family, and I had no idea how to act. The interactions I witnessed with her relatives were totally foreign to me. I have never sat and reminisced about my childhood with anyone. Who would I even do that with? I had never sat down and talked with any grandparent or older person. Now I was constantly surrounded by chatter, emotion, and feelings. I can only describe my reaction to this extended family as uncomfortable, at best.

Because I had sworn off the need for any family connection, I couldn't help but be nervous about what I was getting into. My wife had the typical American family. Her parents divorced while she was a teenager but she continued her bond with both parents throughout.

Her dad is the patriarch of his entire family. Vernon was born in Mississippi and moved to Chicago as a boy with the migration of blacks leaving the south. While he grew up as a poor black child in the Jim Crow era, he still managed to go to Harvard Business School. Since he is a self-made man who has amassed wealth as a private business owner, he decides, and even funds, the majority of the outings the family takes. Her mother is a great cook and designer who loves to travel, and loves her grandkids. My wife's parents are close and have a great deal of impact on her life.

So, I always feel I am being judged or that I'm an outsider. It makes me uneasy when they try to build relationships with me. I believe my wife notices my edgy nature and I'm sure it doesn't make her happy. For me, to trust them as my own family would be a mistake. If I were to depend on them as my family, there is a great chance I would be disappointed. When my wife and I have issues, she can confide in her mother. She can depend upon her father to be there for her if there comes a time when we are at odds. I cannot say that I have the same refuge.

Who can I confide in if I have marital troubles? Who can I depend on for advice about my marriage or my wife? Her father is not my father; her mother is not my mother. They will always side with their daughter, as I would with mine. In the end, if my wife and I got divorced, they would still be her family, but they would no longer be mine. Why would I tie myself to something that can be taken from me? Why would I create a dependence on people who may not be there for me to depend on when I may need them most? I have made that mistake before.

In my mind, I had come to believe that having a family like hers was not important, that it was a negative. But in my heart I have always yearned for it. So why did I not take the opportunity to fully enter into her family? Of course, there were the logical trust issues - that someone would let me down if I let them get too close. But, I had already gotten over that dilemma in my personal relationships, why was this so different? This was a fear of being judged unworthy, of not being accepted. Deep down I knew they would never accept me for who I was, no matter how hard I tried. While my wife may love me, her parents and family would never find me worthy no matter how hard I tried...so why try?

A Childlike Need for Acceptance

As long as I can remember, I have tried to prove myself to others and have been found wanting. No matter how well I took care of my sisters, how well I sang, my mother would not stop leaving us at home alone. Even when I let my sisters eat first and cleaned up after them, she still sent me away. No matter how well I tried to speak or how straight I combed my hair, I could not find a family that wanted to keep me. When I would sneak down the hall of my foster homes at night, I could hear them talking about me, saying I was more trouble than I was worth. I could not get Millie to love me enough to protect me no more than I could get Tom to stop victimizing me. Becoming an Eagle Scout or a track star was not enough to get them to treat me like a son. I always found myself trying to prove my worth, and always had to deal with the pain of being deemed unworthy.

When you are trying to sell yourself, trying to get adopted, trying to get someone to adopt you, keep you, or even give you a second look, you are waiting for someone to find value in you. You are constantly aware of disappointment and still put your hopes on the line. In the end, it is still the same old song; you are left alone and wanting. While you dream of a family, all you really want is to be wanted, to be remembered. I even sank down so deep that I settled for abuse as a replacement for love just to gain acceptance.

At some point, I just gave up on ever having a "family." I knew that my desperation to be wanted, to finally fit into a family unit was a part of my undoing. If I had not been so worried about getting adopted or finding permanent placement, then I would have resisted being violated and abused by a family member. If I had not placed so much value in family, I would have at least fled the Wilson household. Instead, I just stayed, fearing that I would never get another chance at a family; that no other family would want me.

However, old habits die hard. Instead of looking for validation from my spouse or my wife's family members, I found myself working hard to gain the acceptance of others. I know that it is not uncommon for someone to look to others from time to time for value, to feel needed, or admired, or at least appreciated. However, this need for acceptance can become detrimental when taken to the extreme.

Even as a state's attorney, I came to realize that I was still dealing with my childhood need for acceptance, willing to do anything to find validation from others. I was an experienced attorney heading my own unit when I received a new boss. It did not take long for me to realize that she had utter disdain for me. With each interaction, she used a derisive tone, dismissed my input, and spoke down to me. She made it no secret that she did not respect my leadership or my abilities. She began to ridicule me to other division chiefs and even my subordinates. She dismissed my community service and work with foster children as a political ploy for self-promotion. The more I performed, the more critical she became. Even when I was successful in trying homicide cases, she questioned my trial tactics and courtroom presence. Yet, I found myself doing something counter intuitive to my treatment…I still tried to win her favor.

She was the antithesis of everything I valued in a leader, yet I felt compelled to show her my worth. This was not merely because of her position as my supervisor. My issues ran deeper. The more she judged and viewed me in a negative light, the more driven I felt to change her mind. To get her to see the true me. To prove myself to her. I was unaware that I had reverted to my childlike response of selling myself to someone who clearly did not value me. Even in my professional life, I could not escape the impact of my tumultuous childhood. Even with all of my accomplishments, I still craved acceptance. I could not just walk away without proving to her that I was worthy. Deep down inside, I still questioned my own worth.

I continued to bring ideas to her, just to have her dismiss them as nonsense. I worked on projects she chose to discontinue before I could finish them. I watched her take credit for work I completed, even though she had dismissed it as a waste of time. The more I struggled to find favor, the nastier she became. The desire to please this person even manifested itself in physical ways. The stress of this actually caused my blood pressure to rise and my headaches to return in full force. My body became more and more affected by the insecurity I felt. I started doubting my abilities as an attorney, writer, and leader.

This desire for acceptance, the pain caused by not being valued, and the stress that was hurting my body and mind was happening without my notice. I was not aware that I had reverted back to my childhood method of absorbing all the pain and mistreatment thrown my way. I was lucky to have a co-worker and friend point out that I was putting myself through this pain for acceptance that would never come. This friend had prosecuted child abuse and sexual assault cases for years and knew of my past. She was able to recognize how much I had diminished myself just to gain this woman's acceptance. In the end, I quit. This was the best thing I could have done.

I learned that I needed to be constantly vigilant when it came to my self-worth, but being too cautious can cause just as much damage as an over reliance on another's opinion of you. While I had learned to shun family and family relations, I still found myself looking to others for validation and value. I found myself striving to be seen as special, as someone to be remembered. My solution for avoiding grief by limiting family ties was no solution at all. I pursued acceptance in other areas of my life with increased vigor, instead of trusting those who at least tried to bring me into the fold, those that had already extended themselves. Maybe the very thing I was looking for was there all along. Maybe my wife's family did find me worthy of being a part their family.

Inability to Connect

The absence of a connection with my wife's family is not because I have not tried, but some things have become innate. I have had a chance to reconnect with people from my past; one of my sisters, my birth mother's relatives, and one of my foster families. Each time it has been difficult and uncomfortable for me. Each time, I found myself unable to open up enough to create or maintain any connection.

Candy was my baby sister at the time we were removed from my birth mother. Years later, I was able to track her down (thanks to my ex-wife) living in a town near the area where we were born. She had been adopted as an infant and raised in a loving family. Her adopted parents were reticent about letting me meet her and it took several telephone conversations to convince her mother to let me speak with her. In the end we met at a Cracker Barrel near Rolla, Missouri. She was a lovely woman and we spoke for about an hour. She was now married with a husband in the Army and two children of her own. She was able to go to a good college and became a nurse. We exchanged information and parted ways. That was in 1999. She mailed me pictures of her sons some years later and that was pretty much the extent of our contact.

It's not that I disliked her. It was just that there was nothing really to talk about. We had no memories to share and little common ground. It was like meeting a distant cousin. For me, to know that she was OK was more than enough. I guess I didn't do much to keep the relationship going, but I really didn't know how.

This was the same distance I felt for my mother's relatives as well. I had an opportunity to find my grandmother before she passed away. This was also due to the efforts of my first wife. She found my grandmother's phone number and I called her. She was hard of hearing and could not figure out who I was. Eventually she exclaimed "you're that little colored boy, Mary's Boy!" She asked me to come and visit her and I agreed. In my heart, I felt I was making a mistake and setting myself up for failure. I really didn't want to go, but figured I would go out there for an hour just to say hi.

I had put the trip off for as long as I could. I remember arriving at 6 p.m. and driving up to the little shack she lived in. It triggered a great number of childhood memories and emotions. When I arrived, the little shack was overflowing with people. My mother had thirteen brothers and sisters. Most of my aunts and uncles were there waiting for me. The cacophony of movement and sound and activity was just overwhelming. Many of my uncles and aunts were deaf. As such, there were multiple conversations going on, some in sign and others verbal. Some were telling me different stories of my childhood. Others asking me to find my mother. There were pictures on the wall of my mother and all of her family. The smell of the wood stove, the view of the poorly lit room, and the sound of all the conversation was too much to handle.

My grandmother was in a wheelchair, suffering from diabetes and a number of other ailments. While I was expecting cold detachment or mild curiosity, I received love and affection from everyone. My grandmother's first words as I came in were "I was holding on, I knew you would find me before I died." The entire family had been waiting there for me since nine that morning. They were all so proud of me and each wanted to tell me about my mother and why she gave me up. The reasons and facts varied greatly from sibling to sibling, and many spoke in hushed tones, so that my grandmother would not hear. My grandma held onto my hand the entire time I was there. She would not let my hand go until I had to leave. When it was my time to go I told grandmother that I would be back soon. I knew as I left that house that I wasn't coming back. Two years later, I learned that grandma died three months after my visit.

It wasn't that I did not appreciate everyone showing up, or that I wasn't interested in their stories, I just could not find that connection. All of the many questions I may have asked had been laid to rest years earlier. I had given up on ever having this meeting and had cut off any emotions that were tied to my birth family. They had never been there for me, and I figured that I would never see them. I had let that part of my life go. Even surrounded by people I was related to, I could feel no real emotional bond. They were just people from my past with stories about me. I couldn't make myself feel something, especially when I didn't know what it was I was supposed to feel.

Reconnecting

While the foster homes had darkened my outlook for having a loving home, the Wilson's destroyed it. I had to let go of any value for family in order to get by. In order to survive abuse and even foster care, you have to remove the connection to the people around you and your "loved ones." You cannot feel too connected to people that may send you to another home at any time. You cannot maintain an emotional tie to someone who beat and rape you for their pleasure. I had to purge myself of any hope of love and protection to survive. The abuse would have been too much for me to survive if I believed there were people out there that might come and rescue me. If I would have held onto any hope that things would get better, I would have killed myself. Instead, I adapted as best as I knew how. I gave up on everyone around me. After all, no one came for me.

After you have been neglected and let down, you just lose faith in people in general. To really believe that family is a good thing after so many years of being abused and neglected is still difficult. My natural default is to keep people at a distance and avoid a connection. It is better not to know someone too well rather than find out they will not be there when you need them. It's not wholly unrealistic. No family members called to check on me during 9/11 although I was living in D.C. No one from my past calls to wish me a happy birthday or to see if my daughters are healthy. There is no one to fall back on if I can't make my mortgage payment or need a babysitter. I do not expect these things.

It's not that I am an emotionless automaton. I have had no problems establishing a bond with my children. I love my daughters with all of my heart and show them each day. I'm just not that capable of extending those emotions outside of my immediate family. I know I should call the Apsher's more often. I love them. Part of me wishes I could keep in touch with Candy or my birth family, but I really do not have any desire or feelings to have an emotional bond with them. I have made efforts to relax around my in-laws and allow myself to be part of their family to some degree.

Conclusion

Family is not a magical term. It is not something that can be defined by blood relation. A true family is something that is created over time. I thought my lack of desire for a family was because of distain or lack of trust. There is also a lack of confidence in myself and the fact that I never had a foundation to build upon. My childhood rarely provided me with a positive definition of family. I never had a good example of why family would be a necessity and no reason to place any importance on the need for family. It was just something some people were born into. I was never able to enjoy the unconditional love that healthy families share.

This disconnection can be problematic for any child. It can also be a problem for society, in general. If you emotionally disconnect yourself from this world and you also feel anger for the horrible experiences you had to endure, then you may become extraordinarily capable of horrific violence. That may be the path that allows you to commit violent and vicious crimes against others. Too many abused children become abusers.

Too many foster children never feel connected to this world, or valued by society. In both cases, they may have an unquenchable anger for the cruelty endured within their life.

I have learned that I cannot get my validation from others when it is detrimental to me. It's okay to value other's opinions, but not let them tear you down. No one's approval is worth my health and happiness. Moreover, I realize that I cannot base my value on the approval of others. I know my childhood may continue to have an effect on my ability to relate to others and bond with good people. This is something I need to work on, because I need to find value in myself.

I know my lack of faith in family has caused me to miss out on a lot of good things life has to offer. Now that I am a parent, I now know that family is important, and that I must work hard to develop and extend my family. That means taking chances, facing judgment, and dealing with rejection. I know my children need to have a close bond with as many relatives as possible; they deserve it. And I deserve it too. It is a work in progress.

13. Parenthood and the Impact of Abuse

Most of my colleagues joke about slowly becoming their parents. How many times have you told your child "I have had it up to here?" How often do adults criticize the popular music or style of dress? Can you even count the number of times you have told your child that they have it so much easier than you did at their age? In many ways it is true that we mimic our parents. In fact, most of our social ideologies and societal mores are passed down from our parents. We learn what is normal by the way they lived and the way they treated us. Our views on religion, politics, even cooking and sports are often passed down by our parents. Good parenting doesn't change over the years, it gets passed on.

But this little factoid was my NIGHTMARE because I knew that bad parenting could be passed down, too. Psychology classes taught me that abused children often became abusive parents. Children who were neglected as children were more likely to neglect their children. Even those who simply witness household violence are more prone to be violent when they have their own family. I learned that children who were the victims of sexual abuse often become pedophiles themselves. It is considered the cycle of abuse. Each of us can easily replicate our childhood when we become parents. It is heart wrenching to know that most abusers were once victims themselves. Bad parents can have a lasting impact on our lives too, long after they are gone.

215

Where does that leave me? I saw and was the victim of so much. My birth mother placed me in bad and neglectful situations. She chose drugs over me. My adopted parents were my archetype for what parents should not be, using violence as a form of discipline. When I messed up in school, the discipline was swift and exacting, with little or no mercy. I knew I was going to be beaten severely for minor infractions. The physical abuse by Tom was repeated to the point where it became expected. I never had a mother to protect me or a father to show me proper affection.

I was absolutely terrified to start a family. I feared that I would become some violent abuser. I already possessed a quick temper and a lifetime of anger. Could I abuse my children? Would anger rule my parenting? Could I lust after my own children? Could I somehow or in some way take all of the suffering and humiliation I received and pass it down to my children? While I have never had any sexual desire for children, and since I had no idea what made someone a pedophile, I was horrified that I may have had that potential. I knew I'd rather be dead than ever have those feelings, even if I had to take my own life. Deep down inside I prayed that I had not inherited that trait from Tom, and if I had, that I would have the courage to follow through and end the cycle.

There were other things I had to be on the lookout for as I began to focus on creating a family of my own. What kind of parent would I be? What could I do to avoid the mistakes of my parents? Were there hidden triggers to my rage or did I possess some uncovered deviancy that a child would bring out. I prayed that I didn't have to play the role of a distant and stern parent just to avoid interacting with my children. As scared as I was about beginning a family, I really did want to finally have someone in my life who shared my features, my attitudes, and my blood. But I was determined not to allow my children to suffer as I had.

Physical Discipline vs. Abuse

I have seen some parents viciously attacking their children for minor infractions as a way of preventing serious things from happening later. Their view is, if you overlook the small stuff, the big stuff will happen. This is usually a direct result of the way they were punished as children. It worked for me, so it will work for my children. There may not even be any malicious intent, just a need to keep their children in line; to ensure that their kids make it into adulthood. But, there is a difference between discipline and abuse. So how does that line get drawn?

It was Tom's duty to delve out the discipline and Tom did so with gusto. He regularly lost his temper for the smallest things and his anger would escalate once the beatings began. What would begin with eager questioning would turn into yelling. That would then turn into him punching and kicking, and often end with him pummeling me or beating me with any object within reach. The level of discipline did not necessarily match the offense. It was pretty much random or motivated by non-disciplinary desires. These beatings were such a common occurrence that I failed to equate them with abuse. I knew I shouldn't have been beaten so badly, but I began to get used to them. These beatings were a part of the only life I knew and a normal type of discipline. In fact, it took years before I recognized that it was physical abuse.

As a child, I believed Tom loved me, even though he relentlessly beat and pummeled me. I had to believe that the discipline was deserved. Subconsciously I had to accept that he was doing what needed to be done as a parent. That maybe he was toughening me up for what the real world had in store. Maybe it was all right to lose your temper when you disciplined a child. If that punishment was the only form of discipline you received, how could you be expected to teach anything different to your child? This was the lesson in parenting I learned.

Later, as I got older, I came to know that no child should be beaten and punched, ever! Even if Tom believed he was doing the right thing and that a closed fist is acceptable as discipline, I knew better. I knew he was wrong. However, I was still worried that I would succumb to his predilection for physical abuse, just as he inherited it from his parents. This is where I knew how he and I differed. I know it is wrong to hit my children in anger. I am too intelligent to resort to rage and violence to teach a child a lesson.

Handicapping Children

You may think I would be against any type of corporal punishment; that I believe conversations and timeouts would be sufficient to raise a healthy and productive child. That would be a false assumption. I realized that Tom's style of discipline was with malice and ill-will. It was not discipline, but abuse. There was no lesson to be learned or healthy structure in place to keep me in line, just random and anger filled beatings. Some children need a spanking from time to time. I know I sure did! While timeouts may work for some children, I knew I was not one of them.

I was brought into the Wilson family after a difficult start in life. I had been torn from my family, rejected by other families, and witnessed abuse and neglect prior to setting foot in the Wilson household. There is no way a time out would have worked for me. Even enduring this abuse, I was a little shit. For example, I once got into trouble at school during the winter. The teacher called Tom and when the teacher gave me the phone, Tom told me "give your soul to the Lord, because your ass is mine when you get home." I can't remember what I had done, but knew I was going to get a beating.

Despite what I knew was coming, I took a bucket of water to create a patch of ice on the porch. It took a while, and I had to bring several buckets of water to make it real solid. Like clockwork, Tom came home and began building up his rage. He claimed that I was embarrassing him, acting out in school. He began to punch and kick me in the side. My only concern was making it to the porch. And like a Scooby Doo episode he followed me onto the porch, tried to kick me and I ducked. He hit the ice and went completely horizontal, landing on the porch with a crack! He laid there sprawled out on the porch with the wind knocked out of him. I ran out into the middle of the yard hooting and laughing my butt off! This wasn't revenge, or a defensive maneuver; this was just me being devious and ornery! As crazy as that sounds, I was just having fun. I took one hell of a beating that day and again that night. The beatings and abuse had become normal in my life, and I was still a kid. I needed guidance, structure and yes....discipline.

The Switch

I have seen several media stories that link corporal punishment to adult violence. Somehow the method that has been utilized throughout history to discipline children is now the reason for our crime statistics? Amazingly, it is the media that continues to draw this correlation...the media! If there is any one thing that has exacerbated crime in this country, it is the media. The claim is being made that a parent spanking a child increases violence in our communities, not the thousands of murders portrayed on television, the desensitizing of our children, or the glorification of violence...but spankings!

When I speak to most of my professional friends about their childhood, they fondly reminisce about the discipline that was delved out. First of all, this was done by grandparents, aunts, uncles, even neighbors, as well as their parents. Go ahead; ask any of your co-workers, friends, or associates. I guarantee you will find someone that has the "switch" story. Does this ring a bell? You messed up and you were warned, and as a child often does, you ignore or forget the warning. What happens next? You are told that enough is enough and now you have to take your medicine. What was the medicine? Walking out to pick a switch.

Almost everyone will agree that having to go and pick out the instrument of your discipline was devastatingly effective. Everyone that experienced this will tell you how they dragged their feet, crying, reluctant to go outside and select the right switch. They will probably also tell you that they had to pick a good one, too. If they picked one that was too weak or too soft this would garner them even more punishment. They will also tell you about the walk back, how they tested the switch, heard it whistle and cut the air with that 'switching" sound. That was how you knew it was a good one. Then you would slowly walk back, with tears in your eyes and hand the switch to your mother. A spanking, crying, and a stinging bottom were soon to follow.

Depending upon the area where you were raised or your age, you could easily replace that switch with a flip flop, fly swatter, wooden spoon, or that white belt from the disco era with dual holes that whistled when it was swung. The key was, they made you go get the object you were going to be disciplined or spanked with. Now, ask those same people if they thought that was abuse. Ask them if they now think their parents hated them so much back then to torture them in some outrageous fashion? Or did they just think that it was love? Although they didn't like it at the time, each person will tell you they deserved it. And EACH ONE will tell you they are better for it! In fact, just look at their lives and their level of success and happiness. Regardless of the made up statistics, stern and loving discipline as a child kept these people out of jail, stopped them from mouthing off at the cops, and disobeying teachers in school.

In the end, as reprehensible as child abuse is, its prevention should never include chipping away at a parent's right to discipline a child while leaving them with the responsibility to raise their child. You cannot prevent child abuse by taking all belts out of the house, or by keeping a parent in fear of penalties for unknowingly spanking their child too hard, or by forcing all parents to adhere to a specific form of discipline. Each family's background differs greatly and each parent needs to be able to provide the structure and discipline they deem is necessary. The state need only intervene when the line is crossed into malice or reckless behavior.

I believe there is a proper way to discipline your child, and yes that includes spanking! Of course, what I went through was nothing close to normal or acceptable discipline. I encourage parents to discipline their children in whatever non-malicious way they see fit. My purpose is to remind people that children are being abused every day, but parents should have the right to be parents; their children deserve it.

Inherited Sexual Abuse

I do believe in the cycle of sexual abuse; that children who were abused can in turn abuse their children. However, because it is so utterly reprehensible and socially unaccepted in any form or fashion, child sex abuse cannot be blamed entirely on an abuser's childhood. This is not to say that the desire may be created at a young age. A sex abuser knows sexual abuse is wrong. They are aware there is no situation where sexual contact with a minor, their child included, is deemed to be acceptable or understandable.

Even when I was getting beaten, I believed, and still want to believe, Tom only lost control. I believe adults can lose their temper with their children, that they get carried away with their discipline and take it to the extreme. This can happen, especially if there is intoxication or drugs involved. While the discipline may be harsh, it is at least possible that it was not meant to be abuse. Each of us has lost our temper. No, we may not have slammed a child's arm in the door or punched a 10-year-old in the face, but some of us have done things out of anger that we regret.

Sexual assault is something altogether different. There is no loss of control, no drug induced reaction that stimulates your thought. Having the desire to engage in sexual contact with any child, one you brought into this world, or one you agreed to care for, is unconscionable. I find it hard to imagine this being a learned response. I believe early exposure to it may generate an improper desire. The major difference is this one thing…you know it is wrong…you know it is damaging.

While I may have been able to excuse Tom as being heavy handed or just unable to control his temper, I never believed the sexual abuse was warranted or acceptable. Once it started happening, I knew it was wrong, as does every child who has to endure it. No matter how many times they say they are sorry, or that it will never happen again, even if they try to reward you for dealing with it, it never becomes right. It never becomes something you can envision doing to someone else.

While physical abuse is usually predicated by the child doing something wrong, sexual abuse has no such origin. Hands down I know it was the worst thing I have had to deal with. The desire or need to sexually intrude on any child's sexual development is not bred out of a reaction to their childhood, it is a choice. Therefore, while children who are molested may be more likely to molest their children, it is something they choose to perpetuate. Because it is a choice, I would **never** choose to engage in any sexual contact with my children. It has never been a desire; it will never be a desire. I would never choose to impose my childhood angst and confusion on my children. If those urges ever arose, I would do the right thing and leave, even if it meant taking my own life. Since I have lived that life, why would I ever choose to force my children to suffer the same fate?

So, to those children who are going through this horror, there is no excuse for your suffering. To any perpetrators, there is no excuse for your actions. Even if you were exposed to this deviant behavior by some trusted adult in your childhood, your actions were always your own. You chose to violate a child's trust instead of seeking help for your issues. You chose to pass this down to yet another generation, instead of letting it die with you. Your troubled and tortured past does not excuse your choices.

Choosing What I Pass Down

My childhood neglect and abuse can, without a doubt, affect my ability and discernment as a parent. It can even affect how my spouse will parent our children. This does not mean that abuse victims are forever unable to perform the role of parents. Although, it is worth noting that my childhood was less than normal and, as a result, I may face added difficulties in my role as a parent, some of my values and reactions may have been polluted by my suffering. There may be life lessons that I should unlearn, lest another generation suffer. There may also be times when I need to rely on the opinion of my spouse to ensure that I am not being too stern or too protective with my children. Either way, it is always important that I realize that my childhood was not acceptable and as an abuse victim I must NEVER emulate my abuser. I don't have to be like my parents.

I don't ever want my children to experience the pain and downright torture I had to go through. I know I must always remember that I cannot lose control of my temper when disciplining my children. In fact, because of my childhood, my wife is the one who usually delves out any discipline. This is to avoid me being too severe with them. I believe that occasional corporal punishment is a necessary tool in disciplining a child. I believe it should never be administered with anger or malice and, only with discretion and discernment.

As a survivor of sexual and physical abuse I am wary of my children being around too many people. They do not spend many overnight visits with friends, nor do they have a lot of adult caretakers in their lives. At an early age, we have explained to them that only three people need to see them naked, daddy, mommy, and the doctor. As they get older, I am thankfully removed from that list! They are not overly exposed in any graphic detail to the evils that can be done to little children, and they are sheltered from the actions of bad people. They know strangers are not to be trusted and that even loved ones have their boundaries. I will never be someone they need to be wary of. I love them too much.

I always made excuses for Tom's actions. I never want that for my kids. I know children have unconditional love for their parents and I don't want my children to ever have to accept less from me. A child's love should never be a sacrifice, and it should never be accompanied by an excuse. To put it simply, when my kids find out about my childhood, I don't want their reaction to be "oh, that is why Daddy was so distant" or "that is why Daddy wasn't around and spent very little time with us!" I don't want them to finally have an excuse for Daddy's shortcomings. I definitely don't want them to say "well, that explains his horrible and violent temper," or "that explains why he beat us; he was beaten as a child."

My childhood anguish has given me a great deal of compassion for the human plight. There are a multitude of children right now who are going through things that are much worse than my childhood. So while I abhor the thought of my children experiencing any of the physical, mental, or sexual abuse I endured, or the social isolation that accompanied me most of my life, I want them to have compassion for the suffering of others. My goal isn't necessarily to hide what I went through, but to make sure my girls are at least able to benefit from the compassion and understanding that my life taught me, without having to suffer. There are many ways to learn just how hard the world can be.

This means that they are exposed to the homeless. Not only their presence, but their names, why they are there, and what can be done about it. I want them to feel obligated to provide some answers to the sufferings of this world. As they get older, I need them to understand that the abused women living in shelters, or those who have yet to leave their abuser, are not suffering by choice. That those homeless families or people living in tents may not be too lazy to find work. I want them to know mercy and obligation. They should know that while they are fortunate, there are people out there right now in need of assistance. I want my children to know that they must position themselves to be able to help those in need.

I choose to always be the example for my little girls. To let them see a man putting on a suit every day and going to work, even if I am not happy with my job. To let them see a parent that eats after they are fed, even if that means a baloney sandwich instead of the meal that was prepared. To let them see a man who will not just complain about the world, but try to change it, even if that means entering politics. This doesn't mean I am the perfect parent, but I strive to be better. I still have a volatile temper, although my children have seldom witnessed it. I also curse entirely too much, as my daughters will tell you, especially when I am playing video games or driving. I don't blame my childhood for my cursing (thank you very much U.S. Army), but there is no excuse and I constantly strive to do better. My walk with the Lord is a long one.

Instead of using my childhood sufferings as an excuse to be distant, violent or absent from my daughters, I am hoping that I can salvage some good out of that life. Instead of my children inheriting the mistakes of their father, I want them to benefit from the humility and compassion that pain has taught me. I can use what I went through to make my children aware of the world suffering around them so they can make it better. When my children are of age and read this book, I hope they are proud of their Daddy. I hope they see the journey I have walked and the hills I have climbed to get here. There will be no more cycle of abuse, no more family history of neglect and low self-esteem. As a parent, I will learn from my childhood, instead of allowing my daughters to become a victim of it.

14. To Lie

Costly Lies

I remember when I left the Army. I was going through a divorce and drifting aimlessly. I knew that I wanted to go to law school. The problem was that I had no idea of how to do that. I didn't know any lawyers or anyone who was even in higher education. More importantly, I didn't think I could ever get into law school. I graduated from undergrad with all A's, but to me that was a fluke. The school must have been too easy; after all it was a school on a military base. I figured they just taught easy classes.

It was easy to tell people that I was going to be a lawyer. In fact, it was easier to talk about going to law school than it was to apply. If I tried and failed then I would know that I was not good enough. If I just kept talking about it and never tried, then I could still hope that I would have been good enough, even if I never got in. It's kind of like not studying for a test because you were afraid of failing. If you didn't study and failed, it wasn't because you were not smart enough, it was because you didn't really try. However, if you really gave it your all and failed, then that was proof that you were never smart enough. That was a tough reality to face. So I created this fantasy world where I was going to go to law school...eventually.

I shared something in common with many foster and abused

children that I have met in my life: low self-esteem. The reason I seldom ever aspired for greater heights is because in my heart I knew I would never be good enough to succeed. This was coupled with not having access to people who could direct me to the path of success, or tell me what I needed to do to achieve my dreams. So, while I always had dreams of being a lawyer, I honestly never thought I would be one. Oh, on the surface I talked a good game, told people I was just waiting to find the right school, or trying to find the money. I was lying to myself and everyone around who would listen, with no real hopes of ever going to law school.

One day as I walked through the mall in Belleville, Illinois I saw a guy I recognized. Come to find out, we were stationed together in Germany. He was living in St. Louis and going to graduate school. We had engaged in some pretty intelligent conversations working out in the gym while overseas, mostly about community activism and how we would like to change the way our culture and our people were viewed. Of course, he was one of the smartest brothers I had met while in the Army, so it didn't surprise me that he was going to graduate school.

Well, we began to talk and I found out that he was from East St. Louis, and grew up only a few miles from where I grew up. However, our towns could not have been anymore dissimilar. Freeburg was all white and middle class and East St. Louis was all black and incredibly poor. He asked me what I was going to do now that I was out of the Army and I gave my patented answer, "I am going to go to law school." He asked me a question I had never heard before, "How did you do on the LSAT?" I had no idea what that was, not knowing that it was the very test that you MUST take in order to get into law school. I told him that I didn't remember, but probably did OK. At that point I could tell that he had seen through my lie. So, I tried to extricate myself from the conversation and go about my business.

He walked with me and asked me if I had even taken the LSAT

yet? I tried to squirm out of it by saying that I didn't really remember, but thought I had. He replied that if I had taken the test I would have remembered. He told me that the exam was in a month or so and that we should take it together. I said sure, and we exchanged phone numbers. He later called and told me what study guide to buy and where the test was going to be given.

I didn't even go and get the book. The reality of not being good enough was finally setting in, and I didn't need to see proof sent to me in the mail. The Saturday came when the test was to be given and he called me to make sure I was up and on my way. I lied and told him I was on my way, then went to the gym. I received a call four hours later. He sounded quite upset and asked me where I was. I lied and told him that I wasn't prepared but would take it the next go around. I figured that would be the end of it. He would be off to law school and I could continue pretending that I might go one day.

He told me that he took the test and then declined to have his test graded. Then he told me that he signed us both up for an LSAT class at the college that started in a month and that I'd better have my ass there. He even rode with me to the classes to make sure I would attend. We talked on the phone and met, as a result of his bullying and prompting to study our practice books.

Well, test day came and he made me spend the night at his house to ensure I would not back out. By then I had found someone who actually believed in me enough to sacrifice his time and effort to help guide me toward my goal. I was going to at least give it a try. When the scores came back, I actually scored very well and received a number of scholarship offers to some of the top law schools in the country! We both went on to our respective law schools, graduated, passed the BAR the first time and both became attorneys. We chose different schools and found different paths that have taken us to opposites sides of the globe. He chose the Army

JAG and I, the State's Attorney's office.

Marlin Paschal is three years younger than me, with his own story of poverty and being raised without a father. He found the time to look out for a man he hardly knew. He not only showed me my self-worth, but that sometimes all we need is one person to believe in us. He showed me that I had to make sure that I empowered as many people as possible to make our world a better place. He humbled me with his self-sacrifice in order to follow his belief that we were our brother's keeper and that we must work selflessly for those who have been laid low by life's challenges. He taught me the ultimate danger of being an accomplished liar.

The day I met Marlin Paschal in the mall was the day I learned my false reality was merely going to keep me from ever achieving my potential. When I met Marlin that fateful day, he listened and then corrected me. He told me that I wasn't going to law school without doing the right things. To have someone call your bluff in such a strong yet caring way was entirely unexpected. Marlin clearly pointed out that I was not going to law school if I had never taken the entrance test. He volunteered to take it with me. Even when I later reneged on the test date, he was patient enough to see that I was ready for the next exam date.

That was when I realized that the world I had created wasn't just false, it was inhibitive. I had sold myself and others a wonderful bill of goods that made me look like I was achieving everything I ever wanted. I chose to lie about improving my lot in life, rather than face the painful test that I may not be good enough to ever reach my dream, or even good enough for anything good to happen to me. In reality I was going nowhere, and ignoring my lack of direction and effort. My survival technique was destroying me. I was never going to see my true self, and therefore never reach my true potential. I was lying to hide from failures, something I had done my entire life.

Human Nature

I believe lying comes naturally to human beings. I marvel at the ingenious mind of my four-year-old as she tells me that her mother gave her permission to eat seconds of dessert. I ask her, "even though you did not finish your supper?" And she replies without missing a beat that "Mom said it was OK." I could question her further and break her down, after all, I am a trial attorney and know how to cross examine an untruthful witness, but I relent. She is only young once. After her little round belly is full of seconds of ice cream I tell her that lying is wrong and she should always be truthful. "Daddy always knows," I tell her and she apologizes for not telling me the truth. Of course she will do it again, and I will correct her until she learns. This reminds me of everyone's need to create a world that is most pleasing to them, whether it is getting extra desserts or just being viewed as normal.

For years I was a habitual liar (some may say now I am just a paid habitual liar as an attorney). I didn't start lying to cover up my failures and short comings. My entire young life was pretty much one big lie if heard from the right point of view and at the right time. To put it plain and simple, I had to tell myself that I was never forced to have sex with a man, that I had parents who loved me, and that I was of value; that I was going to be somebody. The truth of my life was just too hard to bear. In fact, while I can face the truth now, the reality of my childhood may have been too much to handle. Had I fully accepted the truth of everything I had gone through, I may have given up on life entirely. If I took the time to understand the reality of my childhood, I could never have thought it possible to aspire for any modicum of success.

Learning to Lie

I had learned to lie well before my adoption. I lied to my mother to protect my sisters when they peed the bed or ate her cookies. I lied to my grandmother about my mother's friends. I lied to protect my mother from the social workers. But these lies were to protect my family, not to hide some secret shame. Entering into the foster care system taught me to lie to protect myself. While dealing with social services, I was told to make a scrap book of my family. Now, I had a picture of my mother and my sisters. I was able to even write some details about that side of the family. However, I did not have any idea of who my birth father was. So, the counselor told me to find a magazine and cut out a picture of a black man and tell people that he was my dad! Sounded simple, so I did it. That little lie taught me that I had something to hide, the fact that I didn't know who my father was. In fact, it taught me I even had something to be ashamed of. It taught me that I could lie about these things and they would go away. Little did I know my reasons to lie and hide from my problems would grow exponentially as I navigated through the foster system and with adoption.

When looking for a permanent home, being black did not seem to work well for me. It was easier to be mulatto or even of American Indian decent than it was to be black. I still could not seem to find a family that wanted to keep me. Rejection became something that I could not keep dealing with…another reason to lie. It is oftentimes easier to create a false reality than to realize you are unwanted. As I moved from home to home, waiting to be adopted, I had to tell myself something. I had to make up a reason as to why I was moving on to another home, why my mother or my mother's family was not coming for me, why I was unwanted. While I did not know the truth, I had to make up a reason. So I would make up reasons, I would lie to myself and others. Sometimes I would say that the mom didn't want me at the last home or that they were getting too attached to me, imagining that my birth mom was coming back for me. I would even tell myself that I really wanted to leave and didn't like it there anyway. Anything to excuse the fact that the families didn't want me. I had already begun to lie to myself to ignore my real life. I was already creating my fantasy world.

After I was finally adopted, I found myself in a position where I had a family, my fantasy had come true and someone really wanted me. I didn't have to feel rejection and have to lie to myself anymore. For the first time in my life, I had an opportunity to be "normal." However, normal seemed to come with a price. During the honeymoon phase of my adoption, things were already starting to go awry. Things didn't feel right and seemingly worsened day by day. Tom had already been peeing in the bathroom with me. While that seems innocuous, it did not feel right. Additionally, his temper was already getting the best of him. While the discipline had not reached the level of abuse yet, it was still scary. There was no reason to lie, because no one ever questioned my well-being. I was desperate to have a home, a family, and didn't want to be rejected again.

Lying as Defense - Covering For Your Parents

Soon after the adoption, my world was turned completely upside down. The violence and inappropriate contact began to escalate rapidly and I was completely stunned. I did not know what to do. The man I thought wanted me to be his son was causing me so much pain and fear that I was paralyzed. Each day brought more pain and new humiliation. I did not possess the mental faculties to understand what was happening to me, or why it was happening. However, I realized it was wrong and no one was going to help me. Things were getting worse and I had no way of saving myself. I could not believe these things were happening, and I did not want to believe they were happening. After a while, I had to pretend they were not happening, that I was not being victimized and sodomized by someone who said they loved me.

By lying to myself about what I was going through, I was unwittingly creating an environment that allowed my abuse to continue unabated. Too often, children create a world in which they are not the victim, where their life is normal or where they have control. Some children may even be honor students or superior athletes, in an effort to convince themselves that they are normal and show everyone they have a great family life. This is often done without parental prompting. A child doesn't have to be forced to lie, because it is part of human nature. All children just want to be loved and have a normal happy life, even in the midst of hell. I was so desperate for a normal life that I would lie just to appear like everything was okay.

Tom never prompted me to lie about what was happening. He may have told me what to say to cover up bruises or marks, but if he did, I don't remember specifics. He never told me how or what to say to cover up the sexual abuse. I would go out of my way to hide what was happening to me. I would volunteer excuses just to avoid dealing with the truth. He just abused me and knew that I would never let anyone know. And I always covered for him.

Tom always wanted me to go to band practice with him. Often, when he was done with practice, he would find a reason to be mad at me. I didn't finish my homework, or I wasn't paying attention and learning how to read notes, it was always something. So he would begin beating me on the ride home. I would always try to sit in the back seat, out of his reach, but he would make me sit in the front passenger seat and then the beating would begin. He would punch me while he would drive. The abuse would ramp up until I could not take it anymore, until my face was bloody, or my chest hurt to breath. Then the real pain would start as he took the long way home.

It was always me that explained why Tom and I got home so late after band practice or boy scouts. I would tell Millie that Tom found me stealing or trying to run away to explain my beaten appearance. Or, that Tom had to pull over because I started acting out in the car, to explain why we were so late. I would have to be the one to make up a story to tell Millie, if Tom was in my room late at night or my sister complained about noise from my room. Living in fear, in pain, and in suffering became my life. I had to find a way to cope with the nonstop shock and pain, and still find a way to hide what I was going through. Making it seem like I was a thief or a belligerent child that would jump out of a moving van became a viable option in order to hide that I was being forced to perform degrading sexual acts for what felt like hours at a time. I always lied. I always took the blame. And, everyone always believed me. I even began to believe the lies I created. Anything was better than dealing with my reality.

Myself

Of course the greatest lie I told was to me. In order to survive my ordeal, my life, I had to create my own little alternate reality. I had to lie to myself that the physical abuse was just discipline. I had to imagine that the sexual abuse just didn't happen. My pre-pubescent mind could not even wrap itself around what was happening to me. I wanted to be normal. I wanted to be loved. But, the cost was so high! I went to school, I played outside, and I even went to church, pretending that none of the abuse occurred. I weaved a complex tapestry of lies to stave off the insanity.

I convinced myself that the beatings I received from Tom were my fault, all of it. Tom had high blood pressure. Every time he lost his temper, he would blame it on his high blood pressure. Millie would tell us to stop making father so angry because he could not control himself. In hindsight, high blood pressure was more akin to being the incredible hulk. I would tell myself that the sexual abuse was still better than having no one. That I was really just bringing it on myself by my actions and that I deserved it. That I had done something to make him think I needed that kind of discipline.

I would also lie to myself about my sexual experiences (like most men). When someone would ask when I lost my virginity, I would tell them it was when I was 10 years old to a girl named Cynthia. That was my reasoning for being so sexual at such a young age. After a time, that lie also became a part of my reality. But that was not true either. I had to lie about that, otherwise I would have had to acknowledge that Tom made me have an orgasm at around that age. That he took one of the most special things a man can experience, my first, from me. Even now as I write this I am embarrassed and ashamed. So, I found a way to hide that shame and make myself out to be a lady's man from an early age.

In reality there was no way to resolve the acts I was forced to commit or the physical reaction Tom was able to elicit with my own masculinity. Even now, it is easier to go back to the false world I created, rather than admit to the gory details of the abuse I was forced to endure. Deep down inside, it was my shame that kept me lying to myself. In order to survive my childhood, I had to find a way to reduce the shame I felt. Unfortunately, no amount of lying or fantasy can fully get rid of my shame.

Truth from Fiction

Creating a false reality became second nature to me. When you repeat lies over and over, when you continue to cover and make excuses for your abuse, you start to lose track of what actually happened. In order to make a lie believable, I had to believe it, too. There is no point in telling a story you don't believe. It convinces no one. For me, successfully lying about child abuse was partly a cover up, part denial and part fantasy. I wasn't just lying to others, I was lying to myself.

The more I believed those lies, the more my reality changed into something I could deal with, and how I envisioned what my life should be like. Over time, my lies became my reality and the truth was hidden. My life became a lie, a lie that I wanted to believe. In my world I was not the victim, I just messed up a lot. Once I could convince myself that the abuse never happened, I was eventually able to repress all memories of that abuse. Oh, I would still have to deal with the effects of my abuse, the unnatural desires and reactions that derived from that mistreatment. I just could not remember why I had those aberrant thoughts. Years and years of telling, altering, and denying the facts of my childhood made it difficult to actually recall the truth. Now I was living those lies and my fantasy world had supplanted my reality. No matter how farfetched my fantasy world was.

For instance, I had created a false reality where I fought Tom, where I finally stood up to him in the midst of his violation and made him permanently stop and forego his evil ways. In my memories, I had physically resisted him and made him see that church and God were the ways of repentance. For most of my adult life I walked around with this completely false memory that I had implanted. I wish I could say that it was true, but when I look deep within, I know it didn't really happen that way. There was no final stand, do or die moment, only cowardice and fear. I never wrestled control or earned my freedom, he just slowly stopped. I never put the fear of God into his heart, the assaults just slowly receded. His nighttime visits to my room just became less and less frequent.

The only thing I really did to resist was to get older. The bigger I got, the more difficult I was to manhandle and hurt. This is not to say that I ever punched Tom, I could not bring myself to ever do that because I loved him and he was all I had. I was able to withstand his punches, I was able to duck and dodge until he tired, because I was tall and wiry and getting older and he couldn't do much damage anymore. Heck, now that I am writing this, maybe I just grew up! Since he was a pedophile and I was no longer a nine-year old boy, maybe his drive was no longer there for me.

Because I never dealt with the fact that I couldn't even save myself, I did nothing to ensure that he wasn't abusing anyone else. It is a dreadful thought that he may never have been healed, that he may never have seen the light. He had access to a multitude of little boys through boy scouts, teaching, and the church. Even his grandkids were spending the night on most weekends. It is painful for me to realize that he may have never found God, but instead found other victims.

Only in writing this book am I able to truly remember how the abuse stopped. Because of the false reality I created, I couldn't acknowledge that I didn't play a part in stopping my abuse. My false reality at least provided me with some redemption. Until recently, I was able to lay claim that I had stopped Tom from his evil ways, and that I had stood up in a final stand and brought him to Jesus. The truth is that the false reality I created may have helped him victimize other little boys once he was done with me.

Hard to Believe

This is the damning reality of my abuse. Surviving was difficult and nearly impossible at times. In order to make it through to the next day I HAD to create a separate reality. Otherwise, I would have had to carry the abuse, neglect and emotional damage with me every day. Each new day would have just added to the pile of misery. While this escapism allowed me to go on, it created additional problems over time. Pretending you are not living in hell can work too well over time. I learned to lie so well that no one would ever suspect what I was going through. No one questioned my safety or my wellbeing. I appeared to be a normal boy.

This public image really becomes a problem if you ever divulge your secret. Because things appeared normal, I seemed to have a loving family, all smiles for the family photos. So why would anyone ever think I was being victimized. Not that society wants to believe things like that happen anyway. The few times I tried to tell, no one ever believed me. Those that knew my family could never believe Tom was a pedophile and would never believe I was a victim. I know there are people familiar with the Wilson's that will question my veracity about the abuse I suffered even after reading this book. Some of my family members may deny any of the abuse, even when they saw plenty of signs No one wants to admit that someone they know or are related to could be capable of these acts.

I remember when Rosanne Barr told the public that her dad sexually abused her. Her parents immediately took to the air waves to tell everyone that she was lying. The country didn't know what to think. Even when Casey Anthony took to the stand to explain the molestation by her father, no one wanted to believe her. In fact, it was somehow more palatable for people to think that Casey was responsible for murdering her child than it was to believe that she was molested by her father.

Until they came out, these women appeared to live normal lives and even maintain relationships with their abusers. I mean, when it's your parents, what else can you do? They did such a good job of creating a false world with no outward signs of abuse that their fantasy world became the reality that everyone else saw. When the family looks normal and the child is not a total outcast or mental case, people find it hard to believe abuse occurred. So when someone finally is brave enough to step forward, no one wants to believe them.

No one wants to believe that adults can hurt children in that way, even when we see the reports on television. People definitely do not want to believe that family members can abuse and molest their own children. The fear is that if someone who looks so normal has such hidden demons, then anyone can beat and abuse their children. ANYONE can be a pedophile.

Now I am not saying that it is impossible for someone to lie about being abused. I will forestall the easy question of, "Why in the hell would someone want people to know that they were raped by a loved one?" I am sure false accusations abound. But when a person bares their soul and faces public humiliation of being a victim, they should at least be given the benefit of the doubt. When facts are provided that demonstrate multiple violations in detail, then maybe we should listen. When someone has nothing to gain but everything to lose in their quest to help others who are suffering, then maybe we should take them seriously.

Distortion

Continuing this childhood fantasy world made it difficult to deal with my problems as I grew older. If you learn that the most effective way to deal with the bad in your life is to deny it, then you don't stop. Even more, if you are taught to not only be a liar, but a detailed liar, then it becomes habit forming. It becomes a way of life and a means to make yourself appear better in the eyes of other people and in your own eyes.

By the time I was 18 years of age, I was a full-fledged habitual liar. I realized that in my reality I could be anything I wanted to be. Not only could I be normal, I could be better than normal. I didn't have to be the abused kid in my mind or in the eyes of those around me. As I entered into the Army, I painted a picture of the popular kid and the consummate athlete. The ladies' man. I was a straight "A" student in my world! I created an image that was the polar opposite of who I was as a child. I created a new me, a strong me, a boy that was never a victim and never had any problems in life. In my fantasy world I didn't join the Army out of necessity; I joined because I wanted to. Instead of telling the truth of my failures, I just continued to lie. I would just make up some grandiose story of my success, while ignoring my shortcomings. It worked, so as a child it became a solution to all problems I faced.

I don't think I was fooling anyone but myself. My self-confidence was still low, I was still an undersized man, and I was so confused about who I was that I was petrified around women of any color. It was obvious to those around me that for all my bragging, I was still weak and fearful. The reality I created was at such odds with the person I actually was. It was to the point where my stories became unbelievable. Instead of owning up to the lies, I just ignored the fact that I was merely making a fool of myself and kept right on talking. Deep inside, I had no use for the truth anyway. Better to be thought of as a liar than to be known as a weak victim.

Surviving and Thriving

It is clear that lying was a means of survival for me, my ultimate defense mechanism. It was the only way for me to keep living. So, it would be hypocritical for me to tell a child who has suffered abuse to stop lying, to deal with the reality of their situation. Little minds are not built to deal with that heavy burden. In my opinion, sometimes it is better for little ones to pretend it never happened, to pretend they had a normal childhood, or minimize the ordeal. There is no right or best way to deal with childhood sexual abuse. As a child, it was like a war for me, where survival meant victory.

If you believe someone loves you, yet they sexually and physically abuse you, you must therefore create a world where abuse and sexual deviancy is, in fact, normal and acceptable. By doing this, you can go on believing that you have a somewhat normal childhood and you are loved. This false reality also allows you to coexist with your abuser once the abuse has halted.

This reality doesn't automatically right itself once you enter into adulthood. Once you become a father and your twisted reality has never been challenged or dispelled, just how do you treat your children? If you believe your abuser loved you, then what would be an appropriate level of discipline for your children? What boundaries would you have in place for appropriate contact? If you never figured out what you received from your abuser was not love, then how would you know how to love your kids? That little world you created for survival could have a devastating impact on many innocent lives.

Instead of dealing with the pain or learning from failure, the victim just hides it away or denies that he or she was a part of that negative reality. Indulging further into this fantasy world can cause the victim to create a false sense of morals and mores, where the abuse he or she suffered was not abnormal, but was instead their version of natural law. Abuse and lust supplant discipline and love, deceiving the victim's ability to discern right and wrong, good and bad.

The Truth

How easily does that childhood defense mechanism become a detriment to the very life of the victim? The world that was once created in order to survive horrific treatment has now crippled that person. Years and years of lying now only serve to confuse the truth. Memories become lost or muddled to the point there is no way to determine fantasy from reality. Definitions of concepts such as discipline and love become so skewed as to render that former victim incapable of behaving properly by society's standards. Without a firm grasp on reality, the victim of abuse has no foundation upon which to build a natural and meaningful existence. As such, the pattern of lies that was born out of survival is now constantly woven to blanket any negative or unpleasant reality.

If you are a victim of abuse, if you can do anything, please recognize the truth! What you went through or what you are going through is not normal. It is not something that is acceptable, even if your abuser gets away with it. It would be hypocritical for me to tell you that your shame is irrational, but it is unwarranted. There is nothing that can be done to undo the pain and suffering we had to deal with. But, you must continue to deal with it. Not the gruesome details, but at least dealing with and acknowledging the fact that you were wronged.

The lies each victim must tell as a child are also understandable. For life to continue with some normalcy, I understand the need for secrecy. While it doesn't solve anything, keeping your suffering a secret is also a normal reaction. Many people still have to look at their abuser every day, knowing that any indication or accusation of abuse will cause a civil war within your family. So, you may feel there is no sense in going public with what you have been through. Know that abusers thrive on secrecy; this is what allows them to continue their deviancy, victim after victim,   one hidden act at a time.

Try not to lie to yourself. Recognize a lie for what it is - a denial of the truth. If you can avoid the habit of lying as an adult, then you can disassemble that fantasy world you created as a child. This may even allow you to realize that you were treated badly, that normal loved ones do not treat their children with such distain or lust. Understanding that you were mistreated will help prevent you from repeating that abuse and visiting it upon your children.

Once you come to terms with your mistreatment and the abuse you suffered, you can understand that you are no longer a victim. This means you can deal with life's difficulties and failures as they come, instead of falsifying the truth and hiding away in that fantasy world where you are the hero, and nothing bad ever happens to the hero. When you learn to deal with the bad things in life, you will be able to accept who you are and what you need to do to achieve your goals. Face reality instead of making up excuses for failing to achieve your goals or lying to everyone around you by claiming success where you have yet to even try. Look at what you are trying to do and figure out what you need to do to get there. It may be harder to face reality, but it is the only chance you will have of truly finding happiness and accomplishment. Otherwise, that fantasy world will be more than a hiding place from all of life's tragedies. It will also be a tomb for all of your unfulfilled dreams and accomplishments.

You can even take it one step further and be truthful to others about your trials and abuse. Maybe you can start with a counselor. Or, you can even use a more public forum. If you can ever come forward with your story, it will help others realize they are not an anomaly, they are not alone. If more Americans see how common this abuse is, maybe they will be more willing to acknowledge it and teach children to have standards of how they should be treated and what love really means.

At the very least, tell your spouse so he or she can be aware of triggers and possible problems. I don't get frustrated when my wife tells my daughters not to sit on my lap with their legs open. I don't take it personally, I told her about my past. I hope she trusts me, but always puts my daughters' safety before our relationship. It is difficult to tell someone you love that you were in such a weakened state or that you were not normal; but they deserve to know. At least they can be prepared and choose for themselves whether or not they'll be willing to deal with you.

Ultimately, survival is not enough. You have to find a way to be more, to be successful, and to thrive. My value in myself was so low that I feared being let down even further, even if that meant never trying and just living in my world of what could have been. If I had allowed myself to continue lying to myself and others, I would not be here today, accomplishing and daring to be happy and successful. That missed opportunity would have been more tragic and unjust than all of the combined abuse I ever received at the hands of Tom Wilson and everyone else that has done me harm.

Being truthful to yourself about your past may be the best gift you will ever receive. When you really reflect on your suffering, you will see the same thing I see. While I default to shame for what I was put through, I can't help but feel some modicum of pride at the simple fact that I made it. Somehow, someway, I survived. I can look back on the truth and realize that I no longer have a reason to hide. There should be nothing to be ashamed of. As a child, I managed to endure things that would break most adults. My past shows my strength, not my weakness. I was not broken under the weight of the violations and humiliations; I survived. That much was proven on the day I stopped lying about my past and started revealing my future.

PART III

15. Social Services

I know I may seem somewhat jaded by my experiences with state social services and the counselors and social workers that operate within the agency. To some extent this may be true. In fact, for many years I hated those who were tasked with caring for me and insuring my welfare. I hope that after reading this, you will understand where my anger originated. The pain of being left alone, voiceless and hopeless by an organization tasked to protect, care, and even guide me leaves a dark spot in my view of social workers as a whole. I am also well aware that most of this anger is indeed misplaced.

As an adult, I now see the fault is systemic and lies within the design of the state child welfare system, not the individual workers. This is a top down problem that state governments cause by a lack of funding and a disingenuous approach to caring for the unwanted and troubled children in our communities. Of course, I realize that there are plenty of employees in these government agencies that suffer burnout by being overworked and underpaid. Others may default to apathy for their charges after years of seeing little success and witnessing their work going unrewarded, or seeing children die all too soon. A few simply might not be cut out for that line of work.

However, most of these social workers are talented and caring. Their views of children are so genuine and positive that they find good in every child they come across, no matter how misguided and socially ignorant that child may be. (This is why a prosecutor always avoids placing a social worker on a jury, knowing that they will find some redeeming qualities in ANY defendant, no matter how heinous the crime.)

Workers in social services usually never get to hear the successes of children within the system. Children that cannot find a place in our society are often found on the front page of the newspaper or dead on the street somewhere. A social worker's success stories are oftentimes too few and seldom revealed. This has got to break a person's resolve, causing them to question why they even continue the fight.

I know the job is tough and the hours are long for those counselors who are employed to deal with children in the foster care system. However, these children are dependent upon them. Their caseworker is often the only constant in their lives. They are the only one who truly cares enough to find out their needs and desires. They are their only voice. If their caseworker does not speak up for their interest, then who will?

In my heart I believe my caseworker tried to do her best for me. I know it was hard to find a place for a little black boy in the Midwest during the early 1970's. I know that each time I was sent away from a home, it was her job to try and find me another home. I also know in the end she gave up. As soon as she found a family that was interested in adopting me, it was a wrap. She finally found a place for me, a family that wanted to adopt a foster child, and they were going to make it work. In the end, I was left on my own and alone.

Senseless Death

In September 2008, a seven-year-old girl was discovered by a neighbor stumbling down the street in Lusby, Maryland. She was half-naked, beaten and bloodied, barely able to keep herself upright. She told the neighbors she jumped out of a second story window to escape the abuse of her mother. Within hours, police discovered the bodies of two other children - Jasmine and Minnet Bowman - in the freezer of the house the little girl barely escaped from.

This was the house of Renee Bowman, a single mother of three children who had moved numerous times to end up in this small town. As the facts of this case were brought to light, the tragedy unfolded further. She murdered the two children found in her freezer. The two bodies were severely malnourished and suffered from blunt trauma and asphyxiation. She smothered them both.

Ms. Bowman stood trial for murdering two of her own children and severely beating the surviving child. Evidence was produced that described the lives of these children prior to their gruesome discovery. The surviving child testified that all three children were locked in a room, day in and day out. They were forced to use a bucket for a bathroom. They were beaten with multiple objects, including a wooden shoe and a baseball bat daily. They were choked and battered for even the slightest mistake. Ms. Bowman even told the little survivor that the other two children left because they "thought she was stupid and did not want to see her again." Now alone, the little girl was forced to face the full brunt of Ms. Bowman's wrath.

It was later discovered she had killed the other children more than two years earlier and had even moved with the bodies in her freezer. She showed little remorse for her actions and was eventually convicted of two counts of premeditated murder, as well as counts of child abuse. The main evidence against her was the seven-year-old girl she had not yet killed.

This case in itself was a tragedy and a great shock for the entire state of Maryland and the region. The facts of this case were further exacerbated by the fact that Ms. Bowman was not even the biological parent of these three children. She had been allowed to adopt all three, at separate times! She was paid over $150,000 to care for these children, collecting checks even after their demise. She was even in the process of trying to adopt a little boy to "complete the family!"

These poor little girls died alone, in pain, and voiceless. They were placed in an inferior home with no stability, no food, and no love. They were wards of the District of Columbia and residents of our great state of Maryland. No one came for them. No one cared for them. Three different times Ms. Bowman was able to qualify as an adopted parent, without a proper home or job. Her only source of income came from adopting these children and no one seemed to notice a problem. Social Services and our society failed these children and these children paid the ultimate price for that failure.

No Voice

This story was so painful to hear. Not only was I devastated at the loss of several young lives, I was frustrated to learn of the total lack of oversight, just throwing these unwanted children to anyone who would say 'yes.' It is utterly reprehensible that our children can still suffer such abuse under the care and watchful eye of our state system. These children were just shipped off like domestic livestock or household pets. Once placed, they had no voice and no one to listen to them.

I could not help but be reminded of the way I was treated while in the foster care system; the way I was shipped around, no notice and no idea of what was in store for me. While I do not remember all of the homes I was placed in or the names of the families I lived with, I do recall one common theme. I was never asked to give any input on what was going to happen to me. I wasn't even asked if I was happy or if I felt safe. I was never allowed to communicate that I was being treated unfairly or if I felt loved. My feelings, needs, and desires were discounted or ignored. I never had a choice on staying or going. When it was my time to go, I would just find my bags packed with little or no forewarning. I wasn't even allowed a say in where I was to go next. Whatever family I was sent to was the family I was with…period. All the while I was made to feel as though I should just be grateful to have any home, to have anyone take me in. After a time, I was grateful.

The only time I ever had any input into my future was my final adoption with the Wilson's. But let's put this into proper perspective. By that point I had been through several homes with families that didn't seem to want me. Of course I wanted to be adopted; of course I wanted a family. As I revealed earlier, the abuse and uncomfortable sexual contact had already started. I knew this wasn't the best place for me…but I was made to feel like it was the only place for me. This was as good as it was going to get and it was what I deserved. I knew that whatever happened to me from this point forward was unknown. I knew what it was like to bounce around and not feel wanted, so I would take the unknown any day over that unwanted feeling. I was convinced that some family was better than none at all.

I was in a courtroom when I was asked to confirm if I wanted to be adopted. While I am now quite comfortable in a court of law as an experienced litigator, to a young child this was a scary place to be. While standing right next to the entire Wilson family, what was I going to say even if I didn't want to be adopted? I was placed into a situation where I had no options and no voice.

I was never made aware that I had a choice, or if I said "no," that another home would have been provided. I was not taken into a separate room and asked in private what I thought of the Wilson home. I wasn't told that I didn't have to fear their anger and reprisal if I didn't want to be part of that family. I was never made to feel safe enough to say "no," or valuable enough to protect. At no time during the entire pre-adoption period was I ever asked if I felt safe or loved with the Wilson's.

And then it was over. The adoption was final and I was officially a

Wilson. Social services was no longer liable for anything else that would happen to me. I was just dropped into this situation with no other options and now I had no outlet to call upon. They had washed their hands of me and left me to my fate. I was with the Wilson's less than a year before I was adopted and dismissed. There were no post-adoption monitoring or updates. No spontaneous visits or telephone calls to ensure that I was okay. The honeymoon phase was over and all false pretenses were dropped. Tom no longer had anyone to answer to; I had no contact with my birth family, no contact with any of my foster families, and no contact with social services. Then, the real hell began and there was no one I could turn to.

No Value

I have three daughters. Like most parents, I have tried to teach my daughters from a young age, what is and is not acceptable. My daughters know they should not take candy or food from strangers. They know they should never talk to strange people or get into a car with anyone they don't know. They also know "good touch, bad touch." They know their bodies are special and only mommy and daddy and sometimes a doctor should ever touch or see under their clothing. They know this means aunts, uncles, neighbors, and other family friends are not to touch them in any of their private areas. They know they should speak up immediately if they feel uncomfortable around a person, or if they are asked to do something that doesn't feel right. They know they will never get into trouble for telling on anyone and that someone will always listen to them.

I was never taught these lessons prior to being placed in various homes, and many of the foster youth I have come into contact with were never provided with this valuable knowledge. Why are these same lessons not taught to our foster youth and the wards of our states? After all, these are our children too. These are children of the individual states and this country. Why are these children not armed with this knowledge? Like me, many foster children came out of environments that were less than wholesome and have witnessed and experienced inappropriate behavior from adults in their lives. This is why many of these children are in the system to begin with. Many of these children don't even know what true parental love is and will settle for any affection they can get. Like me, they never learned how a child should be loved.

To a child who has been ripped from their family and siblings, then bounced around from home to home, there are sure to be some social and emotional issues. I have spoken with many former foster youth who share similar horror stories of placement and foster care. After being constantly rejected and moved from family to family, it is easy to lose faith in everything: the system, the families, and more importantly, yourself. If your birth family has rejected you and no one really wants to keep you or love you, how can you be expected to have any love for yourself or even know what love is? You just want someone to fill that void in your life, to find some value in you.

During my time in the foster system, I was never once told what was considered inappropriate or what I should settle for. No one ever told me to be on the lookout for someone who can get mad very easily. I was never told to pay attention to how people talked to me or treated me when I did something wrong. If I had known that people shouldn't violently react to a child's simple mistakes, maybe I would have been more hesitant on being adopted. I was never made aware that my body was private. I was never told no one should watch me get undressed or watch me take a bath at eight years of age. No one communicated with me that a grown man should not want to pee with me and that I should always pee in private. I was never told that no one should put anything up my butt unless a doctor said so. If I had known these things were wrong, maybe I would have never agreed to be adopted.

No one ever told me that I didn't have to go with the Wilson's. That I was special and someone else would be grateful to have such a wonderful and inquisitive little boy. Instead, I was told that I was lucky to be adopted at such a late age. How could I not have accepted a place in the Wilson household? I was never given another choice.

I was never asked about my experiences prior to being in foster care or if I was touched or made to do things I felt were uncomfortable or wrong. There was never any question of what I knew about my body or other people's bodies, or if I had ever seen a naked adult and if so, why? These questions may have alerted social services to my skewed view on love and what is acceptable. Someone may have been made aware of the psychological issues I developed. If they had asked, they definitely would have quickly learned that I didn't know how to be loved.

Social Services Role in my life - Removal

The story of my suffering is mirrored by countless children I have met who suffer daily at the hands of "loved ones" and "caregivers." I have no doubt that our government needs to remove children from the abuse and their abusers. Children who are in need of assistance should be removed from unhealthy homes with good reason. It must be difficult for case workers to gauge when a child should be taken from their parents. There may be obvious reasons for removing a child, such as sexual abuse and malicious physical abuse. There are also other less obvious reasons for removal, such as mental anguish and neglect. It can be a tough call for a social worker to remove a child from their birth parents.

I have no reason to doubt the good intentions for removing me from my home. To see children living in a state of squalor and filth may not be enough to take a child away, but when those same children are repeatedly left to fend for themselves and made to go without proper nourishment, then the choice is clear. I know social services visited my birth mother's house repeatedly. There were even a few visits when they were prevented from entering because I would not open the door. When they were allowed in, they would see that my sisters and I were malnourished and barely clothed. My mother's physical condition was not much better, due to her poor diet and drug habits. I was placed in several foster homes before being permanently removed. Maybe they were trying to give my mother time to get herself together. She just kept choosing drugs and alcohol over her children. To be honest, I'm not sure why they waited so long to take us away.

Repatriation

Courts consider re-establishing the family unit is in the best interest of the child. The goal of most caseworkers is to keep the family together, through parenting classes, financial assistance, and time to establish a healthy lifestyle. Repatriation of children into families they have been removed from is a good suggestion, but should be done with extensive evaluation and care and never be the hard and fast rule. I know this makes social services' role in protecting the child even more complicated and convoluted, but some people may never be ready to be parents. Temporary removal may be successful by giving parents time to get it together, but it can also make the foster care process much more difficult for the child.

Because I had previously been temporarily removed from my mother's care, I really had no idea that this removal was going to be permanent. I have a feeling that my mother didn't know either. There was a false sense of hope that things were going to get back to normal. It took a few years for me to realize that my mom really wasn't going to come back for me. As a result, the disappointment and let down was even more painful after so many years of hope. It would have been better to know ahead of time that this would be it; that there was no chance of going back home. At least I wouldn't have had to live with the misguided feeling that she wanted me back, or that I already had a mom.

In my case, the temporary removal process just prolonged the inevitable. No amount of parenting classes could teach my drug addicted mother how to provide a stable home for her children. All of us were removed multiple times while they gave her repeated chances to do right.

All those chances just dragged the process out. After years of trying and waiting, I guess someone figured out that she wasn't capable of being a good parent to us. For me, this delay greatly reduced my potential for adoption because I got older. By the time everyone realized my mother was not going to get it right, I was no longer that cute little chubby infant. I was walking; I was into things; I had no discipline; and I was attached to my family. While infant children are in demand to be adopted, few people want a child who is old enough to be attached to their birth parents.

Even children born addicted to drugs and alcohol are targets for reintegration into their birth family. Even though the courts may find a mother to be incapable of being an adequate mother, she is oftentimes allowed to remain in contact with her children. I can appreciate the concept of giving people time to get their lives together. However, when you create a life, you have run out of time to get your life together. You should not put a child's welfare at risk while you get yours together. I realize addictions are hard to kick and children are not always planned. If you birth a child who's an addict, you should automatically forfeit your right as a parent to that child. There is no way you can un-ring that bell because the damage has already been done. This may sound harsh, but consider my point of view.

I remember the movie "Losing Isaiah." The thought that a crack addicted mother could throw a crack addicted child into a trash can and still lay claim to that child seemed absurd at the time. Although the mother was able to get clean, find a minimum wage job, and get an apartment, doesn't mean she was able to undo what she had done. The fact that she attempted to regain custody of her child that was now in a loving and healthy environment was appalling. The fact that the race of the child versus the loving parents was even an issue was offensive. The story reeked of one thing...selfishness. Giving preference to a neglectful parent is bad policy.

Which is more important: the needs of a child or the wants of a parent? Which carries more weight: blood relations or good parenting? In cases where a child was removed from danger or neglect and placed in a better environment, serious contemplation should be taken before allowing the negligent parent any contact with that child. Even if that child wants to go back to the birth parent, strong consideration should be placed on more than just the blood relationship shared. If the child is placed in a safe and loving home, how can it be in the best interest of the child to remove him from that home just to place them back with their birth parents? While blood is thicker than water, deeds should always supersede blood! Those that care for children of others selflessly perform the greatest deed.

Some mistakes that a parent makes are just too heinous to recover. Even if they learn from their mistakes, it doesn't mean they will have a stronger claim to their child. My sisters and I had gone through many negative experiences while with our mother. There was nothing our mother could have done to redeem herself. I understand that a parent wants to be around their children, but that should not overrule the best interest of that child. Even if the birth parent lives in regret, it still may be better for the child to remain in the stable environment in which he or she was placed. It should not be a foregone conclusion that the best parent is the one that shares that child's bloodline.

Relatives

So, if the birth parents are not the best place for a child to go, what is the next best thing? Many people believe that blood relatives, grandparents or uncles and aunts are a better option than foster care. I feel that this is good for many reasons. It leaves the child with someone they know and trust. They are not totally removed from their environment. The child also has some contact with their birth family, instead of losing everyone they are related to. While there is merit to this idea, the standards should remain in place. The family member's home should be able to pass the same inspection a regular foster family would have to go through. They should also have to pass a mental and physical examination to ensure they are fit to be foster parents. They should have the same random inspections and visits as any other foster parent even if they already have children of their own.

As a little boy, I know this is what I would have chosen if given the option. I loved my grandmother; she had a house and lots of land. I had plenty of uncles and aunts, some close to my age. While I was the only little black kid, they still showed me affection, I was still family. But, I realize that leaving me with my relatives may not have been that much better than leaving me with my mom. They were all pretty impoverished and probably wouldn't have been able to afford to care for me and my sisters. There was also a strong likelihood that if we were placed with a close relative, my mother would have contact with us. Since social services had given my mother several chances, I am sure they decided it was best that we all be given a new start...and a new family.

Home Selection

When it does become necessary for a child to be permanently removed from the birth family, where does the child go? The obvious answer is a foster home. However, vetting a foster home is replete with its own special set of problems. It is common knowledge that people get paid for caring for a foster child. The money provided is not supposed to be a means of income for the foster parent, but many families are using foster children for just that.

Believe it or not, some families do it solely for the money. I know many foster children who are kicked out of the home the moment the checks stop coming in. Because there is ample payment to house foster children or even adopt them, more care should be placed in ensuring the home is the best place for a child to prosper and feel valued, even if it is only temporary. Any money paid out to the family should be utilized for the child's well-being. If a family depends upon that foster care stipend to pay their rent or mortgage, the child doesn't need to be there. If the family is already on government assistance, why would it be reasonable to place a child in that home?

I have visited multiple foster homes that were filthy and overcrowded, housing many foster children. I have visited homes where the foster children were locked out of the home if no adult was present. I've seen foster homes in such a state of disrepair that the house was deemed uninhabitable. It's a wonder they ever qualified to be foster homes. When someone is aware they are going to be inspected by social services, the house is made clean and tidy. However, like many of the houses I visited, there were obvious signs that the house was not fit to house any children.

Foster parents and potential adoptive parents undergo screening to ensure they are physically and mentally fit. In fact, when Tom went through his screening, it was discovered that he had a tumor on his lung. This was later removed and he credited me for "saving his life." While I believe the physical evaluation is adequate, I have little faith in the psychological evaluation. Not only because of my experiences, but also because I have met too many children and former foster youth who have related horror stories to me of their mistreatment by their foster parents. Unless the parent admits to being a pedophile or has been charged with child abuse or sex crimes, there is no test that can ensure that parent is not going to be a danger to a child brought into that home.

I'm sure that even by current standards, Tom appeared to be more than psychologically qualified to be a foster or adoptive parent. He was into scouting, he was into church, he was a kindergarten teacher, and played in a marching band. I am sure he told the evaluators that he just wanted to rescue a little black boy from the orphanage and fold him into the family unit. What no evaluation could have discovered was that Tom was searching for someone special. He was looking for that little boy that had nowhere else to go and no one else to go to. That little boy whom he could intimidate and brainwash into believing anything. That little boy who could eventually believe physical abuse is love and sexual molestation is acceptable. He was looking for a victim, and where better to find a victim, than in foster care.

As far as I am concerned the mental evaluation is not nearly enough. Until there is a more determinative way to find out a person's inner thoughts, close oversight and accountability will have to do. Random visits and questions may uncover any ruse that the foster parents may use to lull social services into complacency. Social services should make sure that the living conditions are acceptable and the child is receiving the benefit of the stipend. While it is important for children to find a home, it's not enough that a family simply wants to adopt or be a foster family. They must meet standards and continue to meet them after placement. This is the same treatment you would want for your daughter or son, should some tragedy befall you.

Siblings

It may become necessary for children to be removed from their birth family for their protection and safety. It was unimaginably difficult to be ripped from all I knew, my mother, my home, my relatives. Why did they take me from my sisters too? While enduring this trauma, having any family member is better than just being alone. I can still feel the effects of being separated from my sisters.

Only as an adult can I now begin to comprehend why social services didn't place us together. It may have been difficult for them to find a home big enough for all of us. I understand this because Candy was an infant and she had the best chance of being adopted immediately. Heather, Holly, and I were thought to be fetal alcohol babies with special needs. I also now realize that a black child may have made it difficult for us to be placed as a group. My attempts to understand still do not ease my pain and guilt. They could have at least kept us in the same area. They could have updated me as to my sisters' safety. It would have given me some respite if I had known they were safe, even while I suffered through my fate.

Not being with my little sisters was even more painful than not having my mother. I know it's not rational to feel any guilt for the condition of my sisters, but feelings are rarely grounded in logic. I was old enough to remember my sisters and my obligation to them. I was supposed to protect and care for them when mommy was not around. I wasn't able to do that. I didn't even know we weren't going to see each other again. Sometimes, the only way to get rid of that longing and guilt is to bury it. I couldn't bear to think of them, so I tried not to. I worked on putting them out of my mind, forgetting about my family. I had to forget about my birth family in order to just survive whatever family I was placed with. As I grew older, it also became more and more difficult to feel anything as far as family is concerned.

This kind of emotional removal or distancing became habit forming. Once I had to go through tough circumstances at the hands of my adopted father, I began to devalue family and emotional ties altogether. Letting go of "family" allowed me to deal with the disappointment of being rejected, let down, and abused. It also made it harder for me to experience any emotional bond in the future. The ability to experience emotional feelings has been difficult to repair once I allowed it to be destroyed.

I believe my life would not have been as difficult had I been able to remain in contact with my sisters. It is good to have a sense of family as you mature. When you value that intimate connection between loved ones, you have a better chance of establishing mature and lasting relationships. The loneliness and lack of familial contact I felt as a foster child has followed me into adulthood. I have spent countless hours just trying to undo this distance lest I miss out on the greatest reason for living...my family.

16. Abused Children in the Foster System

Children are placed in the foster care and adoption system for a variety of reasons. Many children are put up for adoption due to unwanted pregnancies, poverty, and youth of the parents. Others are removed from homes for neglect or an inability to properly provide for their child or children. Still, others are in the system due to physical abuse, and many children are victims of sexual abuse at the hands of loved ones. These child victims of sexual abuse must be handled differently from other children in the social services system. There should be dedicated social workers trained to handle these special cases. These counselors should have a smaller case load that focuses solely on fulfilling the needs of these damaged and confused children.

Victims of sexual abuse will need a greater amount of services and attention in order to provide them with a chance at becoming successful adults. The problems of rejection and disappointment all foster children must endure are compounded by issues of mistrust and a skewed sense of normalcy. These needs must be addressed before and during the placement process. There needs to be an honest assessment with the child that allows them to be aware of their challenges and things they must deal with. They must learn to protect their mental wellbeing instead of pretending nothing is wrong.

Every child entering the foster care system should be thoroughly evaluated to discern any hidden experiences the child has been through. Once any sexual abuse has been uncovered, there should be immediate and constant psychological intervention as a guide. The child must be made to understand that what happened was not their fault. They must also be allowed to honestly explore their feelings of what they went through to ensure they understand what is acceptable and how a loved one should truly treat them.

Preparing Parents

As difficult as it may be to place children with a history of sexual abuse, it is important to ensure that potential foster parents are made fully aware of the trials the child has endured. Parents willing to care for these special children should be knowledgeable on how to deal with this type of trauma. These parents must be informed that there is a chance that this abuse could resurface as the child matures. They should be on the lookout for behaviors and possible identifiers that would suggest the child is acting out or emulating the sexual abuse they suffered earlier. Foster parents should also be ready to address any negative behaviors the child may demonstrate as soon as they recognize them, and be mindful of the possible issues that can arise if they already have children in their home.

Even before entering foster care, I had witnessed a great deal of sexual activity. I was also made to engage in sexual activity myself. Sometimes it was by myself, other times it included my little sister. My sexuality was awakened entirely too early, before I could even begin to understand what I was doing or why I wanted to do it. This curiosity was only exacerbated by my age. It seemed the older I got, the more I wanted to play around with girls. I didn't know why, I just wanted to. By the time I was with the Apsher's, I was always ready to play doctor or hide and go get it with girls of my own age. While this can be seen as innocent fun, or regular childhood curiosity, it can also be viewed as a sickness when you are the foster child. No parent wants their foster child messing with their daughter.

If the Apsher's would have known I had already been sexually violated as a little boy, they might have seen the signs of my curiosity when I was with them. Even more important, they may have been able to help me realize that it was not proper to play with girls that way and probably would have reinforced it with counseling and prayer. I would have known then that my curiosity was too advanced for my age and that I should have talked about it instead of just playing in the dark with girls. If this would have been brought out earlier I would have known that it wasn't right to play those games. It would have been one less issue to deal with as an adult.

I know it is important not to stigmatize a child or identify that child as a bad egg or as a deviant, but it is equally important to be realistic about the possible problems the foster family may face. If the parents are not aware the child was a victim of sexual abuse, they will not be on the lookout for behaviors that may lead to deviant or even dangerous acting out. If the child's issues are not fully disclosed, the family will not understand that the child's enhanced sexual curiosity should be expected because of what he or she went through prior to placement. This ignorance can also endanger other children in the household, if the child acts out more severely. This is not to say the child will be a rapist, but to be honest, if he does not receive the proper treatment and care, he could be. If we can be honest early on we can put a definite stop to the possibility of a cycle of abuse.

Reality

In the end, children are extraordinarily resilient. Instead of misleading them by inferring that their birth parents are going to come eventually or that they were just being removed for a short time, they should be told the truth as soon as they are old enough to understand. It is also important for a child to know why he or she is being taken away. If these questions are left unanswered, a child will internalize their situation and blame themselves for what happened. Even worse, they may just create their own fantasy world where they can hide from reality.

Children need to be made aware of where they are and why they are there. It's okay to be vague to a small child, but as they grow, they should be told the truth instead of being allowed to make up reasons for their situation. If they don't know who their dad is, let them know their dad is unknown. Don't tell them their parents died in a car crash if they were just drug addicts that couldn't care for them. Don't tell them they're not black or they just came out different than their sisters if their mom cheated on her husband. Just tell them the truth. It's going to come out sooner or later. Later is much more damaging and harder to deal with after years of lying and fantasy.

These children need to be made aware of their life's path. They need to know they are different, but it's okay to be different. They need to know they have a say in what is going to happen to them. They need to know there is someone who is looking out for their best interest and cares about their wants and needs. They need to know their differences make them special and any family would be lucky to have them for their own. They need to be taught that they deserve the best treatment and should not settle for anything less. They need to know they have options and those options need to be vetted and prepared, whether it be back with their birth parents, family members, foster home, or permanent placement.

No child should be a burden or a paycheck in the foster system. Foster parents need to be made aware they are expected to provide for the needs of the child. To ensure this is accomplished, random site visits should be the norm. Children need to be a part of the process, having input on when and where they will go next. Even if they are adopted, there should be some communication and oversight to give the child a voice, for their protection. Allowing them a small voice in their own fate will give them some sense of value and importance in their lives.

If someone would have taught me that I had value and that I should have expectations from my caregivers, things would have been different. If I had known my body is my own and no one should touch me the wrong way, I would not have the scars I now bear. If I was told that foster kids get free college, I would not have been so desperate to be adopted. If someone would have reassured me that I would always have a home, I may not have even said yes to the Wilson's. I most certainly would have had the courage to report my abuse instead of suffering those indignities in silence.

Children that have been abandoned and discarded, lack any sense of self-esteem. Children that have been beaten and abused, molested and assaulted, feel they are worthless. Children who have been moved around from home to home, rejected, and cast aside, are sure their lives are meaningless and no one cares about their future. children in social services are there through no fault of their own. They are not the bottom of the barrel, wastrels who will most likely be a drain on society. They have inner strength that would shame most adults. They have endured things that would break most men. They deserve to be treated better and have someone they can trust. Hopefully that person is their parent or adopted family, or even their social worker. If they are yours to care for until a fit parental figure can be found, please give them value.

Foster Care's Future

President Barack Obama and First lady Michelle Obama brought attention to a troubling problem: Foster Care Group Homes. During their earliest volunteer work covered by the media, they exposed the poor living conditions in a DC group home, which occurs in many throughout our nation. The Obama's painted walls and hung curtains at bare windows, but this was just the surface of many problems found in foster care group homes.

Children living in group homes range in ages from toddlers through high school age. This opens the door for younger children to be exposed to behaviors that are inappropriate for their age. It also puts them at risk of physical, emotional, and sexual abuse. The noise level and lack of proper supervision has also been a problem raised by visitors and some who have been placed in this environment. Another concern raised with group homes is they do not allow children and youth to experience a sense of family. Group homes are staffed with shift workers so there is little chance of developing meaningful relationships with adults. Building trust and a sense of security requires consistency, which is lacking in this situation.

Individual foster care homes may appear to be the best option. But, are foster care parents adequately trained? Is it in the best interest of children to be moved from home to home? Do foster care children separated from their siblings benefit from the experience, or is it just another loss and emotional upheaval which they must overcome? There are foster care parents who simply want to be 'a bridge over troubled waters' for children and youth caught in the jaws of the system. However, there are some who become foster care parents to pay their own bills or fill their pockets. Money motivates them to open their doors to those who truly need a home. The system does not seem to be designed to discriminate between the two. Either case may cause emotional suffering for the child or youth. It is difficult for a child to be snatched from a stable, loving foster care home, and even more traumatic to be placed in an unloving and ill-motivated one.

It may be time to resurrect the orphanage with a new design. Orphanages could be a permanent placement with trained and dedicated people. They could be designed as a family-centered home, similar to a well-run boarding school with at least two educationally qualified live-in adults, a full-time psychologist, nurse, social worker, and state certified teachers on staff. However, the children could attend public school, eliminating the cost of a full teacher staff, but there would be a need for certified teachers for tutorial purposes. There could be set homework time, recreation and activities, life skills training, chores, and family meals everyday (breakfast and dinner). Even though there may need to be some restrictions on food distribution, I believe it is important for children to be allowed to snack at leisure. A place where a fridge and its contents or a pantry was open for children and youth to freely attain food could be set aside. This encourages the sense of belonging, sharing, and making good decisions. Also, computers and other electronics could be provided for educational and fun time purposes.

A family-oriented campus with recreational facilities would greatly benefit foster care children and possibly reduce costs to the state. Children and youth would gain from a supervised facility where healthy relationships are fostered between the permanent staff and children residing in age appropriate settings. In the end, how would you want your child to be housed if tragedy thrust them into the foster care system? It may seem harsh, but allowing these children to face the reality that they will not be adopted, while providing them a permanent and consistent home would help these children to continue their journey into adulthood without the added disappointment of being moved from home to home or neglected by foster parents once the state stops paying for foster care.

17. Closure

While I was still working as a State's Attorney, I remember a special young man who wrote his judge a letter. He was locked up for petty criminal offenses and basically had spent his young adult life in and out of jail. He wrote the judge to explain why he was in his current situation, not asking for leniency or providing an excuse, merely telling the judge how he landed in jail. He disclosed that he had been a victim of sexual abuse during his early teen years. His abuser was a friend of the family that often visited and even stayed at his house from time to time.

He stated that he would avoid coming home whenever he saw the abuser's vehicle parked at his house. This lead to the boy spending nights away from his family, out in the street. Needless to say, with little supervision he began to miss school and get into trouble. By the time he was 16-years-old he was in the juvenile system, committing petty crimes of theft and burglary. He avoided his abuser as well as he could, but could not totally escape his grasp. He did not think his parents would believe him, so he eventually just stopped coming home.

After investigating this inmate's claims, my co-worker decided to help this young man contact his abuser and hopefully bring him to justice. The young man began writing his abuser from jail, "reminiscing' about their sexual activities. The abuser began to take great joy in remembering his victimization of this young soul, regaling the young man with his version of events, and confirming his role. This correspondence went back and forth for months, while the prosecutor's office gathered evidence of the violations this young man was forced to endure.

The office was able to gather enough evidence through those letters to convict the abuser of several counts of sexual assault. This process took quite a few months, allowing the young man to leave prison, find meaningful employment, and even start a family. By the time his abuser was up for trial for his crimes, the young man had a new child and was well on his way to recovery. He even participated in the sentencing, telling the judge of the damage he had incurred because of the vile and heinous acts committed by his abuser, now known as the Defendant. After years of mental anguish, this young man was finally vindicated for his suffering and his abuser was locked away, never to be in a position to abuse a child ever again.

This young man was able to trace much of the pain and destruction in his life to this one man. His disconnection from his parents, his juvenile run-ins with the law, his life on the streets, and his lack of education could all be attributed to the actions of this one man. The young man had lost so much because of the abuse he had suffered. His driving force was bringing this man to justice; making this man pay for the suffering he caused. He finally achieved his goal. His abuser was finally made accountable for his actions, and was brought to justice and punished. This brave boy was able to force himself to relive specific acts of abuse and write them down. He was even able to engage in correspondence with his abuser, just to draw out specific acts of abuse. The actions of this young man placed his abuser in a position where he was forced to plead guilty; having no defense or argument for his actions. This boy almost single-handedly brought his abuser to justice.

Yet, this brave young boy committed suicide a few weeks after his abuser was sent to prison. He never left a suicide note, but he did have a conversation with his sister the night before he took his own life. He told her how empty he felt. He had waited a lifetime to get revenge, to see his abuser publically outed and punished. He had always held onto the notion that punishing the man who abused him would provide some sense of closure. If he could prove that he was victimized, that his mistakes were predicated on the abuse of a trusted family friend, then everything would be better. Unfortunately, that was wishful and naïve thinking. That thinking cost that young man his very own life. He was looking for one thing that punishing his abuser could never provide…closure.

Why Me?

Almost every victim of child abuse that I have spoken with has an overwhelming desire for answers to their life's trials and tribulations. They are consumed by a lack of understanding, causality, the need to know why they were singled out. Even though they are no longer in a position to be a victim, they are still reliving the victimization. Trying to determine "why" they were abused. This all-consuming need to find logic in their suffering can have a catastrophic outcome if it is not tempered with reality. In reality there is no amount of knowledge that can undo what has already occurred, or make any sense of what happened in their lives. Placing so much value in finding an answer may become a driving force in a victim's life, but it will never provide meaning or closure.

Shortly before he died, Tom felt the need to confide in me about his childhood. He told me about his uncle. How he loved his uncle, how fun his uncle was, and how his uncle molested him when he was 12-years-old. He explained that it happened quite a few times over the course of two years. He told me that, as a little boy, he was an outcast and had few friends. He told me how his uncle seemed more like a friend than a relative, and how crushed he was after the first time he was molested. Of course, Tom cried and apologized many times during that conversation. He told me how ashamed he felt and how he wished he could undo everything that had happened.

I wasn't sure why he told me these things, because after I left for the Army, I really stopped caring about "why" and just tried to bury my childhood deep down in my memory. If it were not for Tom's impending death, I would not have even stayed around to listen to his reasoning. It seemed like he was trying to relieve himself of a terrible burden. That by telling me these things he could somehow undo the harm he caused. He wasn't telling me these things for my benefit; he was admitting all of these things to make himself feel better. During his battle with cancer he chose to divulge information that he could have just taken to the grave.

If I was looking to Tom to provide closure, awaiting the day when I could finally confront him and find the answers for the years of suffering, his explanation was most certainly a letdown. In the end, discovering that Tom was molested by his uncle did nothing to help me. Did that undo the pain he caused? Did that make me stop questioning my sexuality or allow me to regain my trust in people? Finding out why he did what he did changed nothing. My time in the Army had made me realize that there was nothing he could have said that would have changed my life or changed what he put me through. Instead of asking him why he did it, I just let it go. I was not going to give him the power to provide that closure. That was something I had to do for myself.

Who Are My Parents?

I have spoken with many foster children who are consumed with finding their birth family. Being around other children with normal families often causes these children who are outside of societal norms to question "why" or "why me?" They look different than their foster parents or foster siblings. They do not share the same last name. Some may be of a different color than their foster parents. Some even have memories of their birth family, the way their mother looked, how their sisters and brothers sounded.

I remember being asked "what's it like to not know your real parents?" or "what's it like to live as a foster child?" It is questions like this that differentiate you in your own eyes and the eyes of your peers. I was surrounded by constant reminders that I was "different." It is no wonder that a foster child develops an overwhelming curiosity as to origins of their birth.

Unfortunately, I have also heard countless stories of children who have been adopted into a beautiful and loving home that still harbor anger and resentment at their situation. Although they have everything a child could want, they are still not satisfied because they are adopted. Others have been placed in a nurturing and giving foster home, safe and well fed, with a guarantee of free college and a bright future. Yet they still yearn to know their real parents and want to know why they were placed into foster care. I am sure these are normal reactions to being different or having a different life.

I have seen these questions lead to great anger, anxiety and misery. I've met countless children who placed such emphasis on what they didn't have, or what they were missing, that they ended up feeling sorry for themselves, even when they had everything life had to offer at their fingertips.

I know most adopted and foster parents rue the day when their child starts questioning them about their past. Often, these parents have no answers, just the love and desire to provide a good home for the child. No matter how nice the parents are, they realize they will never replace the blood relative. They are never going to look like the child or be the child's birth parents. The child can then become easily distracted with questions about their past that remain unanswered. Many become fixated on finding their "REAL" parents.

At some point in their life, a foster teenager may even turn their back on that couple that cared, clothed and nurtured them, all in the search for their "real" family. The child doesn't understand that their real family is the one that cared enough about them to care for, to provide for, to keep safe and give them direction and purpose. The love their foster parent provided goes beyond a blood relation. In the end, the people who raised them with love and care are their parents, no matter who conceived them. Time after time, the angry teen is looking for one thing…CLOSURE.

The Risk

As I grew older, I had formulated a specific view of my mother and her reason for letting me go. In my mind, my mother was young and poor. Since she had no support and little education she felt it was best to let me go into a system that she believed would do a better job of supporting me and caring for me. In my mind, she regretted that decision and would have come to get me if she could have found me. Even when I was suffering most, I could always fall back on the thought that my mother wanted me; that she was looking for me and would come rescue me.

Of course, I eventually realized that my birth mother was not coming. Nevertheless I still romanticized her life and her reasoning. That was wrong as well. I learned that my birth mother never tried to come rescue me and didn't really look for me. In fact, she became pregnant again shortly after we were taken from her! But she didn't stop there. She went on to have 13 other children, in addition to the four of us that were taken from her. She wasted no time moving on without me.

I discovered that for years she lived only a few hours away from me. During all of my abuse and neglect, she was starting new families, getting married and getting high. In the end, all of her children were taken away from her by the state. Many of her children were born with mental and physical ailments stemming from her continued drug abuse. She left behind a long trail of pain and misery. Once I realized just how destructive my mother's life was, I let go of ever tracking down her whereabouts. As indifferent as it sounds, I was actually relieved to hear that her troubled life had probably come to an end. Even when I learned from her sisters that she changed her name and might still be alive, I did not try to find her. I resented the path she had chosen, the damage she had caused, not just to me, but to quite a few of my brothers and sisters. I also knew that had I located her, I would have naturally tried to reach out and save her instead of focusing on building my own future.

The few answers she would have been able to provide would never have been worth the trouble of finding her. There is no reason she could have provided that would have clarified why she allowed us to starve, allowed her friends to molest us, allowed us to be taken away and split apart. There is nothing that she could have done to lessen the pain or mitigate the damage that was thrust upon me. Regardless of what was revealed, I would still have those same scars on my face, the same low self-esteem, and that ever present self-doubt.

But what if the opposite had occurred? What if I had found my mother and she had finally gotten her life together, had a nice house and a good job? What if she was married with a family and her children well fed and taken care of, with all of the love and structure any child would need for a happy and productive childhood? What if her children were all college bound with a great future, while I was bounced around, kicked around, and forgotten, abused, battered and unwanted?

To have seen the great life I could have had if my mother had gotten herself together and kept me would only have exacerbated the pain and injustice I already experienced in my life. To find out I was just a momentary lapse of reason that was forgotten and swept under the rug would have been devastating to my young mind.

I'm not saying that there is no point in searching for your birth parents, but sometimes reaching your ultimate goal of finding out about your past may even interfere or destroy your future. With so many struggles that foster children face, allowing the potential of something so unpredictable to enter their lives may be too much of a gamble. Why set yourself up for failure with the possibility that you will rekindle a relationship with a person who chose to give you up? What are the chances you will find someone who actually wants to find you? What if you find them in a situation that is so nice that you feel hate and envy, or so bad that they will become a burden and heavy weight around your neck? I learned that seeking out answers to my past was not as important as finding my future.

I came to understand that you may be by yourself or you can have people around you that care and support you. While these people are not related to you, they are there for you nonetheless. Sometimes, believing your parents would have loved you if they could has to be enough, instead of finding out that they not only had no value in you, but had no value in themselves. There really is no need to search for someone to fill in those blanks for you. No one can fill in those empty spaces in your heart. These are yours to fill in. I decided not to look for my birth mother to make my life better. It is my life to make better. Do not let these unanswered questions derail your life and prevent you from excelling. Do not let the past delineate your future!

Closure is something I had to find within. I realized I could close the bad chapters in my life at any time. I didn't need to sit around and hope that someone was going to give me some answers that would make my life all better. It was within me all along. I survived, under abusive and painful situations. I survived the neglect. I survived without being around blood relatives. I survived with foster care. I survived alone and humiliated. The closure happened when I decided to end that chapter and move on.

More importantly, I have found that closure is not all it's cracked up to be. To most, closure is just another way of saying, "I found out something I did not know." In the end, it is what it is. I will always have unanswered questions and blank spots in my life. While that seems unfair, that is my life and the cards I was dealt. To focus on the questions that may never be answered is only a distraction. Especially when the answers will do nothing to change my past, or my current situation. If I keep looking backwards, it is very hard to move forward...and very easy to get tripped up.

10,000 Hills

18. Message to Survivors

The more I speak out about my story, the more people ask me what made the difference in my life. How did I manage to make it out of the darkness and achieve something? This is always such a hard question to answer for many reasons. First, I have never thought of my accomplishments as being particularly noteworthy. I am proud of the things I have done, but I have never thought of myself as being successful. I am still trying to climb up that ladder. Second, while I have met a number of nice people, was cared for by a few good families in foster care, and enjoyed many pleasant experiences, I have never been able to identify any one person or thing in my life that "made all of the difference." Finally, I have never wanted to exclude anyone from the possibility of succeeding by suggesting that my way to success was the only way

I know that the life of each child is different, that the troubles and struggles each foster child or abused child faces are unique. I also know that many of us share some things in common. We can learn from our successes, not just replicate our failures. I can recall some of the things that helped me to weather the storm and come out from under the shadow of my childhood trauma. While my life is unique, I know some of the things that helped me through can be used by others as well. I do not believe that any one thing can make all of the difference, but I can share some of the things that I have done to arm myself for what lies ahead.

Using Your Mind

I can't tell you the number of my high school classmates who were amazed to find out that I graduated cum laude from undergraduate school, or the number of friends that attended law school after finding out I was able to make it through. They knew me from my high school days, and were surprised I had successfully followed the path of education. I cannot hold a grudge against them for underestimating me. I had underestimated myself.

My high school grades suffered from my environment, my home life, and because I had long since given up on becoming anything. My guidance counselor told me that there was little opportunity for me in college. Emotionally, I was stunted and given no direction. I was miserable with my hands and had poor marks in shop class, so I was not even going to make headway in a trade school. Like many children I met, I was never made aware of any foster care college opportunities. My only option was the Army. After all, college isn't for everyone.

However, it wasn't that college wasn't for me; it was that I had never learned to apply myself. I know many people sit in a classroom, never study a lick, yet somehow they get good grades. While others, like me, perform miserably even when we try. Not everyone is gifted, but that does not mean they cannot obtain a good education. It is not really a requisite intelligence level that allows you to succeed in higher education; it is your desire to learn. That means, even if you struggle to get average grades, you can still do well in college, once you understand how you learn.

Many of my law school classmates were incredibly gifted. They never had to study a day in their high school or college careers. However, since I was not gifted, I learned what it took for me to comprehend and retain. I had to work very hard, to write down anything I wanted to commit to memory and repeat the ideas in my head. I had to first understand the big picture, what things mattered, and then reduce them to their essential ingredients. Once I understood the policies behind the ideas, the ideas were easy to remember.

Not every child learns the same way. However, if you never learn to apply yourself, then it will be difficult to move forward. It doesn't matter if you were good in school or if you struggled. To put it plainly, even if you do not get great grades, keep on trying.

Patience and a continual focus on the importance of education and learning will move you continually in the right direction. There might be a few more years of college, or even a few years of working before you even get into college. I didn't even start college until I was 24, and it was a community college. I wanted to go to college, and I wanted to learn.

I am not saying that college is the only form of education. There are a number of trades and skills that can be attained by learning and applying yourself. These jobs can lead to self-sufficiency and independence greater than a college education. Individuals who work with their hands and apply themselves to learning their craft can make just as much money as those with professional degrees. But you have to learn to apply yourself by becoming educated.

For me, getting an education was more than a way to find value in myself. It was a way for others to see value in me. This was something I yearned for my entire life, and I noticed that education carried value. For those who start out with little or no value, education can help fill some of that void. Beyond value, I know my education is what has set me free. Not free from my childhood, (that is still a work in progress) but free to determine my own destiny. Free to influence policy and politics. Free to write this book and influence others. It has allowed me to gain rank and stature. It has freed me to be able to understand and articulate ideas that can change the world around me. No matter where you are in this world, education is always valued.

But my opportunity for education did not come easy. When you do not have a support system in place, college is a long, costly process. I worked a lot of jobs to pay for my education - fast food, movie rental, soldier, network engineer, bouncer, and law clerk. I worked with the goal of attaining a professional degree. It was depressing to see my high school classmates go on to college, while the military was my only option. To see them focusing solely on education while I focused on survival. Make no mistake; I worked jobs that I absolutely hated! I worked for people who had no respect for their subordinates. However, each menial job, each long night, each small paycheck was one step closer to achieving my goals - attaining a college degree and learn skills that would carry me through my adult life.

You should not measure your success by those around you. Just because others are off to a running start, doesn't mean that you cannot catch up and achieve your goals. It just may take some additional time.

I do not feel that I have reached my pinnacle yet, or that I have completed all of my education. If you ask me what I want to do when I grow up, I would unabashedly tell you that I don't know yet. But I will keep moving forward. I have learned to use my years of struggle to work to my advantage. I try to focus all of my angst and frustration into something useful - passion and drive. I feel that my rough childhood prepared me for the battlefield that life presents; that my struggles and solitude allow me to persevere under duress. Whatever path you choose to take, be sure to learn something along the way. Don't settle for people telling you that college "isn't for you," but at the same time, don't ever believe that attaining a degree is the only way out. You must keep aspiring for greatness and train to be a subject matter expert at whatever you choose to do.

How to be Alone

Taking the steps to ensure that I gained an education brought more than value or status, it also brought independence. As I matured into adulthood, I became accustomed to surviving on my own and not depending on others to help or even catch me when I fell. I joined the Army on my own. I went to college on my own. I moved to Washington DC and entered Howard University School of Law School on my own. There was no room for sorrow about having to fend for myself. The motivation and commitment was always been up to me, and me alone.

When it was time for me to graduate from law school I had no intention of participating in the actual ceremony. I am not big on pomp and ceremony, and I didn't really want my classmates to know about my life, to know that I was lacking any real family. That was a part of me that I didn't care to be made public. In the end, my girlfriend (now my wife) talked me into participating.

It was kind of embarrassing that I didn't need many of the tickets set aside for the graduates. The only people present for me were my girlfriend, her parents and her brother, who didn't even know me that well. When they called my name, there was a momentary pause. Other graduates had tons of family there, and when their names were called, it was a raucous sound of cheering and excitement. You could definitely tell where their family was sitting. These kids were getting their Juris Doctorate; they were graduating from Howard University School of Law and their families were ecstatic for their accomplishments. For me, there were no cat calls or people yelling out my name, there was just that momentary silence, until my girlfriend's family began to cheer and then the audience chimed in.

But I made it. I graduated. *I did it. Even being alone, I did it.* I walked across that stage and took hold of *MY* diploma. No one could take the credit or share in the glory; that accomplishment was mine and mine alone. I did not depend on anyone to help me pay for it, to help me study, to help me live while in school. I did it on my own. Of course I thank God for granting me the ability to be there and the fortitude to make it through. No one can take that accomplishment away from me. Being alone did not mean that I could not succeed.

Being by yourself can be difficult. An absence of friends and family, loved ones, or relationships can cause anyone to miss out on some wonderful experiences; miss out on life. However, learning to be alone doesn't always have to be bad. Once I learned to live alone and be happy with myself, it was much easier to be happy with someone else. If you are not happy with yourself, then you will find it nearly impossible to be happy with *anyone* else. I had identified the key to my destiny...and my happiness.

I understood that learning to stand alone meant that I did not need to be with someone, that I would be with someone because I wanted to; not out of dependence, but out of choice. Granted, there were trust issues, but those could be overcome with determination and self-realization. While trusting people did not come naturally to me, I began to work on being more trusting.

It is not that I don't value the opinions of others. Like I said, deep inside I still yearn for the admiration of others based upon my accomplishments. In fact, sometimes the opinions of others can help you better yourself. We all have a self-image that needs a reality check from others from time to time. I cannot be lessened by another's opinion of me for I know I am a good person, a regular person with faults and inner greatness. I have learned to live with me, and sometimes only me. I have too far to fall and no one to catch me. Please do not confuse this for some great inner confidence or strength; it is just accepting who I am.

This meant that I didn't have to be married or in a relationship to feel complete. I got married because I want to be with my wife (most of the time!). I don't have to have someone beside me to justify who I am or to make me somebody. I won't lose my job, or commit suicide because others may view me as weak or pitiful. I have been through much worse (just like many of you).

Learning how to be alone did not preclude me from being an attentive father. The abuse I suffered from my childhood may have distorted my view of family to some extent, but it didn't destroy my ability to love. I may not be the most romantic spouse; I may not have an unconditional trust in my wife or the other adults in my life; but I am a loving and dedicated husband, and father. I have a family. The one I created. I am the base of my family tree. The greatest legacy I will leave behind is right here in my house with me - my children. Although I started life alone, and survived alone, I will not end this life alone.

Another's Perspective

Although I said that there was no single thing that has made all of the difference, I would be remiss to leave out one of the greatest lessons I learned in my life; the one lesson that has kept me going when I felt that I had nothing left; the one thing that allowed me to navigate the obstacles and hills that were always in my way. While Tom Wilson was easily the most destructive force in my young life, he also imparted the most valuable lesson that I would ever learn. No matter how hard your life may be or what you have been through, there are always others whose lives are infinitely more difficult. One of the best ways to deal with your difficult life is to help those who are less fortunate; to see life through their eyes and from their perspective.

Tom forced me to volunteer to work for the Missouri School for the Blind as a young boy. I was being abused and molested by that man, but he thought I needed to do community service. Granted, this was not something that I did willingly, but I was too young to refuse his commands. This was not the soup kitchen or food pantry type of volunteering; this was up close and personal. This was a school for blind and handicapped children. Their disabilities ran the gamut, from blind and deaf, to wheelchair bound and autistic children. Tom actually started a handicapped scout troop, which was no small feat, since the children's needs were varied and complicated.

Spending time every week with these boys gave me the strength to see that my hell was manageable in comparison to the lives they led. I was able to realize that my hell may one day end, but they would still be wed to their wheelchair for a lifetime unable to see a morning sunrise or the meal they were going to eat. Some of the kids were teenagers. They had fully functional minds and all of the normal feelings and desires of teenagers. However, some of their disabilities left them unable to even use the bathroom by themselves. Others could not speak and would have to sign to communicate. Since some of them were also blind, this made for a challenging life. To see a 17-year-old boy in tears because he was unable to tell us that he needed to urinate until it was too late was heartbreaking.

I was depressed because I was an unwanted child who missed his mother. But, these kids would tell me stories of the way they lived. How their parents came to visit less and less each year. Some were abandoned and wards of the state, just as I was. Some were born blind and could not comprehend the color red or their own appearance. Others were not born blind but became blind by some tragedy. One boy told me of how he was an unwanted infant who was thrown in a dumpster shortly after birth. Unfortunately, a curtain rod went into his skull and left him permanently blind. Another boy told me of how he was shot in the head by police after wielding a pellet gun during a botched robbery when he was a young teen. He said he only wanted to be with his father who was incarcerated for a similar crime.

I watched these kids attack life with zeal and excitement. I learned that they ate clockwise, positioning their food the same way every meal so they would know where the different foods were located and could feed themselves. I watched them run track with leather gloves and a guide rope. They played kickball with a ball that had a bell inside it. I remember a deaf mute who was relegated to using a wheelchair go camping and try to cook scrambled eggs and pancakes. Watching these kids, most of who were going to be dependent upon other people for their entire lives, make the most out of a sunny day reminded me that my life was still worth seizing.

When you work with handicapped people you realize that your issues are not so monumental. As a child, seeing kids my own age negotiate their physical ailments and utilize the faculties still at their disposal, demonstrated to me that I did not always have to be a victim, that I would not always be helpless, and that I could survive these trials and leave the tortures behind. Many of the handicapped children would have willingly traded places with me just to have the opportunity to walk, see the snow fall or have the hope of someday living on their own. Seeing their resilience shamed me into being something better, even at a young age.

I realized that being a foster child or even a victim of abuse paled in comparison to the circumstances in which some of these children were born. When we focus on the things that are missing, we often discount the opportunities we have. Now, this is not to say that I never had pity parties or felt sorry for myself. Of course, there were many times that I could not imagine life being any worse for anyone else. That suicide would be a better option than living my life. But during some of my lowest points, I would notice some child struggling with his wheelchair in the store. Or I would see a young man with Down's syndrome working the cash register at a fast food restaurant. And it would always bring me back to those days when I was working at the blind school.

Even now, this is the one lesson I find myself continually falling back on when times get tough, when my mind unwillingly slips into those spaces where I can only feel bleak and destitute. I will see someone struggling with their situation, be it handicapped, or impoverished, or worse. And, I am reminded of my blessings and the opportunities I still have. God forbid that I waste these blessings by being dismal and miserable, because there is no guarantee that I will not be in a wheelchair or blind tomorrow, or worse. Depending on another's perspective, my life is great.

So, if you have children that are complaining about not being able to find their parents, if you are an adult who has suffered as an abused child and are thinking that life is not worth living, go and volunteer to help the handicapped. It won't make your problems go away or erase your past, but it will put your challenges and pain in a proper perspective. It will show you that your challenges can be overcome. You will then see where the battle lines are clearly drawn, that you have everything inside of you to achieve greatness, that all you have to do is keep on walking forward.

These children can bring a new perspective to your life. It will show you that the things that have happened to you can be overcome, or that the impact can be minimized. After all, it is not what has happened to you that controls you; it is the perspective with which those things are viewed. If you realize that although you are alone, you are not a failure, that although no one seems to believe in you, you can still succeed because you believe in yourself. If you realize that your past cannot be changed, but that your suffering is over and you are now free to move on, maybe you will choose to move on. Helping others will help you remember that there are those who have suffered just as you have, and survived. There are those who are much worse off than you will ever be, and they are living each day to the fullest.

19. 10,000 Hills

As a unit chief in the state's attorney's office, I was blessed to be given a single administrative aide to help me and my attorneys. Jean was just awesome, dependable to the point of making me almost helpless. She also had to deal with tragedy, close and personal to her. I remember her telling me that her mother-in-law had passed away. I could tell that she was in pain and did not pry into the facts, but allowed her to grieve as she chose. Years later, Jean told me the details of her mother-in-law's death.

It was early December and her mother-in-law had already purchased Christmas presents for her grandchildren and the rest of the family. That evening, she put a roast in the oven and got ready for a family dinner. Then she took out a pistol that was secured for emergencies and ended her life. This was a shock to everyone and took the family by complete surprise. However, in retrospect, it was clear that this woman, this mother, this grandmother and wife had led a life of misery and pain. She was on constant medication for depression and anxiety. She vacillated from happiness to being sullen and withdrawn in the space of a conversation. Her condition stemmed from the sexual abuse she suffered as a child, at the hands of a loved one. For years, she quietly carried this pain and only shared it later on in her life. By then, so much damage had been done that she was a shell of the woman she could have been. Even though she was miserable and sad, even though the weight of the betrayal and suffering buckled her knees, she still pushed on in agonizing silence. She was 68-years-old.

Before It's Too Late

While this story is tragic, it is even more painful to know that this lady fought her battle alone. She carried this heavy weight deep down inside for all of those years without finding a way to free herself of it. I know how painful the abuse is, and how easy it is to become grateful and that it just isn't happening anymore. I know how preferable it is to keep it inside, hoping that no one else will ever know the humiliation and victimization you have felt.

Once I joined the Army, I thought I was going to be able to totally recreate myself. I thought that I would be in a position where I would never have to feel like a victim again. I figured all that abuse was behind me and as long as I looked to the future, then everything would be okay, or at least better. I tried to ignore the years of neglect and suffering and pretend they never happened. The problem was, that it did happen, not once or a few times, but for years. It happened as a child, when my mind was too young to even appreciate the damage that was done. I just focused on the physical damage. How could I possibly know what kind of harm was being done to my emotions, my values, my spirit, and my ability to properly interact with people? I just thought I could keep on living, and that any life would be better than my childhood.

So I just went forward, carrying my cross. From the outside, it was working. However, inside the damage wasn't clearly identifiable, instead of a cross, it was a cancer. It was growing inside of me and influencing my life in ways I never realized or ever could have imagined. I couldn't see how my judgment was being skewed, how my views of love and the world around me were broken, how my self-confidence, standards and expectations for myself were never at a healthy level. Just like my childhood, I continued to just push on through. Day by day the negative impact of my childhood increased.

Things were going wrong in my life that I could not explain. I had outburst feelings of angst, distrust, and rage that were unexpected and uncontrollable. I could not enjoy the successes in my life. Certain things would trigger episodes of emotions that I could never have predicted. A random song would come on the radio and cause me to tear up and openly weep. A unique scent would cause me to immediately get angry. The design of a room or setting would cause me to lapse into a state of depression. Random things would elicit memories of my victimization or feelings of being so very lost and alone. I could not understand why I was experiencing these dramatic mood swings and chalked it up to some mental instability. We are all a little crazy sometimes, I thought.

I was pretending that I was normal. More to the point, I was pretending that I had a normal childhood or that nothing from my childhood could ever affect me now. And I was wrong. Of course I had good days and a marginally pleasant adult life, but I see that it could have been so much better. I had settled for surviving and never focused on doing more. I could have done so much more. I could have been so much happier. I could have enjoyed my successes more, instead of waiting for the other shoe to fall. I could have let good people into my life, instead of not trusting those that showed me love. I could have kept bad people out of my life, instead of trying to save them. Instead of going through years of negativity and pessimism, I could have looked forward to what life had to offer. I needed to acknowledge that I had some broken parts that needed to be fixed.

To Me

I view my life as a series of hills -- thousands of major struggles that began early in life. As soon as I would rise up and deal with one challenge, another would be there before me. If it wasn't hunger, it was seeing my mom with other men. If it wasn't helping my sisters, it was losing them. If it wasn't being unwanted, it was being wanted for the wrong reasons. And these challenges were there every day, in some form or fashion. Always one more challenge in front of me. Always one more hill to climb.

To some this may seem depressing or melodramatic because it denotes a life of misery and strife. Even if this is not your life, there are some who are forced to keep dealing with these tribulations; forced to keep walking these hills, just to survive. To me, and many others, this is what life was. It starts off rough and continues to be a difficult journey, fraught with trials, dangers, and temptation. I started off poor and neglected, and then I was saved from that only to lose my sisters and my home. I was placed in one home, only to be moved to another and another, yearning for permanency, only to find that permanent placement to be nothing short of Hell. And then to escape and realize that my childhood and the very defenses I developed to survive were stunting my ability to grow as a person, still slowly killing me from the inside. One obstacle after another, each seemingly more difficult to traverse or overcome. Each hill becoming just a little bigger, a little steeper.

The Campaign Trail

But it is not all gloom and doom. Once I realized I was still being affected by my childhood, it became a matter of addressing my issues. I could no longer accept that I was as good as I was going to get, that surviving my childhood was enough. I had to hold myself accountable for all my shortcomings and try to find a different and better way to deal with life. I had to learn to grow and be better...happier.

I began this book by describing my "special day," but there is no doubt that it did not just happen. The amount of work put into making that day possible is almost impossible to put into words. The walking, talking, platform development, and getting my message out to the citizens took an enormous amount of time and effort. I was trying to become the first

African-American ever to represent my county in ANY state office. I had to start out as a virtual unknown in my own community but somehow win this election.

But gaining this office took much more than my hard work. Yes, I served my country; sure, I earned my Juris Doctorate; I even created my own grant position as a prosecutor and later created and managed my division in the state's attorney's office. These were all things I did on my own. Of course people gave me chances, but at best, most people just got out of my way and allowed me to succeed or fail on my own. I did not have to depend on anyone else or care what others thought of me, I just had to keep pushing myself. As long as I had me, I had a chance.

Being a prosecutor allowed me to save lives and speak up for the victims. It also gave me a chance to work with defendants and inspire them to do greater things than commit criminal offenses. I worked so hard to help individuals, but those in need just kept coming. There were always more victims, more misguided children, and more vicious criminals with tragic childhoods. Each day became more frustrating because I could not save them all. Not as long as the current policies were in place. I noticed most of the lawmakers had never spent a day in jail, in a foster home, or had to live as a victim. There was no connection to those who were suffering the most. I wanted to do something more, to give foster kids and victims of sexual abuse a voice on a larger scale. The only way to change the policies was to become a lawmaker, instead of just enforcing the laws.

I had grown enough as a person to realize that I had to step up until someone better could take my place. Someone who was more qualified to take the mantle of leadership and speak for those less fortunate souls that no one wants to acknowledge. Politics is something entirely different and oddly foreign. Qualifications and experience unfortunately have very little bearing on getting elected. All of my childhood struggles and adult successes mean very little in the political world. In order to win an election,

I needed something more, much more than I alone could provide.

It is plain to see how my childhood molded some of my adult characteristics. I have hopefully explained the painful lasting effects of child abuse in my life and how dealing with my suffering is ongoing and continuous. The coping mechanisms and survival techniques I have developed were my means of survival. However, none of these characteristics would help me with this challenge. In fact, most of them would hinder any chance I would ever have to become an elected official.

While I felt my childhood and dedication to community service was something that was needed in today's political world, I knew nothing about politics. Beyond voting, I was a neophyte in the political realm. I had no financial backing and only a limited understanding of community organizing. I did not even know how to register my campaign or what it would take to win an election. In fact, the only thing I did know was that I could not do it on my own. Unlike all of my other challenges, this mission forced me to eschew my survival tactics, let down my guard, and for the first time in my adult life, trust and even depend on others.

I had to rely on Greg and Matt for organization. This meant allowing casual friends to have an impact on my life. They were subject matter experts on political campaigns that I had to trust. I let them control every facet of my campaign, even if I personally disagreed. While my internal mechanisms were screaming that they could be sabotaging my chances, I had to shut that mistrust out and hope and take a chance.

I also had to go to my father-in-law to ask for financial assistance in beginning my campaign. This went against everything I had learned as a child. Relying on "family" was something I had learned to avoid long ago. Without Vernon's help, however, I could never have gotten my election committee up and running. This meant putting aside my instincts and actually asking a family member to invest in me, something no one had ever done for me before. Greg created a campaign packet with spreadsheets, charts, and calculations to demonstrate that I could actually win, and my father-in-law came through without even reading it! He even convinced many of his friends to donate to my cause. This was the seed money I needed to get my campaign off the ground.

However, this initial investment was not nearly enough to ensure a chance at victory. The loner attitude I had developed over the years had to be set aside in order to raise sufficient funds. This meant I had to approach people I had known professionally for years and do something I never thought I would ever do -ask them for a favor. And not just any favor; I had to ask them for money! While I had friends and professional acquaintances, I had gotten by without asking for anything. That way I would never be hurt or disappointed. Now, not only did I have to face the fear of rejection, I had to deal with the possibility that people I thought were my friends would not be there for me.

The people around me came through in spades. Not only did my friends donate, but professional acquaintances also gave freely. Of course, there were a few people that did not help out, but there were many others that gave in small and big amounts. I even had people from high school help - people that used to call me "nigger" donated on Facebook!

Once the campaign began to build, I also had to deal with another unknown barrier. As anyone who has run for office can tell you, the greatest sacrifice is your family. Because I was spending so much time working on my bid for office, I was not always able to fully contribute to my family's well-being. I was spending so much time in the community, that I could not always make my half of the bills or spend time caring for my children. I had to depend on my wife. I had to trust Nicole to have my back during this time. This was a huge departure from the lessons my mother and Millie had taught me; that I should never trust or depend upon any woman to care for me. Yet, in order to achieve my goal I had to set aside this defense mechanism and put my trust in this woman. While she was not overly involved in my campaign, she took care of my girls. She kept up with everyone's homework, took them to all of their events and never complained when I was unable to provide my share of the bills. She always had the girls looking beautiful for every outing and meet-and-greet, even when I could not be there with them. She even bought me a beautiful watch on the day of election, to show she was proud of me whether I won or lost.

I learned long ago not to place much stock in what others thought of me, that their opinions should not matter enough to stop me from achieving my goals. Of course, I secretly wanted to be accepted, but I learned never to expect that I would be accepted. Instead, I learned to get along without any social groups or organizations, just doing things by myself. But, even money and an organized campaign is not enough for a new comer to win a political election because people are always the bottom line. By running for office, I was doing exactly what I had taught myself never to do…rely on the opinions of others. More than that, I was begging them to find me worthy of their support! That is just what running for office means. I had to tell people why I thought I was qualified and allow them to determine if I had done enough to earn their trust. I had to put my future in the hands of others, in the hope that they found me worthy. I had to rely on many people I had never even met to decide my fate! This was in direct contravention to my most ingrained and basic instincts. This was by far the hardest barrier to bring down.

Seeking to become the first African-American to be elected to state office from my county meant that I had to open myself up to the possibility of racism and people judging me solely because of my color. This was something I had moved far away from; something I had shielded myself from through education and success. I never wanted to be in a position again where the word "nigger" could impact my life. Now I was opening myself to be inhibited and negatively affected by racism. I could lose just because I was black! I had to once again try to change the minds of some people who were going to judge me because of my skin color. I did not try to convince them that I was not black (although some thought I was Hispanic). I had to hold my head up and embrace my race, proudly putting my brown face on all of my signs. I would meet racism head on, and accept whatever happened.

When I began my bid for office, I never realized that I would have to trust people to judge me fairly. It did not dawn on me that I was stepping into the public eye solely for people to let me know how they felt about me. And if they did not like me, I would fail at something that I had sunk my heart and soul into accomplishing. Unlike anything else I had ever done, as a public servant, people's opinions DO matter. Their thoughts and feelings about you DO count. I had to learn to invite and accept people's opinions on my accomplishments and on my views. I could no longer dismiss what others thought because I was asking for their judgment. I was asking for their acceptance.

In the process, I found that I could care what others thought without letting it hurt me. Even if they did not accept me or support me, it did not mean they looked down on me, just that they did not think I was qualified. Or they supported someone else. Some of the opinions I received helped craft my platform and my position. I could allow these opinions to influence me.

This race forced me to set aside many of the survival techniques I had developed and work through my short-comings and self-doubts. I learned how to be a better me. Many people voted for other candidates they thought were more qualified; some just didn't like what I represented and did not vote for me. But when the final vote was counted, I had won my election. This victory meant so much more to me than a political seat. It was a defining moment in my life because I had broken through so many personal barriers and grown past my reliance on these defense mechanisms.

Even if I had not been successful, I had allowed myself to trust friends, to rely on family members, and I had the courage to allow the opinions of others to dictate a portion of my future. Best of all, I took a chance and honestly believed that I was good enough and that I deserved to be successful.

This is not meant to be a political book, but my election did mark a turning point in my life. Not that I could not have been happy if I had lost, but I didn't lose! I set my sights high and reached my goals, with the help and trust of hundreds of people. I was able to do this because I decided I had to grow and leave my past behind. Not just the abuse, but the residual effects of a lifetime's worth of suffering and pain. I have found that it is not enough for me to just survive. Yes, there are still plenty of hills in front of me, but I know they are leading somewhere. I will not continue in some fruitless and directionless struggle. I am walking with purpose.

10,000 Hills
While some of the views I have may seem pessimistic or even cold-hearted, they have helped me find a way to survive childhood abuse. The views I shared are not "one-size-fits-all" but they have allowed me to find a way. That is what most of us are looking for...a way. That is all that I am trying to provide - a view or light at the end of the proverbial tunnel. I see my views as pragmatic and practical, but not necessarily the best option for everyone. While some things only brought on more problems, I have found others things that worked for me.

I know that each person who struggled with abuse and neglect or endured a troubled life in the foster care system had a life different than mine. I know there are people who have suffered unimaginable horrors that would have broken me. I know that I am no guru on surviving harsh realities. However, working with many former foster youth and victims of physical and sexual abuse has helped me to recognize some struggles that are common to many of us. Although our situations are different, our sufferings are different, and our lives have turned out differently, there are certain things that many of us share, other issues we all share. That is why I share my point of view and my reality of these common problems.

I pray that this book at a minimum serves to remind people that abused foster children do exist. There are children out there right now who have been going through things that make my childhood look like a walk in the park. There are thousands of examples of young children who are beaten, battered, molested, raped, hurt, emotionally scarred, let down and neglected…all at the hands of "loved ones." And yet, they still go forward. They do this with no light at the end of the tunnel. They just keep on keepin' on.

It is a tragedy that many of our youth have to go through the horrors of child abuse and neglect. We compound that tragedy when we allow these children to slip away into anonymity. These resilient little, compassionate children are heroes in their own right and deserve the accolades and honors that accompany that title. In reality it doesn't seem to pan out that way for abused and foster children in this society. They are mostly marginalized and dismissed as waifs, fodder, and wastrels. How can we simply discard all of this potential that can benefit our society? Who better to run the department of social services than someone who has survived the foster care system and attained a college diploma, on their own! Who would be a more compassionate leader than someone who has suffered at the hands of loved ones and knows that there are people out there in need? All of that passion and compassion that accompanies a life of childhood suffering can be a great benefit to our society if we provide a path for these children to be politicians, judges, and professionals.

I want each person who has suffered at the hands of a loved one to know they are not alone and that there is a way to make it through. I want them to know that they will be alright. That they will not always be a victim and things will get better. They may not ever be "normal" but what the hell does normal mean, anyway? Who is to say what normal is? My goal is not to be normal anymore, it is to be happy. My goal is to be proud of my journey, and it is to leave a legacy that is greater than I can ever be.

Realize that all of the challenges you have overcome in your life demonstrate your resilience. Not your perfection, but your tenacity. Be aware, the obstacles you faced as a child would have broken most adults. Yet, you survived it, day after day, night after night. You mentally dealt with the disappointment, the letdown, the neglect, and the abuse. You faced these challenges alone and some of you did all of this as a child!

If I can give hope to the hopeless, stop someone from taking their life, or just motivate someone to relate a story that is more compelling and better written than mine, I will be happy. If I can get others to write and talk about their suffering, to show the world how common my life story really is, then I can die knowing that every single humiliation, every vile act that was forced upon me, every evil and nasty deed that I was ever forced to commit, every bit of pain, disappointment and loneliness, was worth it.

If I can get others to see that their past does not delineate their future; that the effects of their abuse does not have to follow them throughout their lives; that they can have more, then this was all worth it. In the end, even if you have trust issues and don't like letting people inside your emotional walls, you can still have a family. Even if you never had parents that actually loved you, you can still be a good parent. All the suffering you went through does not have to be passed on, and you can find happiness in the lives you bring into this world and the family you create. You can be the base of your own family tree, a tree that branches out for generations, spreading happiness and compassion for years to come.

I hope that after reading this book, you will understand that child abuse has a continuing effect, as it has in my life. But I realize that my challenges are not impossible to overcome, they are not impassable, and they are not mountains…just more hills to climb. I don't say that light-heartedly. That doesn't mean that it's all easy and downhill. It means that I have suffered and struggled before, and I will continue to deal with my issues, but I will move forward whether I succeed or fail.

If this book seems confusing and contradictory, that is because some of my life is just that…confusing and contradictory. Feeling that my birth mother loved me, even though I know deep down inside that she did not love me enough; Believing that Tom's love was true on some level, even though I know I am just making excuses for him; Eschewing therapy but instead relying on psychological understanding of my reactions,; these are some of the contradictory feelings I relay to you. But they are just that, my feelings.

To some, it may appear that I have gone through a great deal of self-diagnosis in this book. That may be true. I know that I can't speak for everyone, but I know that most people who have lived through traumatic events spend a large part of their lives in forms of self-diagnosis. I cannot speak for every foster child or abuse victim when I try to tell my experiences. But I have spoken with numerous foster children and adult victims, all of whom share backgrounds and struggles similar to mine. Some of the advice I have given may not apply to them. There is no single solution.

After reading this book, you may feel that I am not that well-adjusted. And you may be correct. Since I am not sure what "normal" is, I just try to find happiness. My life is a work in progress, and I am progressing. Some of my issues may be completely gone over time, others may dissipate to nuisance background noise, while others may always be only a trip wire away from being triggered. Either way, what you have read is a part of who I am, what I have experienced, and what I still struggle to overcome.

I realize that some may read this story and doubt the facts, but that's okay, I did not write this for them anyway. I also know that some of the targets for this book are too young to read it, but I hope that someone shares it with them one day. And, I want those who are still carrying this burden to know that you don't need to be ashamed of what happened to you, even if you never tell a soul. I want you to realize and know that it gets better, but that you may need some help along the way; that your childhood coping mechanisms that helped you survive may become detrimental as you mature, and may hinder your ability to thrive. I know too many others who share our story, and I want you to know that you are not alone. You are never alone.

When I look behind me, all I see are the hills I have climbed, the things I have overcome, and my accomplishments. When I look to my front, all I see are new challenges to overcome, more hills that I WILL climb. Even when childhood issues rear their ugly heads, I will just keep trudging along. It may not be an easy path but I am up to the challenge, and I will be happy. It may be a challenging and steep climb, but there are no mountains. It's just another hill. I have climbed so many already, some bigger, and some smaller. All I have to do is keep walking. No matter how long the journey or how steep the incline, I know I will make it...and so will you.

Greater Angels

I rise, ignoring that pain and sorrow that threatens to fill each day. Why, after all of my suffering do I still work for a greater good, why do I still try? Simple. Though it seems at times my pain and misery will overcome my life, I have suffered too much for that. Since I know a life of abject misery and horrifying abuse, there is one thing I see with utter clarity…that I cannot knowingly allow others to suffer the way I have suffered. Each bit of agony and humiliation I have had to deal with serves as a reminder of just how cruel people can be to one another. Just how dangerous a system can be when it thinks that money can be the bottom line of government; people are always the bottom line. It is people that matter.

See, no matter how much rage and anger I may possess, no matter how degrading and dehumanizing my childhood may have been, I still know basic right from wrong. Of course I still deal with my inner demons; of course I have to be constantly vigilant lest my self-pity or anger get the better of me. Of course I have to constantly remind myself that I must lower my guard and allow other people to get to know some portion of who I am in order to operate in this world. To survive with what happened to me takes constant effort, so I do not weaken and fall to my lesser demons. However, there is something more.

When you have been the object of ruinous lust and affection, the target of physical and mental abuse; and when you have been the subject of repeated rejection and neglect, you get a first-hand glimpse of what real pain is. When your entire childhood has been filled with betrayal and misery, you cannot help but feel compassion for the human condition.

The pain I felt as a child was nearly unbearable and drove me close to the edge of my humanity time and time again. Hours of abuse fueled months and years of internal misery and self-hatred. Knowing just what human beings are capable of and experiencing what damage adults can inject into the life of an innocent and dependent child is enlightening. I have found that many people remain blissfully unaware of the abuse suffered by our children. Most refuse to believe just how violent and degrading a child's life can be. I know the truth, and the more I work to stop the mistreatment of children, the more I have found that my story is far from unique.

To that end, I would never want to cause any of the pain I have suffered. It is a driving force in my life to be remembered for something good, or at least not be remembered at all, before I am a source of pain in anybody's life. As much as my rage and inner demons threaten to consume me, my knowledge of the human condition and the suffering around me reminds me of what damage those demons can do.
I refuse to be the cause of that much pain.

So, in the end, the same suffering that could drive me to the edge of violence and a sociopathic view of the world, is also the same motivation that pushes me to always help those who are suffering. The humiliation and self-loathing I feel for being a victim of sexual abuse also pushes me to rise to a position that can actually change what our children go through. It is that anger about violence in our community that motivated me to become a lawyer and a prosecutor.

At times, I wake from a night of dreams of what Tom made me do, how he beat me until I begged, with visions so real, so vivid, that I awaken to the taste and smell of an unwashed genitalia. That teary-eyed humiliation reminds me that others are waking to the same sensations, only they are not dreaming. Their nights are still filled with the horrors that are now only memories in my head. That there are children that are right now, this very moment, going through things that I could only imagine, things that make my life look easy in comparison. That fuels the need to focus my energy on finding a way to come to the aide of those still suffering.

When a song or smell invokes an influx of memories of abandonment and abuse, being cast aside by an addicted mother, rejected by families, and left to the whims of a man who used me to serve his sexual needs; When that pain becomes unbearable and my heart yearns for release from the suffering and indignity; When, in those weak moments, I feel that death would be of little consequence when compared to having to continue to bear the burden of what I have gone through – I realize there are adults out there right now whose childhood will cause their demise. They will take their own lives, by a single act or the more painful method of a slow death by addiction. The thought that there are others who feel worse than I do at my lowest, emboldens me to do something to alleviate their pain

306

and misery. Even if that means bearing my soul and weaknesses to the ridicules of the world, just so they do not feel alone.

The impact of my childhood is both my damnation and my savior, my lesser demons and my greater angels. I am not perfect and I will never claim to be, but for now I will try to use my suffering as motivation and my life as a lesson.

I choose to follow my greater angels, and so should you.

Psalms 82:3-4

"Give justice to the poor and the orphan;
Uphold the rights of the oppressed and the destitute.
Rescue the poor and helpless;
Deliver them from the grasp of evil people."

-Thanks Pastor Mike and Pastor Chris

Made in the USA
Coppell, TX
06 April 2023

15337860R00177